CONCEPT OF PROGRAMMING LANGUAGE

Harsh Marwah

ANMOL PUBLICATIONS PVT. LTD.
NEW DELHI-110 002 (INDIA)

ANMOL PUBLICATIONS PVT. LTD.
Regd. Office: 4360/4, Ansari Road, Daryaganj,
New Delhi-110002 (India)
Tel.: 23278000, 23261597, 23286875, 23255577
Fax: 91-11-23280289
Email: anmolpub@gmail.com
Visit us at: www.anmolpublications.com

Branch Office: No. 1015, Ist Main Road, BSK IIIrd Stage
IIIrd Phase, IIIrd Block, Bangalore-560 085 (India)
Tel.: 080-41723429 • Fax: 080-26723604
Email: anmolpublicationsbangalore@gmail.com

Concept of Programming Language

First Edition, 2010

ISBN 978-81-261-4474-7

PRINTED IN INDIA

Printed at Mehra Offset Press, Delhi.

Contents

Preface

Concept of Programming Language is a truly well-written textbook for the students of UPTU. To increase capacity to express ideas - the depth at which we can program, just like the way we think, is highly influenced by the expressive power of the language in which we communicate our thoughts.

An Improved background for choosing appropriate language - if you know more about programming languages, you have a better idea what to choose when development time comes. An Increased ability to learn new languages - continuous learning in the field of software engineering is very much essential.

This textbook is good for any college student or professional trying to get a feel of how the most popular programming languages have evolved in the past 4 decades, and what sets these languages apart. The quality of this book is that it explains the history behind each language which goes into a detail description of how each language evolved over the years.

Author

Chapter 1

Introduction

CONCEPTUAL OVERVIEW

AWK is a pattern-matching programme for processing files, especially when they are databases. The new version of awk, called nawk, provides additional capabilities. Every modern Unix system comes with a version of new awk, and its use is recommended over old awk.

Different systems vary in what the two versions are called. Some have oawk and awk, for the old and new versions, respectively. Others have awk and nawk. Still others only have awk, which is the new version. This example shows what happens if your awk is the old one:

```
$ awk 1 /dev/null
awk: syntax error near line 1
awk: bailing out near line 1
```

awk exits silently if it is the new version. Source code for the latest version of awk, from Bell Labs, can be downloaded starting at Brian Kernighan's home page: (–) Which is their in most lab. Michael Brennan's mawk is available via anonymous **FTP** (.) Frequency transfer protocol on every site of awk. Finally, the Free Software Foundation has a version of awk called gawk, which are available in great demand. All three programmes implement "new"awk. Thus, references below such as "nawk only," apply to all three. gawk has additional features.

With original awk, *you can*:

- Think of a text file as made up of records and fields in a textual database.
- Perform arithmetic and string operations.

- Use programming constructs such as loops and conditionals.
- Produce formatted reports.

With nawk, *you can also*:

- Define your own functions.
- Execute Unix commands from a script.
- Process the results of Unix commands.
- Process command-line arguments more gracefully.
- Work more easily with multiple input streams.
- Flush open output files and pipes.

In addition, with GNU awk (gawk), *you can*:

- Use regular expressions to separate records, as well as fields.
- Skip to the start of the next file, not just the next record.
- Perform more powerful string substitutions.
- Retrieve and format system time values.

COMMAND-LINE SYNTAX

The syntax for invoking awk has two forms:

```
awk [options] 'script' var=value file(s)
awk [options] -f scriptfile var=value file(s)
```

You can specify a *script* directly on the command line, or you can store a script in a *scriptfile* and specify it with *-f*. nawk allows multiple *-f* scripts. Variables can be assigned a value on the command line. The value can be a literal, a shell variable ($*name*), or a command substitution ('cmd'), but the value is available only after the **BEGIN** statement is executed.

awk operates on one or more *files*. If none are specified (or if - is specified), awk reads from the standard input.

The recognized options are:

-Ffs

Set the field separator to *fs*. This is the same as setting the system variable FS. Original awk allows the field separator to be only a single character. Nawk allows *fs* to be a regular expression.

Each input line, or record, is divided into fields by whitespace (blanks or tabs) or by some other user-definable record separator. Fields are referred to by the variables $1, $2,..., $*n*. $0 refers to the entire record.

-v var=value

Assign a *value* to variable *var*. This allows assignment before the script begins execution (available in nawk only).

To print the first three (colon-separated) fields of each record on separate lines:

```
awk -F: '{ print $1; print $2; print $3 }' /
etc/passwd
```

PATTERNS AND PROCEDURES

awk scripts consist of patterns and procedures:

```
pattern { procedure }
```

Both are optional. If *pattern* is missing, { *procedure* } is applied to all lines; if { *procedure* } is missing, the matched line is printed.

Patterns

A pattern can be any of the following:

```
/regular expression/
relational expression
pattern-matching expression
BEGIN
END
```

- Expressions can be composed of quoted strings, numbers, operators, functions, defined variables, or any of the predefined variables described later in the section "Built-in Variables."
- Regular expressions use the extended set of metacharacters and are described in Chapter, *Pattern Matching*.
- ^ and $ refer to the beginning and end of a string (such as the fields), respectively, rather than the beginning and end of a line.
  In particular, these metacharacters will *not* match at a newline embedded in the middle of a string.
- Relational expressions use the relational operators listed in the section "Operators" later in this chapter.

For example, 2 > 1 selects lines for which the second field is greater than the first.

- Comparisons can be either string or numeric. Thus, depending on the types of data in 1 and 2,awk does either a numeric or a string comparison. This can change from one record to the next.
- Pattern-matching expressions use the operators ~ (match) and !~ (don't match). See the section "Operators" later in this chapter.
- The **BEGIN** pattern lets you specify procedures that take place *before* the first input line is processed.
- The **END** pattern lets you specify procedures that take place *after* the last input record is read.
- In nawk, **BEGIN** and **END** patterns may appear multiple times. The procedures are merged as if there had been one large procedure.

Except for **BEGIN** and **END**, patterns can be combined with the Boolean operators || (or), && (and), and ! (not). A range of lines can also be specified using comma-separated patterns:

```
pattern,pattern
```

Procedures

Procedures consist of one or more commands, functions, or variable assignments, separated by newlines or semicolons, and contained within curly braces.

Commands fall into five groups:

- Variable or array assignments
- Printing commands
- Built-in functions
- Control-flow commands
- User-defined functions (nawk only)

Simple Pattern-Procedure Examples

- Print first field of each line:

```
{ print $1 }
```

- Print all lines that contain *pattern*:

```
/pattern/
```

- Print first field of lines that contain *pattern*:

```
/pattern/ { print $1 }
```

- Select records containing more than two fields:

```
NF > 2
```

- Interpret input records as a group of lines up to a blank line. Each line is a single field.

```
BEGIN { FS = "\n"; RS = ""}
```

- Print fields 2 and 3 in switched order, but only on lines whose first field matches the string "**URGENT**":

```
$1 ~ /URGENT/ { print $3, $2 }
```

- Count and print the number of *pattern* found:
- */pattern/* {++x }

```
END { print x }
```

- Add numbers in second column and print total:

```
{ total += $2 }
END { print "column total is", total}
```

- Print lines that contain less than 20 characters:

```
length($0) < 20
```

- Print each line that begins with *Name:* and that contains exactly seven fields:

```
NF == 7 &&/^Name:/
```

- Print the fields of each input record in reverse order, one per line:

```
{
  for (i = NF; i => 1; i-)
    print $i
    }
```

BUILT-IN VARIABLES

Version	Variable	Description
awk	FILENAME	Current filename
	FS	Field separator (a space)
	NF	Number of fields in current record
	NR	Number of the current record
	OFMT	Output format for numbers and for conversion to ("%.6g") string

	OFS	Output field separator (a space)
	ORS	Output record separator (a newline)
	RS	Record separator (a newline)
	$0	Entire input record
	$*n*	*n*th field in current record; fields are separated by FS
nawk	ARGC	Number of arguments on command line
	ARGV	An array containing the command-line arguments, indexed from 0 to ARGC - 1
	CONVFMT	String conversion format for numbers ("%.6g") (POSIX)
	ENVIRON	An associative array of environment variables
	FNR	Like NR, but relative to the current file
	RLENGTH	Length of the string matched by match() function
	RSTART	First position in the string matched by match() function
	SUBSEP	Separator character for array subscripts ("\034")
gawk	ARGIND	Index in ARGV of current input file
	ERRNO	A string indicating the error when a redirection fails for getline or if close() fails
	FIELDWIDTHS	A space-separated list of field widths to use for splitting up the record, instead of FS
	IGNORECASE	When true, all regular expression matches, string comparisons, and calls to index()s ignore case
	RT	The text matched by RS, which can be a regular expression in gawk

OPERATORS

The following programming lists the operators, in order of increasing precedence, that are available in awk.

Note: while ** and **= are common extensions, they are not part of **POSIX** awk.

Symbol	Meaning
= += -= *=/= %= ^= **=	Assignment
?:	C conditional expression (nawk only)
||	Logical OR (short-circuit)
&&	Logical AND (short-circuit)
	in Array membership (nawk only)
~ !~	Match regular expression and negation
< ⇐ > ⇒ != ==	Relational operators
	(blank)Concatenation
+ –	Addition, subtraction
*/ %	Multiplication, division, and modulus (remainder)
+ – !	Unary plus and minus, and logical negation
^ **	Exponentiation
++ —	Increment and decrement, either prefix or postfix
$	Field reference

VARIABLES AND ARRAY ASSIGNMENTS

Variables can be assigned a value with an = sign.

For example:

```
FS = ","
```

Expressions using the operators +, –,/, and % (modulo) can be assigned to variables. Arrays can be created with the split() function (see below), or they can simply be named in an assignment statement. Array elements can be subscripted with numbers (*array*,..., *array*[*n*]) or with strings.

Arrays subscripted by strings are called *associative arrays*. For example, to count the number of widgets you have, you could use the following script: In fact, all arrays in awk are associative; numeric subscripts are converted to strings before using them as array subscripts. Associative arrays are one of awk's most powerful features.

```
/widget/ { count["widget"]++}  Count widgets
END { print count["widget"]}   Print the
                               count
```

You can use the special for loop to read all the elements of an associative array:

```
for (item in array)
        process array[item]
```

The index of the array is available as item, while the value of an element of the array can be referenced as array[item]. You can use the operator in to see if an element exists by testing to see if its index exists (nawk only):

```
if (index in array)
```

This sequence tests that array[index] exists, but you cannot use it to test the value of the element referenced by array[index]. You can also delete individual elements of the array using the delete statement (nawk only).

Escape Sequences

Within string and regular expression constants, the following escape sequences may be used. The \x escape sequence is a common extension; it is not part of **POSIX** awk.

Sequence	Meaning	Sequence	Meaning
\a	Alert (bell)	\v	Vertical tab
\b	Backspace	\\	Literal backslash
\f	Form feed	*nnn*	Octal value *nnn*
\n	Newline	\x*nn*	Hexadecimal value *nn*
\r	Carriage return	\"	Literal double quote (in strings)
\t	Tab	\/	Literal slash (in regular expressions)

USER-DEFINED FUNCTIONS

Nawk allows you to define your own functions. This makes it easy to encapsulate sequences of steps that need to be repeated into a single place, and reuse the code from anywhere in your programme. Note: for user-defined functions, no space is allowed between the function name and the left parenthesis when the function is called.

The following function capitalizes each word in a string. It has one parameter, named input, and five local variables, which are written as extra parameters.

```
 # capitalize each word in a string
 function capitalize(input, result, words, n,
i, w)
 {
        result = ""
        n = split(input, words, " ")
        for (i = 1; i <= n; i++) {
             w = words[i]
             w = toupper(substr(w, 1, 1))
                 substr(w, 2)
             if (i > 1)
                     result = result " "
             result = result w
        }
        return result
    }
    # main programme, for testing
    { print capitalize($0)}
```

With this input data:

A test line with words and numbers like 12 on it.

This programme produces:

A Test Line With Words And Numbers Like 12 on it.

Group Listing of awk Functions and Commands

Table. Classifies Awk Functions and Commands

Arithmetic Programme-Functions	String Functions	Control Flow Statements	I/O Processing	Time	Ming Functions
atan2[3]	gensub[4]	break	close[3]	strftime[4]	delete[3]
cos[3]	gsub[3]	continue	fflush[5]	systime[4]	function[3]
exp	index	do/while[3]	getline[3]		system[3]

int	length	exit	next
log	match[3]	for	nextfile[5]
rand[3]	split	if	print
sin[3]	sprintf	return[3]	printf
sqrt	sub[3]	while	
srand[3]	substr		
	tolower[3]		
	toupper[3]		

[3] Available in nawk.
[4] Available in gawk.
[5] Available in Bell Labs awk and gawk.

IMPLEMENTATION LIMITS

Many versions of awk have various implementation limits, on things such as:

- Number of fields per record
- Number of characters per input record
- Number of characters per output record
- Number of characters per field
- Number of characters per printf string
- Number of characters in literal string
- Number of characters in character class
- Number of files open
- Number of pipes open
- The ability to handle 8-bit characters and characters that are all zero (**ASCII NUL**)

gawk does not have limits on any of these items, other than those imposed by the machine architecture and/or the operating system.

FUNCTIONS AND COMMANDS

The following alphabetical list of keywords and functions includes all that are available in awk, nawk, and gawk. nawk includes all old awk functions and keywords, plus some additional ones (marked as {N}). gawk includes all nawk functions and keywords, plus some additional ones (marked as {G}). Items marked with {B} are available in the Bell Labs awk. Items that aren't marked with a symbol are available in all versions.

atan2

atan2(y, x)

Return the arctangent of *y*/*x* in radians. {N}

break

zzz break

Exit from a while, for, or do loop.

close

close(filename-expr)

close(command-expr)

In most implementations of awk, you can have only 10 files open simultaneously and one pipe. Therefore, nawk provides a close function that allows you to close a file or a pipe. It takes as an argument the same expression that opened the pipe or file. This expression must be identical, character by character, to the one that opened the file or pipe; even whitespace is significant. {N}

continue

continue

Begin next iteration of while, for, or do loop.

cos

cos(x)

Return the cosine of *x*, an angle in radians. {N}

delete

delete array[element]

delete array

Delete *elcment* from *array*. The brackets are typed literally. The second form is a common extension, which deletes *all* elements of the array at one shot. {N}

do

do

statement

while (expr)

Looping statement. Execute *statement*, then evaluate *expr* and, if true, execute *statement* again. A series of statements must be put within braces. {N}

exit

exit [expr]

Exit from script, reading no new input. The END

procedure, if it exists, will be executed. An optional *expr* becomes awk's return value.

exp

```
exp(x)
```

Return exponential of *x* (e^x).

fflush

```
fflush([output-expr])
```

Flush any buffers associated with open output file or pipe *output-expr*. {B}

gawk extends this function. If no *output-expr* is supplied, it flushes standard output. If *output-expr* is the null string (""), it flushes all open files and pipes. {G}

for

```
for (init-expr; test-expr; incr-expr)
statement
```

C-style looping construct. *init-expr* assigns the initial value of a counter variable. *test-expr* is a relational expression that is evaluated each time before executing the *statement*. When *test-expr* is false, the loop is exited. *incr-expr* increments the counter variable after each pass. All the expressions are optional. A missing *test-expr* is considered to be true. A series of statements must be put within braces.

for

```
for (item in array)
      statement
```

Special loop designed for reading associative arrays. For each element of the array, the *statement* is executed; the element can be referenced by*array*[*item*]. A series of statements must be put within braces.

function

```
function name(parameter-list)
statements
{
}
```

Create *name* as a user-defined function consisting of awk *statements* that apply to the specified list of parameters. No space is allowed between *name*and the left paren when the function is called. {N} getline

```
getline [var] [< file]
    or
command | getline [var]
```

Read next line of input. Original awk doesn't support the syntax to open multiple input streams. The first form reads input from *file*; the second form reads the output of *command*. Both forms read one record at a time, and each time the statement is executed, it gets the next record of input.

The record is assigned to $0 and is parsed into fields, setting **NF**, **NR** and **FNR**. If *var* is specified, the result is assigned to *var*, and $0 and **NF** aren't changed. Thus, if the result is assigned to a variable, the current record doesn't change.

getline is actually a function and returns 1 if it reads a record successfully, 0 if end-of-file is encountered, and –1 if it's otherwise unsuccessful. {N}

gensub

```
gensub(r, s, h [, t])
```

General substitution function. Substitute *s* for matches of the regular expression *r* in the string *t*. If *h* is a number, replace the *h*th match. If it is "g" or"G", substitute globally. If *t* is not supplied, $0 is used. Return the new string value. The original *t* is *not* modified. (Compare gsub and sub.) {G}

gsub

```
gsub(r, s [, t])
```

Globally substitute *s* for each match of the regular expression *r* in the string *t*. If *t* is not supplied, defaults to $0. Return the number of substitutions. {N}

if

```
if (condition)
  statement
[else
    statement]
```

If *condition* is true, do *statement(s)*; otherwise do *statement* in the optional else clause. The *condition* can be an expression using any of the relational operators <, ⇐, ==, !=, ⇒, or >, as well as the array membership operator in, and the pattern-matching operators ~ and !~ (e.g., if ($1 ~/[Aa].*/)). A series of statements must be put within braces. Another if can directly follow an else in order to produce a chain of tests or decisions.

index

`index(str, substr)`

Return the position (starting at 1) of *substr* in *str*, or zero if *substr* is not present in *str*.

int

`int(x)`

Return integer value of *x* by truncating any fractional part.

length

`length([arg])`

Return length of *arg*, or the length of $0 if no argument.

log

`log(x)`

Return the natural logarithm (base *e*) of *x*.

match

`match(s, r)`

Function that matches the pattern, specified by the regular expression *r*, in the string *s*, and returns either the position in *s*, where the match begins, or 0 if no occurrences are found. Sets the values of **RSTART** and **RLENGTH** to the start and length of the match, respectively. {N}

next

`next`

Read next input line and start new cycle through pattern/ procedures statements.

nextfile

`nextfile`

Stop processing the current input file and start new cycle through pattern/procedures statements, beginning with the first record of the next file. {B} {G}

print

`print [ output-expr[,...]] [ dest-expr ]`

Evaluate the *output-expr* and direct it to standard output, followed by the value of ORS. Each comma-separated *output-expr* is separated in the output by the value of OFS. With no *output-expr*, print $0.

Output Redirections

dest-expr is an optional expression that directs the output to a file or pipe.

> file

Directs the output to a file, overwriting its previous contents.

>> *file*

Appends the output to a file, preserving its previous contents. In both cases, the file is created if it does not already exist.

| command

Directs the output as the input to a Unix command. Be careful not to mix > and >> for the same file. Once a file has been opened with >, subsequent output statements continue to append to the file until it is closed.

Remember to call close() when you have finished with a file or pipe. If you don't, eventually you will hit the system limit on the number of simultaneously open files.

printf

printf(format [, expr-list]) [dest-expr]

An alternative output statement borrowed from the C language. It can produce formatted output and also output data without automatically producing a newline. *format* is a string of format specifications and constants. *expr-list* is a list of arguments corresponding to format specifiers.

Format follows the conventions of the C-language *printf*(3S) library function. Here are a few of the most common formats:

%s	A string.
%d	A decimal number.
%*n.m*f	A floating-point number; *n* = total number of digits. *m* = number of digits after decimal point.
%[–]*nc*	*n* specifies minimum field length for format type *c*, while - left-justifies value in field; otherwise, value is right-justified.

Like any string, *format* can also contain embedded escape sequences: \n (newline) or \t (tab) being the most common.

Spaces and literal text can be placed in the *format* argument by quoting the entire argument. If there are multiple expressions to be printed, there should be multiple formats specified.

Example: Using the script.

```
{ printf("The sum on line %d is %.0f.\n", NR,
$1+$2)}
```

The following input line:

```
5    5
```

Produces this output, followed by a newline:

```
The sum on line 1 is 10.
```

rand

rand()

Generate a random number between 0 and 1. This function returns the same series of numbers each time the script is executed, unless the random number generator is seeded using srand(). {N}

return

return [expr]

Used within a user-defined function to exit the function, returning value of *expr*. The return value of a function is undefined if *expr* is not provided. {N}

sin

sin(x)

Return the sine of *x*, an angle in radians. {N}

split

split(*string, array* [, *sep*])

Split *string* into elements of array *array*[1],...,*array*[*n*]. The string is split at each occurrence of separator *sep*. If *sep* is not specified, FS is used. The number of array elements created is returned.

sprintf

sprintf(*format* [, *expressions*])

Return the formatted value of one or more *expressions*, using the specified *format* (see printf). Data is formatted but not printed. {N}

sqrt

sqrt(*arg*)

Return square root of *arg*.

srand

`srand([expr])`

Use optional *expr* to set a new seed for the random number generator. Default is the time of day. Return value is the old seed. {N}

strftime

`strftime([format [,timestamp]])`

Format *timestamp* according to *format*. Return the formatted string. The *timestamp* is a time-of-day value in seconds since midnight, January 1, 1970, UTC. The *format* string is similar to that of sprintf. (See the Example for systime.) If *timestamp* is omitted, it defaults to the current time. If *format*is omitted, it defaults to a value that produces output similar to that of date. {G}

sub

`sub(r, s [, t])`

Substitute *s* for first match of the regular expression *r* in the string *t*. If *t* is not supplied, defaults to $0. Return 1 if successful; 0 otherwise. {N}

substr

`substr(string, beg [, len])`

Return substring of *string* at beginning position *beg* and the characters that follow to maximum specified length *len*. If no length is given, use the rest of the string.

system

`system(command)`

Function that executes the specified *command* and returns its status. The status of the executed command typically indicates success or failure. A value of 0 means that the command executed successfully. A nonzero value indicates a failure of some sort. The documentation for the command you're running will give you the details.

The output of the command is *not* available for processing within the awk script. Use *command* | getline to read the output of a command into the script. {N}

systime

`systime()`

Return a time-of-day value in seconds since midnight, January 1, 1970, UTC. {G} *Example*: Log the start and end times of a data-processing programme:

```
BEGIN {
        now = systime()
        mesg = strftime("Started at %m/%d/%Y
        %H:%M:%S", now)
        print mesg
}
process data ...
END {
        now = systime()
        mesg = strftime("Ended at %m/%d/%Y
      %H:%M:%S", now)
        print mesg
}
```

Tolower

`tolower(str)`

Translate all uppercase characters in *str* to lowercase and return the new string.[6] {N}

[6] Very early versions of nawk don't support tolower() and toupper(). However, they are now part of the **POSIX** specification forawk, and are included in the SVR4 nawk.

toupper

`toupper(str)`

Translate all lowercase characters in *str* to uppercase and return the new string. {N}

while

```
while (condition)
statement
```

Do *statement* while *condition* is true (see if for a description of allowable conditions). A series of statements must be put within braces.

Printf Formats

Format specifiers for printf and sprintf have the following form:

`%[flag][width][.precision]letter`

The control letter is required. The format conversion control letters are as follows.

Character	Description
c	ASCII character
d	Decimal integer
i	Decimal integer (added in POSIX)
e	Floating-point format ([–]*d.precision*e[+–]*dd*)
E	Floating-point format ([–]*d.precision*E[+–]*dd*)
f	Floating-point format ([–]*ddd.precision*)
g	e or f conversion, whichever is shortest, with trailing zeros removed
G	E or f conversion, whichever is shortest, with trailing zeros removed
o	Unsigned octal value
s	String
x	Unsigned hexadecimal number; uses a-f for 10 to 15
X	Unsigned hexadecimal number; uses A-F for 10 to 15
%	Literal %

The optional flag is one of the following:

Character	Description
–	Left-justify the formatted value within the field.
space	Prefix positive values with a space and negative values with a minus.
+	Always prefix numeric values with a sign, even if the value is positive.
#	Use an alternate form: %o has a preceding 0; %x and %X are prefixed with 0x and 0X, respectively; %e, %E, and %f always have a decimal point in the result; and %g and %G do not have trailing zeros removed.
0	Pad output with zeros, not spaces. This happens only when the field width is wider than the converted result.

The optional *width* is the minimum number of characters to output. The result will be padded to this size if it is smaller. The 0 flag causes padding with zeros; otherwise, padding is with spaces.

The *precision* is optional. Its meaning varies by control letter, as shown in this table.

Conversion	Precision Means
%d, %i, %o %u, %x, %X	The minimum number of digits to print
%e, %E, %f	The number of digits to the right of the decimal point
%g, %G	The maximum number of significant digits
%s	The maximum number of characters to print

Chapter 2

ABC of Programming Language

ABC LANGUAGE

ABC is an interactive programming language and environment for personal computing, originally intended as a good replacement for **BASIC**. It was designed by first doing a *task analysis* of the programming task. ABC is easy to learn (an hour or so for someone who has already programmed), and yet easy to use. Originally intended as a language for beginners, it has evolved into a powerful tool for beginners and experts alike.

Here is an example function *words* to collect the set of all words in a document:

```
HOW TO RETURN words document:
  PUT {} IN collection
  FOR line IN document:
     FOR word IN split line:
       IF word not.in collection:
         INSERT word IN collection
     RETURN collection
```

Some features of the language:

- A powerful collection of only 5 data types that can easily be combined.
- Strong typing, yet without declarations.
- No limitations (such as max int), apart from sheer exhaustion of memory.
- Refinements to support top-down programming.
- Nesting by indentation.
- Programmes typically one fourth or one fifth the size of the equivalent Pascal or C.

Some features of the environment:

- No need for files: procedures and functions and global variables remain after logging out
- One consistent face is shown to the user at all times, whether executing commands, editing, or entering input to a programme.
- Generalized undo mechanism.

THE LANGUAGE

ABC is an imperative language originally designed as a replacement for **BASIC**: interactive, very easy to learn, but structured, high-level, and easy to use. ABC has been designed iteratively, and the present version is the 4th iteration. The previous versions were called B (not to be confused with the predecessor of C). It is suitable for general everyday programming, the sort of programming that you would use **BASIC**, Pascal, or AWK for. It is not a systems-programming language. It is an excellent teaching language, and because it is interactive, excellent for prototyping. It is much faster than Unix 'bc' for doing quick calculations.

ABC programmes are typically very compact, around a quarter to a fifth the size of the equivalent Pascal or C programme. However, this is not at the cost of readability, on the contrary in fact (see the examples below).

ABC is simple to learn due to the small number of types in the language (five).

If you already know Pascal or something similar you can learn the whole language in an hour or so. It is easy to use because the data-types are very high-level.

The five types are:

- *Numbers*: Unbounded length, with exact arithmetic the rule
- *Texts (strings)*: Also unbounded length
- *Compounds*: Records without field names
- *Lists*: Sorted collections of any one type of items (bags or multi-sets)
- *Tables*: Generalised arrays with any one type of keys, any one type of items (finite mappings).

THE ENVIRONMENT

The implementation includes a programming environment that makes producing programmes very much easier, since it knows a lot about the language, and can therefore do much of the work for you. For instance, if you type a W, the system suggests a command completion for you:

```
W?RITE ?
```

If that is what you want, you press [tab], and carry on typing the expression; if you wanted **WHILE,** you type an H, and the system changes the suggestion to match:

```
WH?ILE ?:
```

This mechanism works for commands you define yourself too. Similarly, if you type an open bracket or quote, you get the closing bracket or quote for free. You can ignore the suggestions if you want, and just type the commands full out. There is support for workspaces for developing different programmes.

Within each workspace variables are persistent, so that if you stop using ABC and come back later, your variables are still there as you left them. This obviates the need for file-handling facilities: there is no conceptual difference between a variable and a file in ABC.

The language is strongly-typed, but without declarations. Types are determined from context.

EXAMPLE

The (second) best way to appreciate the power of ABC is to see some examples (the first is to use it). In what follows, >>> is the prompt from ABC.

There are five types in the language: Two basic — Numbers and Texts — and three structured — Compounds, Lists, and Tables.

Numbers

Numbers are unbounded, and stored exact:

```
    >>> WRITE 2**1000
37 10 71 50 86 07 18 62 67 32 09 48 42 50 49
06 00 01 81 05 61 40 48 11 70 55 33 60 74 43
```

```
75 03 88
69 03 51 05 11 24 93 61 22 49 31 98 37 88 15
69 58 58 12 75 94 67 29 17 55 31 46 82 51 87
14 52 85
69 23 14 04 35 98 45 77 57 46 98 57 48 03 93
45 67 77 48 24 23 09 85 42 10 74 60 50 62 37
11 41 87
79 54 18 21 53 04 64 74 98 35 81 94 12 67 39
87 67 55 91 65 54 39 46 07 70 62 91 45 71
19 64  77 68
65 42 16 76 60 42 98 31 65 26 24 38 68 37 20
56 68 06 93 76
  >>> PUT 1/(2**1000) IN x
  >>> WRITE 1 + 1/x
37 10 71 50 86 07 18 62 67 32 09 48 42 50 49
06 00 01 81 05 61 40 48 11 70 55 33 60 74
43 75 03 88
37 03 51 05 11 24 93 61 22 49 31 98 37 88 15
69 58 58 12 75 94 67 29 17 55 31 46 82 51 87
14 52 85
69 23 14 04 35 98 45 77 57 46 98 57 48 03 93
45 67 77 48 24 23 09 85 42 10 74 60 50 62 37
11 41 87
79 54 18 21 53 04 64 74 98 35 81 94 12 67 39
87 67 55 91 65 54 39 46 07 70 62 91 45 71 19
64 77 68
65 42 16 76 60 42 98 31 65 26 24 38 68 37 20
56 68 06 93 77
```

Non-exact numbers use machine-precision:

```
  >>> WRITE root 2
  1.414213562373095
```

Texts

Texts (strings of characters) are also unbounded:

```
  >>> PUT ("ha " ^^ 3) ^ ("ho " ^^ 3) IN
laugh
  >>> WRITE laugh
  ha ha ha ho ho ho
```

```
>>> WRITE #laugh
18
>>> PUT "Hello! "^^1000 IN greeting
>>> WRITE #greeting
7000
>>> WRITE greeting|4
Hell
>>> WRITE greeting@4|3
lo!
```

Lists

Lists are sorted lists of values of any one other type:

```
>>> WRITE {1..10}
{1; 2; 3; 4; 5; 6; 7; 8; 9; 10}
>>> PUT {1..10} IN l
>>> REMOVE 5 FROM l
>>> INSERT 4 IN l
>>> INSERT pi IN l
>>> WRITE l
{1; 2; 3; 3.141592653589793; 4; 4; 6; 7; 8;
9; 10}
```

You can have lists of any type, so here is a list of lists:

```
>>> PUT {} IN ll
>>> FOR i IN {1..3}:
        INSERT {1..i} IN ll
>>> WRITE ll
{{1}; {1; 2}; {1; 2; 3}}
>>> FOR l IN ll:
        WRITE l /
{1}
{1; 2}
{1; 2; 3}
>>> WRITE #ll
3
```

Compounds

Compounds are like records or structures, but without field names:

```
>>> PUT ("Square root of 2", root 2) IN c
```

```
>>> WRITE c
("Square root of 2", 1.414213562373095)
>>> PUT c IN name, value
>>> WRITE name
Square root of 2
>>> WRITE value
1.414213562373095
```

Tables

Programming resemble arrays:

```
>>> PUT {} IN tel
>>> PUT 4054 IN tel["Jennifer"]
>>> PUT 4098 IN tel["Timo"]
>>> PUT 4134 IN tel["Guido"]
>>> WRITE tel["Jennifer"]
4054
```

You can write all ABC values out. Tables are kept sorted on the keys:

```
>>> WRITE tel
{["Guido"]: 4134; ["Jennifer"]: 4054;
["Timo"]: 4098}
```

The *keys* function returns a list:

```
>>> WRITE keys tel
{"Guido"; "Jennifer"; "Timo"}
>>> FOR name IN keys tel:
      WRITE name, ":", tel[name]/
Guido: 4134
Jennifer: 4054
Timo: 4098
```

PROGRAMME EXAMPLE

The best way to appreciate the power of ABC is to see some examples (the first is to use it). In the examples, >>> is the prompt from ABC.

Some of these articles are followed by a link to a source file for the programme.

These source files were produced by using the 'abc -p' option for packing a workspace. To unpack it in your own workspaces, save the file as F, choose the name of your new workspace W, and say:

```
abc -u -w W F
```

(you may freely choose the names W and F, but avoid using an existing workspace name for W).

A Telephone List

This uses the programming data-type. In use, tables resemble arrays:

```
>>> PUT {} IN tel
>>> PUT 4054 IN tel["Jennifer"]
>>> PUT 4098 IN tel["Timo"]
>>> PUT 4134 IN tel["Guido"]
>>> WRITE tel["Jennifer"]
4054
```

You can write all ABC values out. Tables are kept sorted on the keys:

```
>>> WRITE tel
{["Guido"]: 4134; ["Jennifer"]: 4054; ["Timo"]:
4098}
```

The *keys* function returns a list:

```
>>> WRITE keys tel
{"Guido"; "Jennifer"; "Timo"}
>>> FOR name IN keys tel:
        WRITE name, ":", tel[name]/
Guido: 4134
Jennifer: 4054
Timo: 4098
```

You can define your own commands:

```
HOW TO DISPLAY t:
    FOR name IN keys t:
        WRITE name<<10, t[name]/
>>> DISPLAY tel
Guido 4134
Jennifer 4054
Timo 4098
```

To find the user of a given number, you can use a quantifier:

```
>>> IF SOME name IN keys tel HAS tel[name]
```

```
  = 4054:
WRITE name
    Jennifer
```

Or create the inverse programming:

```
>>> PUT {} IN subscriber
>>> FOR name IN keys tel:
        PUT name IN subscriber[tel[name]]
>>> WRITE subscriber[4054]
Jennifer
>>> WRITE subscriber
{[4054]: "Jennifer"; [4098]: "Timo"; [4134]:
"Guido"}
```

Commands and functions are polymorphic:

```
>>> DISPLAY subscriber
4054        Jennifer
4098        Timo
4134        Guido
```

Functions may return any type. Note that indentation is significant - there are no BEGIN-END's or {}'s:

```
HOW TO RETURN inverse t:
   PUT {} IN inv
FOR k IN keys t:
   PUT k IN inv[t[k]]
RETURN inv
>>> WRITE inverse tel
{[4054]: "Jennifer"; [4098]: "Timo"; [4134]:
"Guido"}
>>> DISPLAY inverse inverse tel
Guido 4134
```

A Cross-reference Indexer

Text files' are represented as tables of numbers to strings:

```
HOW TO DISPLAY t:
    FOR name IN keys t:
       WRITE name<<10, t[name]/
>>> DISPLAY poem
1          I've never seen a purple cow
2          I hope I never see one
```

```
3          But I can tell you anyhow
4          I'd rather see than be one
```

The following function takes such a document, and returns the cross-reference index of the document.

A programming from words to lists of line-numbers:

```
HOW TO RETURN index doc:
   PUT {} IN where
   FOR line.no IN keys doc:
       TREAT LINE
   RETURN where
TREAT LINE:
   FOR word IN split doc[line.no]:
       IF word not.in keys where:
          PUT {} IN where[word]
       INSERT line.no IN where[word]
```

TREAT LINE here is a refinement, directly supporting stepwise-refinement. 'split' is a function that splits a string into its space-separated words:

```
>>> WRITE split "Hello world"
{[1]: "Hello"; [2]: "world"}
>>> DISPLAY index poem
But          {3}
I            {2; 2; 3}
I'd          {4}
I've         {1}
a            {1}
anyhow       {3}
be           {4}
can          {3}
cow          {1}
hope         {2}
never        {1; 2}
one          { 2; 4}
purple       {1}
rather       {4}
see          {2; 4}
seen         {1}
```

An Adventure Game (source)

Adventure style games are very popular in computing circles, and I'm going to develop a small one here. Because of space I will have to leave out many of the advanced features of most adventure games, but it will give you an idea of how it looks in ABC. And of course it will be obvious how the bells and whistles can quickly be added on.

As I'm sure you know, a (textual) adventure programme works by describing a scene. You then give instructions on where to go, or what to do, and it responds by telling you what happened as a result.

For instance, if it says

```
You are standing by a building at the end
of a road.
```

A spring flows from the building.

and you reply

```
> enter building
```

it might reply

```
You are inside a building, a well house
for a spring.
There is a bottle here.
There are some keys here.
```

after which the dialogue might proceed as follows:

```
> take keys
> leave the building
Please use 1 or 2 word sentences.
> leave
You are outside the building.
> go west
You are standing by a stream.
> go south
You are at a small slit that the stream
runs down.
A dry river bed carries on ahead.
> go down
You don't seem to be able to go that
way.
```

```
    > south
    You have found a metal grate fixed
  into the ground.
    > down
    Sorry, you can't do that.
    > open grate
    The grate is open.
    You are at a hole in the ground.
    There is a metal grate lying on the
  ground.
    > down
    You are in a dim chamber.
    A hole in the ceiling shows the sky
  above.
```

and so on.

The main programme making up this adventure looks like this:

```
HOW TO ADVENTURE:
    START
  GET command
  WHILE command <> "quit":
    OBEY command
    GET command
  FINISH
```

START will initialise some variables, like the place where the player is, and what the player is holding. FINISH will print out the score and so on. GET will print the prompt, read a line, strip off spaces, and reduce it to lower-case:

```
HOW TO GET command:
    GET LINE
    WHILE command = "": GET LINE
GET LINE:
    WRITE "> "
    READ command RAW
    PUT lower stripped command IN command
```

OBEY has to split a command into its constituent words, and then decide what action needs to be taken for that command:

```
HOW TO OBEY command:
```

```
SPLIT command INTO verb AND object
SELECT:
   verb = "": PASS
    special command: TRY TO MOVE command
    verb = "move": TRY TO MOVE object
   verb = "take": TRY TO TAKE object
   verb = "drop": TRY TO DROP object
    verb = "kill": TRY TO KILL object
    verb = "what": INVENTORY
    ELSE: CAN'T DO verb, object
```

SPLIT does what its name suggests: splits the command into its constituent words, and makes sure it only consists of one or two words:

```
HOW TO SPLIT command INTO verb AND object:
  PUT split command IN words
  SELECT:
     #words = 1: PUT words item 1, "" IN
    verb, object
     #words = 2: PUT words item 1, words
    item 2 IN verb, object
     ELSE:
        WRITE "Please use 1 or 2 word
       sentences."/
        PUT "", "" IN verb, object
```

A nice feature is to allow synonyms for commands, to allow "go west" and "proceed west" and "move west" all to mean the same thing.

We can do that by having a programming of synonyms:

```
>>> WRITE synonyms["move"]
{"go"; "proceed"}
```

and then adding in SPLIT:

```
SHARE synonyms
...
IF SOME word IN keys synonyms HAS verb
      in synonyms[word]: PUT word IN verb
```

Moving Places

In this adventure, each place has a name, which is a short

description you get each time you visit it after the first time ("You are x", such as "outside the building" above). Then, each place has a long description used for describing it the first time you go there. Such a description is stored as a programming of lines, for instance.

```
>>> WRITE description["inside large hall"]
{[1]: "This is a large hall."; [2]: "There
is an exit to the west."}
```

To display such a message neatly, we can define the following command:

```
HOW TO DISPLAY message:
   FOR line IN message:
      WRITE line /
>>> DISPLAY description["inside large hall"]
This is a large hall.
There is an exit to the west.
```

Then there is a map of all locations, which gives for each location a programming of directions that the player can go in, and where that direction leads to.

```
>>> WRITE map["inside the building"]
{["out"]: "outside the building"}
>>> WRITE map["outside the building"]
{["in"]: "inside the building"; ["south"]:
"standing by the stream";
["west"]: "in the forest"}
```

We can play a nasty trick on the player:

```
>>> WRITE map["in the forest"]
{["east"]: "in the forest"; ["north"]:
"in the forest";
["south"]: "in the forest"; ["west"]:
"standing by the stream"}
```

Moving is attempted by means of the command TRY TO MOVE. All commands beginning TRY TO first check that the conditions for the action are acceptable, and only then do the action. The current location is held in *place*:

TRY TO MOVE *checks that the direction asked for is in the map for the current place:*

```
HOW TO TRY TO MOVE direction:
```

```
        SHARE map, place
        SELECT:
            direction = "":
              WRITE "Where to?"/
            direction in keys map[place]:
  MOVE TO map[place][direction]
ELSE:
  WRITE "You don't seem to be able to go that
   way"/
```

MOVE TO does the actual moving. For now here is a simple version, but it will get more involved later.

```
HOW TO MOVE TO there:
   SHARE place
   PUT there IN place
  DESCRIBE place
```

(**DESCRIBE** describes a place and the objects to be found there; you'll see it shortly.)

In **OBEY**, *you will have noticed the lines*:

```
SELECT:
   special command: TRY TO MOVE command
```

This is to allow the player to say *south* instead of *go south,* by seeing if the command is already in the map for the current place:

```
HOW TO REPORT special command:
   SHARE map, place
   REPORT command in keys map[place]
```

Notice that it also allows you to use commands instead of directions in the map. For instance, when at the grate, you can open the grate by having two places, an open grate and a closed grate:

```
>>> WRITE map["at closed grate"]
{["north"]: "at slit"; ["open grate"]: "at
open grate"}
```

Taking and Dropping Objects

Different objects are left lying about at various places. These are recorded in a programming *objects.* Just as with places, each object has a simple name, to be used when the player wants to know what is being carried, and a longer description when an object is first found.

```
>>> WRITE objects["inside the building"]
{"bottle"; "keys"}
>>> WRITE description["keys"]
There are some keys here.
```

Now I can show you **DESCRIBE.** It remembers which places have already been described (and therefore visited), and only gives the long description the first time:

```
HOW TO DESCRIBE place:
  SHARE description, objects, visited
  SELECT:
    place in visited:
        WRITE "You are ", place /
    ELSE:
        DISPLAY description[place]
        INSERT place IN visited
  FOR object IN objects for place:
      DISPLAY description[object]
```

Notice here the line "**FOR** object **IN** objects for place:". Not every place may be recorded in the objects programming, so it is a shorthand to save repeated checks to see if it is:

```
HOW TO RETURN property for thing:
   SELECT:
     thing in keys property: RETURN
     property[thing]
       ELSE: RETURN {}
```

You'll find it used again later on.

Then there is a list of what the player is carrying, called *holding,* which is initially empty. To find out what is being carried, the player can ask for an inventory:

```
HOW TO INVENTORY:
   SHARE holding
    SELECT:
     holding = {}:
         WRITE "You aren't carrying anything"
         /
     ELSE:
```

```
        WRITE "You are carrying: "
        LIST holding
```

This uses a useful command to neatly print a list of objects:

```
    HOW TO LIST things:
        PUT "" IN separator
        FOR object IN things:
            WRITE separator, object
            PUT ", " IN separator
        WRITE /
>>> LIST objects["inside the building"]
bottle, keys
```

Another useful tool is a test to see if an object is currently being carried:

```
HOW TO REPORT carrying object:
    SHARE holding
    REPORT object in holding
```

and another to test if an object is present:

```
HOW TO REPORT present object:
    SHARE objects, place
    REPORT object in objects for place
```

TRY TO TAKE can now check that the object is present, that it's not already being carried and so on, before actually taking it:

```
HOW TO TRY TO TAKE object:
    SHARE holding
    SELECT:
        object = "":
            WRITE "Which object?"/
        carrying object:
            WRITE "You're already carrying it!"
            /
        NOT present object:
            WRITE "I see no `object`."/
        #holding > 6:
            WRITE "You can't carry any more."
            /
        ELSE:
            TAKE object
```

TAKE looks like this, again a simple version for now:

```
HOW TO TAKE object:
    SHARE holding, objects, place
    REMOVE object FROM objects[place]
    INSERT object IN holding
```

TRY TO DROP is similar:

```
HOW TO TRY TO DROP object:
    SELECT:
      object = "": WRITE "Which object?"
      /
      NOT carrying object: WRITE "You're
      not holding it!"/
      ELSE: DROP object
      HOW TO DROP object:
      SHARE holding, objects, place
      REMOVE object FROM holding
      INCLUDE object IN objects FOR
    place
```

The command INCLUDE adds an item to a programming:

```
  HOW TO INCLUDE object IN property FOR
thing:
    IF thing not.in keys property:
        PUT {} IN property[thing]
    INSERT object IN property[thing]
```

Conditions and Side Effects

One of the tricks of adventure games is that certain actions are not possible unless you are at a certain place, or you are carrying a certain thing, and some actions have unexpected side-effects.

For instance, you shouldn't be able to open the grate if you aren't carrying the keys.

So we can alter MOVE TO to check for this:

```
HOW TO MOVE TO there:
  SHARE place
  SELECT:
    opening.grate AND NOT carrying "keys":
      WRITE "I don't seem able to open the
```

```
      grate"/
   ELSE:
      PUT there IN place
      DESCRIBE place
   opening.grate:
      REPORT (place, there) = ("at closed
    grate", "at open grate")
```

Similarly, somewhere in the cave there is a bird, but you can only catch it if you're carrying the cage. Furthermore, the jangling of the keys frightens it.

So we can alter TAKE to do this:

```
HOW TO TAKE object:
   SHARE holding, objects, place
   SELECT:
      object = "bird" AND carrying "keys":
         WRITE "The bird flutters off in
         fright."/
      object = "bird" AND NOT carrying
      "cage":
         WRITE "You don't seem able to
         catch the bird."/
   ELSE:
      REMOVE object FROM objects[place]
      INSERT object IN holding
```

An example of a side-effect is that dropping the bird is the only way to scare off the snake (should you meet it):

```
HOW TO DROP object:
   SHARE holding, objects, place
   IF object = "bird" AND present "snake":
      WRITE "With a great flurry the bird
      attacks the snake."/
      WRITE "The snake flees into the
   darkness."/
      REMOVE "snake" FROM objects[place]
      REMOVE object FROM holding
      INCLUDE object IN objects FOR place
```

(Obviously, TAKE should also be changed to prevent you from trying to take the snake.)

Removing Objects with Extreme Prejudice

Now you've seen that there are living creatures in the cave. Certain of them are undesirable to the player's well-being and score, and in the brutal tradition of adventure games must be eliminated.

Of course some are harmless, but computers only do what they are told...

```
HOW TO TRY TO KILL object:
  SELECT:
  object = "":
    WRITE "Which object?"/
  (NOT present object) AND (NOT carrying object):
    WRITE "I see no `object`"/
  ELSE:
    KILL object
HOW TO KILL object:
  SHARE holding, objects, place
  SELECT:
  object = "bird":
    WRITE "How cruel! The poor bird dies with a mournful peep."/
    ELIMINATE
    INCLUDE "dead bird" IN objects FOR place
  object = "snake":
    WRITE "Attacking the snake is both dangerous and ineffective."/
  ELSE: It's not a living creature
    WRITE "It's already dead!"/
ELIMINATE:
  SELECT:
  carrying object: REMOVE object FROM holding
  present object: REMOVE object FROM objects[place]
```

Odds and Ends

Well, that's the body of the adventure. Of course, lots of extra places, objects, beings and commands must be added, but that's just a case of more of the same. In **OBEY**, if it can't obey your command, it invokes **CAN'T DO**. As a nicety this prints funny remarks for certain commands.

For instance, if you're at the stream, you might try "swim":

```
>>> DISPLAY funny["swim"]
The water would get into my circuits.
HOW TO CAN'T DO verb:
    SHARE funny
   SELECT:
    verb in keys funny: DISPLAY funny[verb]
    ELSE:
      WRITE "Sorry, you can't do that"/
```

As a final touch, you might want to add the commands "save" and "restore" to **OBEY**, so you can save a game, and come back later to it (or so you can try something, and if it fails restore it and try something else). This is remarkably easy. Since the state of the game is reflected by a small number of variables, you can just put them in another variable:

```
HOW TO SAVE:
  SHARE saved, holding, objects, place
  PUT holding, objects, place IN saved
HOW TO RESTORE:
  SHARE saved, holding, objects, place
  PUT saved IN holding, objects, place
```

Grammar Analysis (Source)

What follows is a brief description of some of the tools it use, with an example. Some of what follows is also presented in the book, though at a more relaxed pace).

Grammars

The representation that I use is more or less a direct transcription of what a grammar is. I use a programming whose keys are texts (i.e. strings) representing the nonterminals of the language, and whose items are sets of alternatives. Each alternative is a sequence of texts, representing terminals and nonterminals.

So here is a how-to that displays a grammar in this form:

```
HOW TO DISPLAY grammar:
```

```
FOR name IN keys grammar:
  WRITE "`name`: "/
  FOR alt IN grammar[name]:
    WRITE " "
    FOR symbol IN alt:
      WRITE symbol, " "
    WRITE /
```

and as example:

```
DISPLAY sentence
ADJ:
    EMPTY
    clev er
    shy
BOY:
    John
    Kevin
EMPTY:
GIRL:
    Mary
    Susan
OBJ:
    SUBJ
SENT:
    SUBJ loves OBJ
SUBJ:
    ADJ BOY
    ADJ GIRL
```

You can generate a random phrase from a grammar with the following:

```
HOW TO GENERATE sym FROM grammar:
  SELECT:
    sym in keys grammar: \ Nonterminal
        FOR new IN choice grammar[sym]:
            GENERATE new FROM grammar
    ELSE: \ Terminal symbol
       WRITE sym, " "
GENERATE "SENT" FROM sentence
Susan loves clever John
```

Sets

Here are some necessary functions on sets. Set union:

```
HOW TO RETURN set1 with set2: \ Union
   FOR x IN set2:
      IF x not.in set1:
         INSERT x IN set1
   RETURN set1
```

Set difference:

```
HOW TO RETURN set1 less set2: \ Difference
   FOR x IN set2:
      IF x in set1:
         REMOVE x FROM set1
   RETURN set1
```

Here is a function that collects all symbols used in the rules of a grammar:

```
HOW TO RETURN used grammar: \Collect all
used symbols
   PUT {} IN all
   FOR rule IN grammar:
      FOR alt IN rule:
         FOR sym IN alt:
            IF sym not.in all:
               INSERT sym IN all
   RETURN all
>>> WRITE used sentence
{"ADJ"; "BOY"; "EMPTY"; "GIRL"; "John";
"Kevin"; "Mary";
"OBJ"; "SUBJ"; "Susan"; "clever"; "loves";
"shy"}
```

The terminals of the grammar are all the symbols less the nonterminals:

```
WRITE (used sentence) less keys sentence
{"John"; "Kevin"; "Mary"; "Susan"; "clever";
"loves"; "shy"}
```

and the unused nonterminals (such as the root symbol) are the nonterminals less the used symbols:

>>> WRITE (keys sentence) less used sentence

{"SENT"}

For neater output, the function "listed" converts a set to a text:

```
HOW TO RETURN listed set:
  PUT "" IN line
  FOR element IN set:
     PUT line ^ "`element` " IN line
RETURN line
WRITE listed ((used sentence) less keys
sentence)
John Kevin Mary Susan clever loves shy
```

A useful set is the set of nonterminals that can generate empty. This is generated by repeatedly doing a pass over the rules that we don't know yet can generate empty, until we find no more:

```
HOW TO RETURN empties grammar:
  PUT keys grammar, {} IN to.do, empties
  WHILE SOME name IN to.do HAS empty.rule:
     INSERT name IN empties
     REMOVE name FROM to.do
  RETURN empties
empty.rule:
  REPORT SOME alt IN grammar[name] HAS
empty.alt
empty.alt:
  REPORT EACH sym IN alt HAS sym in empties
>>> WRITE listed empties sentence
ADJ EMPTY
```

Relations

Relations between symbols of the grammar are the essential element of the grammar tools. A relation is represented whose keys are symbols, and whose items are sets of symbols. For instance, if symbol b follows symbol a in some rule, "b" will be in the set for follows["a"], so you can say, for instance:

```
IF "b" in follows["a"]:
```

Relations are sparse (i.e. a symbol is not in the keys of the relation if the set of elements is empty), so we use the following to access a relation:

```
HOW TO RETURN relation for k: \relation[k]
for sparse relations
  IF k in keys relation:
    RETURN relation[k]
RETURN {}
```

To add an element to a relation, we use this:

```
HOW TO ADD element TO relation FOR thing:
    IF thing not.in keys relation: \First
   time
      PUT {} IN relation[thing]
   IF element not.in relation[thing]:
      INSERT element IN relation[thing]
```

though you may prefer

```
HOW TO ADD element TO relation FOR thing:
    PUT (relation for thing) with {element}
     IN relation[thing]
```

For instance:

>>> **ADD** "b" **TO** follows **FOR** "a"

We'll display a relation with:

```
HOW TO SHOW relation:
 FOR k IN keys relation:
 WRITE "`k`: ", listed relation[k]/
```

Here are some general functions on relations.

The inverse:

```
HOW TO RETURN inverse relation:
    PUT {} IN inv
     FOR k IN keys relation:
         FOR x IN relation[k]:
             ADD k TO inv FOR x
   RETURN inv
```

The product of two relations (a P c iff a R1 b and b R2 c):

```
HOW TO RETURN r1 prod r2: \product of relations
  PUT {} IN prod
  FOR c IN keys r2:
    FOR b IN r2[c]:
      IF b in keys r1:
```

```
        FOR a IN r1[b]:
            ADD a TO prod FOR c
    RETURN prod
```

The closure:

```
HOW TO RETURN closure r:
  FOR i IN keys r:
      FOR j IN keys r:
          IF i in r[j]:
            PUT r[i] with r[j] IN r[j]
    RETURN r
```

To make a relation reflexive, we use the following. Since relations are sparse, we also have to pass the set of symbols that it must be reflexive over:

```
HOW TO RETURN symbols reflexive relation: \make
the relation reflexive
  FOR sym IN symbols:
    ADD sym TO relation FOR sym
  RETURN relation
```

Some Examples of Relations

To collect the *direct* followers for each symbol, we walk along each alternative, collecting adjacent symbols.

There is one catch: in a rule like:

```
SENT: the ADJ PERSON
```

"the" and "**ADJ**" are adjacent, but if "**ADJ**" can generate empty, then so are "the" and "**PERSON**":

```
HOW TO RETURN followers grammar:
  PUT {}, empties grammar IN foll, empty
FOR rule IN grammar:
   FOR alt IN rule:
     TREAT ALT
  RETURN foll
TREAT ALT:
  FOR i IN {1..#alt-1}:
     PUT alt item i IN this
     TREAT PART
     TREAT PART:
       FOR j IN {i+1..#alt}:
```

```
            PUT alt item j IN next
            ADD next TO foll FOR this
            IF next not.in empty: QUIT
    SHOW followers sentence
    ADJ: BOY GIRL
    SUBJ: loves
    loves: OBJ
```

To collect the direct starter symbols of each rule, you also have to deal with symbols that produce empty:

```
HOW TO RETURN heads grammar:
  PUT {}, empties grammar IN heads, empty
  FOR name IN keys grammar:
      FOR alt IN grammar[name]:
        TREAT ALT
  RETURN heads
TREAT ALT:
    FOR i IN {1..#alt}:
        PUT alt item i IN head
        ADD head TO heads FOR name
        IF head not.in empty: QUIT
SHOW heads sentence
ADJ: EMPTY clever shy
BOY: John Kevin
GIRL: Mary Susan
OBJ: SUBJ
SENT: SUBJ
SUBJ: ADJ BOY GIRL
```

Similarly for the direct enders:

```
      HOW TO RETURN tails grammar:
     PUT {}, empties grammar IN tails, empty
     FOR name IN keys grammar:
         FOR alt IN grammar[name]:
            TREAT ALT
    RETURN tails
TREAT ALT:
    FOR i' IN {-#alt..-1}:
       PUT -i' IN i
        PUT alt item i IN tail
```

```
        ADD tail TO tails FOR name
        IF tail not.in empty: QUIT
```

The closure of the head relation represents all symbols that can start a rule, either directly or indirectly:

```
SHOW closure heads sentence
ADJ: EMPTY clever shy
BOY: John Kevin
GIRL: Mary Susan
OBJ: ADJ BOY EMPTY GIRL John Kevin Mary SUBJ
     Susan clever shy
SENT: ADJ BOY EMPTY GIRL John Kevin Mary SUBJ
Susan clever shy
SUBJ: ADJ BOY EMPTY GIRL John Kevin Mary
     Susan clever shy
```

Symbol b may follow symbol a in a phrase if b follows a in an alternative, or if B follows A in an alternative and b is in heads*(B) and a is in tails*(A). This is expressed as the product **`head*. follow . inverse(tail*).`**

Now we have enough to define a command that prints for each symbol in an alternative what may follow that symbol at that point:

```
HOW TO SHOW LOCAL FOLLOWERS grammar:
PUT (used grammar) with keys grammar IN symbols
PUT symbols reflexive (closure heads grammar)
   IN head.star
PUT symbols reflexive (closure tails grammar)
   IN tail.star
PUT followers grammar IN follow
PUT (head.star prod follow) prod (inverse
   tail.star) IN deep.follow
FOR parent IN keys grammar:
FOR alt IN grammar[parent]:
   TREAT ALT
TREAT ALT:
   ANNOUNCE ALT
   FOR i IN {1..#alt}:
      TREAT SYM
TREAT SYM:
```

```
PUT alt item i IN sym
WRITE " `sym`: ", listed local.follow /
local.follow:
  PUT {} IN foll
   FOR j IN {i+1..#alt}:
     PUT alt item j IN next
     PUT foll with (head.star for next) IN
   foll
     IF next not.in empty:
        RETURN foll
    RETURN foll with (deep.follow for parent)
ANNOUNCE ALT:
     WRITE "`parent`: ", listed alt /
```

This prints each alternative separately, followed by each symbol of the alternative indented one to a line followed by the symbols that can follow it at that point.

For example:

```
SHOW LOCAL FOLLOWERS sentence
ADJ: EMPTY
EMPTY: BOY GIRL John Kevin Mary Susan
ADJ: clever
clever: BOY GIRL John Kevin Mary Susan
ADJ: shy
shy: BOY GIRL John Kevin Mary Susan
BOY: John
John: loves
BOY: Kevin
Kevin: loves
EMPTY:
GIRL: Mary
Mary: loves
GIRL: Susan
Susan: loves
OBJ: SUBJ
SUBJ:
SENT: SUBJ loves OBJ
SUBJ: loves
loves: ADJ BOY EMPTY GIRL John Kevin Mary OBJ
```

```
SUBJ Susan clever shy
OBJ:
SUBJ: ADJ BOY
ADJ: BOY John Kevin
BOY: loves
SUBJ: ADJ GIRL
ADJ: GIRL Mary Susan
```

Logic Programming

In his article "(Extremely) Simple Logic Programming in *B*", Tim Budd presented a programme in *B* (the forerunner of ABC) for solving the "Farmer, Wolf, Goat and Cabbage in a boat trying to get to the other side of the river without eating each other" problem. The problem involves the four named trying to cross a river with a boat that can only take two of them at a time, with the added complication that only the farmer can row, and that the goat will eat the cabbage, and the wolf will eat the goat, if they are left without the farmer's supervision.

Tim's programme uses backtracking, and in the way it is formulated takes advantage of the fact that functions in *B* have no side-effects, in effect doing the backtracking automatically for you. However, the programme does have the 'side effect' of writing the results out as it goes along, rather than returning the result. When pointing this out, Tim says:

This is a two-edged sword, however, since in some cases one would like to modify the global environment and that then becomes more difficult.

In other words, if the effect you want to have is more than just writing your answer out, bad luck. The purpose of this article is to show that it is not at all difficult to write such a programme, both using ABC's automatic backtracking*and* returning a result.

Just for interest's sake, I shall also modify some other aspects of Tim's programme, to compare how different approaches to data-structures affect the programme, but this in no way affects the main point of the article, which is to demonstrate returning results in a backtracking programme.

A Solution: First of all, I'm going to alter how the positions of the participants are represented: Tim used a compound like (1, 1, 1, 1) to represent all four participants being on the north bank: each field was the position of one participant in the order: farmer, wolf, goat, cabbage; a zero represented the south bank.

Rather than represent north and south by 1 and 0, I shall use the texts "N" and "S" (I would have used "north" and "south", but this makes some of the lines below wider than will fit on the page). Tim said that he chose the integers to make the conversion from one to the other easier. For the text representation, we have to alter the definition of the function *opposite*:

```
HOW TO RETURN opposite position:
RETURN {["N"]: "S"; ["S"]: "N"}[position]
```

Just to test it:

```
WRITE opposite "N"
S
WRITE opposite "S"
N
```

Now a more explicit data-structure can be used to represent the positions,

```
{["cabbage"]: "N"; ["farmer"]: "N"; ["goat"]:
"N"; ["wolf"]: "N"}.
```

Next we need an easy method of altering the set of positions when a boat-load goes to the opposite bank. If we represent a boat-load by a list of who is in the boat, for instance {"farmer"; "goat"} then we can use the following function to take a position and a list of travellers and return the new position:

```
HOW TO RETURN position altered.for occupants:
  FOR occupant IN occupants:
    PUT opposite position[occupant] IN
  position[occupant]
    RETURN position
>>> PUT {} IN start
>>> FOR participant IN {"farmer"; "goat";
"wolf"; "cabbage"}:
```

```
      PUT "N" IN start[participant]
>>> WRITE start altered.for {"farmer"; "goat"}
{["cabbage"]: "N"; ["farmer"]: "S"; ["goat"]:
"S"; ["wolf"]: "N"}
```

We also need a way to see if a given position is 'safe', that is to say that the goat is not left alone with the cabbage, and that the wolf is not left alone with the goat:

```
HOW TO REPORT safe pos:
  REPORT farmer.with.goat OR
goat.out.of.mischief
farmer.with.goat:
  REPORT pos["farmer"] = pos["goat"]
goat.out.of.mischief:
  REPORT pos["cabbage"] <> pos["goat"] <>
pos["wolf"]
```

(Notice the shorthand c<>g<>w instead of c<>g **AND** g<>w. Another way of writing the same is g not.in {c; w}.)

Now, the new version of the programme to solve the river problem, instead of printing out its results as it goes along, will return the answer as a value. This result is a sequence of boat-loads necessary to solve the problem. Sequences are typically represented in ABC as tables with the elements of the sequence as items, and integers as keys. Elements are then added to the sequence with a command such as

```
      PUT element IN sequence[#sequence]
```

so that the first element is stored at key [0], the second at [1], and so on.

In this programme, the result is a sequence of boat-loads and so it will be represented as a programming with integers as indexes, and boat-loads as elements. The only difference is that the boat-loads are produced by the programme in reverse order to how they will be printed out, and so the elements will be added at the *head* of the sequence.

This can be done with the command PUT element IN path[-#path], which we can make into a function:

```
HOW TO RETURN path with element:
    PUT element IN path[-#path]
    RETURN path
```

An example of a sequence of boat-loads is

```
{[-2]: {"farmer"; "goat"}; [-1]: {"farmer"};
[0]: {"wolf"; "farmer"}}
```

representing the farmer taking the goat across the river, returning alone, and then taking the wolf.

The programme either succeeds, and produces such a path, or the (sub-)problem has no solution, and so it should fail. To represent these two cases, the programme returns a compound, consisting of a text, either "success" or "failure" indicating whether it has succeeded or not, and then the path, empty for failure, and the solution for success. (At first I had the programme only return a path, and used an `impossible' path, such as {[1]: {}} to represent failure. I quickly saw this as a typical programmer's kludge, and replaced it with the cleaner solution here.).

To make life easier, let's have a command to print out the result (this is just a simple version, it could be made prettier):

```
HOW TO PRINT result.and.path:
  PUT result.and.path IN result, path
SELECT:
    result = "failure":
      WRITE "No solution"/
ELSE:
  FOR move IN path:
      WRITE "Move", move /
```

The original programme took as parameter the target position of the four, and then searched *backwards* to see if there was a way that that position could be reached from the start position (which was 'hard-wired' in the programme). It was necessary to search backwards, because, like the new version, it produced its answers backwards, and so the two backwardses cancelled each other out. Another change I have made to the original programme is to make both the start and the target positions parameters, and to make the programme search from the start position for a path to the target position. As I have already said, it produces its answers backwards, but stores them in the result backwards, so that they still come out the right way round.

The final change is that now 'allowable' boat-loads are not hard-wired in the programme, but represented as a list: a maximum of two can fit in the boat (it's a very large cabbage), and furthermore only the farmer can row:

```
>>> PUT {} IN allowable
>>> INSERT {"farmer"} IN allowable
>>> FOR other IN {"cabbage"; "goat"; "wolf"}:
        INSERT {"farmer"; other} IN allowable
```

We can now write a function that returns which boat-loads are possible from the current position:

```
HOW TO RETURN possible.from position:
  SHARE allowable
  PUT {} IN result
  FOR boat.load IN allowable:
    IF EACH occupant IN boat.load HAS
  on.same.side:
        INSERT boat.load IN result
    RETURN result
  on.same.side:
    REPORT position[occupant] = position[min
  boat.load]
```

So now, after that introduction to the data-types, we can see the programme proper. You'll notice comparing it with Tim's original, that the main body is more or less the same, except that results are being returned rather than tests being reported. The main difference is in the refinement to try the next move. Tim's programme tried each of four refinements until one succeeded.

The new version tries each of the allowable boat-loads until one succeeds. If none succeeds, it fails. A marginal issue is how to treat the case where the aim is reachable, but not safe in itself. Tim's version accepted it, and printed the result; this version by reversing the order of the first two IF commands, does not accept it.

```
HOW TO RETURN position path.to aim:
  SHARE looking
  IF position in looking OR NOT safe position:
  RETURN failure
```

```
  IF position = aim: RETURN success
  INSERT position IN looking
  RETURN next.move
 next.move:
  FOR boat.load IN possible.from position:
    PUT new.position path.to aim IN result,
  path'
    IF result <> "failure": RETURN result,
  path' with boat.load
    RETURN failure
 new.position: RETURN position altered.for
boat.load
 success: RETURN "success", {}
 failure: RETURN "failure", {}
```

(Remember that *looking* is used to prevent the programme searching for a solution to a position it is already trying to solve — otherwise you can get an infinite loop.)

Now to try it out:

```
>>> PUT {}, {} IN start, aim
>>> FOR occupant IN {"farmer"; "goat"; "wolf";
 "cabbage"}:
   PUT "N", "S" IN start[occupant], aim
  [occupant]
>>> PUT {} IN looking
>>> PRINT start path.to aim
Move {"farmer"; "goat"}
Move {"farmer"}
Move {"cabbage"; "farmer"}
Move {"farmer"; "goat"}
Move {"farmer"; "wolf"}
Move {"farmer"}
Move {"farmer"; "goat"}
```

Now to try it with a different aim: the farmer has to get the cabbage to the other side (to sell it to the hungry computer programmer who lives there):

```
>>> PUT start IN aim
>>> PUT "S" IN aim["cabbage"]
>>> PRINT start path.to aim
```

```
Move {"farmer"; "goat"}
Move {"farmer"}
Move {"cabbage"; "farmer"}
Move {"farmer"; "goat"}
```

Now, finally, the farmer is fed up with goats, cabbages and wolves, and wants to be alone on the other side:

```
>>> PUT start IN aim
>>> PUT "S" IN aim["farmer"]
>>> PRINT start path.to aim
No solution
```

Producing the Result Forwards

The question arises as to *why* the programme produces the result backwards. The answer for Tim's version of the programme is that you don't know until you've reached the goal whether the current position is on a successful path, and so you can't write anything until then.

With the new version you do have the option of producing the results forwards. To do it you have to pass to *path.to* not only the current position, but how you got to it (as a path). Just to show you how it would look, here is *path.to* altered in that way. The function *with* would also have to be altered to append elements to the path, rather than prepend them.

```
HOW TO RETURN (route, position) path.to aim:
  SHARE looking
  IF position in looking OR NOT safe position:
  RETURN failure
  IF position = aim: RETURN success
  INSERT position IN looking
  RETURN next.move
next.move:
  FOR boat.load IN possible.from position:
    PUT (new.route, new.position) path.to aim
    IN result, path'
    IF result <> "failure": RETURN result,
  path'
  RETURN failure
new.route: RETURN route with boat.load
```

```
  new.position: RETURN position altered.for
 boat.load
  success: RETURN "success", route
  failure: RETURN "failure", {}
```

You would then have to call it as:

```
PRINT ({}, start) path.to aim
```

However, you may notice that *route* here contains more or less the complementary information to what *looking* contains.

If you represent a path as the sequence of positions, instead of the sequence of moves, you can do away with *looking* altogether, with the choice of shareing *route* or passing it as a parameter:

```
HOW TO RETURN (route, position) path.to aim:
  IF position in route OR NOT safe position:
RETURN failure
  PUT route with position IN route
  IF position = aim: RETURN success
  RETURN next.move
next.move:
  FOR boat.load IN possible.from position:
   PUT (route, new.position) path.to aim IN
result, path'
  IF result <> "failure": RETURN result,
path'
    RETURN failure
  new.position: RETURN position altered.for
 boat.load
  success: RETURN "success", route
  failure: RETURN "failure", {}
```

This means that you get as output the states rather than the moves you have to make:

```
  >>> PRINT ({}, start) path.to aim
  {["cabbage"]: "N"; ["farmer"]: "N"; ["goat"]:
  "N"; ["wolf"]: "N"}
  {["cabbage"]: "N"; ["farmer"]: "S"; ["goat"]:
  "S"; ["wolf"]: "N"}
  {["cabbage"]: "N"; ["farmer"]: "N"; ["goat"]:
```

```
"S"; ["wolf"]: "N"}
{["cabbage"]: "S"; ["farmer"]: "S"; ["goat"]:
"S"; ["wolf"]: "N"}
{["cabbage"]: "S"; ["farmer"]: "N"; ["goat"]:
"N"; ["wolf"]: "N"}
{["cabbage"]: "S"; ["farmer"]: "S"; ["goat"]:
"N"; ["wolf"]: "S"}
{["cabbage"]: "S"; ["farmer"]: "N"; ["goat"]:
"N"; ["wolf"]: "S"}
{["cabbage"]: "S"; ["farmer"]: "S"; ["goat"]:
"S"; ["wolf"]: "S"}
```

However, for the rest of this article I will stick with the reverse method.

Another Possible Representation

You may remark in *path.to* that there is no dependency within the how-to on exactly how a position is represented. What would we have to change if we represented it as, for instance, {["N"]: {"farmer"; "goat"}; ["S"]: {"cabbage"; "wolf"}}, a representation that more closely represents the real state of affairs?

Well, the main change would come in altered.for, which would look like this:

```
HOW TO RETURN positions altered.for occupants:
  FOR occupant IN occupants:
     SELECT:
        SOME place IN keys positions HAS
        occupant in positions[place]:
           REMOVE occupant FROM
        positions[place]
           INSERT occupant IN positions
        [opposite place]
     RETURN positions
 >>> PUT {["S"]: {}} IN banks
 >>> PUT {"farmer"; "goat"; "cabbage"; "wolf"}
 IN banks["N"]
 >>> WRITE banks altered.for {"goat";
"cabbage"}
```

```
{["N"]: {"farmer"; "wolf"}; ["S"]: {"cabbage";
"goat"}}
```

A corresponding change also has to be made to possible from. The only other thing that must be changed is the test safe, but it can be expressed even more simply now, since we can use a list of illegal positions:

```
>>> PUT {} IN illegal
>>> INSERT {"goat"; "cabbage"} IN illegal
>>> INSERT {"goat"; "wolf"} IN illegal
>>> INSERT {"goat"; "cabbage"; "wolf"}
IN illegal
```

and then use this test:

```
HOW TO REPORT safe position:
   SHARE illegal
   REPORT NO place IN position HAS place in
   illegal
```

Multiple Paths

An interesting change to consider is returning not just one solution, but *all* solutions to the problem. Clearly then, *path.to* must return not just one path, but all paths solving the problem, so we'll call it *paths.to*. In this case we don't need to return the 'success' or 'failure' indication: if it fails, it just returns the empty list: no solutions found. If the list is non-empty, then it succeeded.

So PRINT *will look like this:*

```
HOW TO PRINT paths:
  SELECT:
    paths = {}:
      WRITE "No solution"/
    ELSE:
      FOR i IN {1..#paths}:
          WRITE "Solution", i /
          FOR move IN paths item i:
            WRITE "Move", move /
```

The main part of *paths.to* is again hardly different from its predecessor. If the current position is where we wanted to go, then the result is the single empty path {{}}. If the routine fails, it returns no paths, i.e. {}. Otherwise, for each possible new position from the current position, it gets all paths from the new position to the aim. For each of these paths it adds the boat-load that created the new position to the front of the path. Obviously, if no paths are possible then it will not add the boat-load to any path.

```
HOW TO RETURN position paths.to aim:
  SHARE looking
  IF position in looking OR NOT safe position:
  RETURN failure
  IF position = aim: RETURN success
  INSERT position IN looking
  RETURN all.paths
 all.paths:
  PUT {} IN results
  FOR boat.load IN possible.from position:
    PUT new.position paths.to aim IN paths
    FOR path IN paths:
      INSERT path with boat.load IN results
  RETURN results
 new.position: RETURN position altered.for
boat.load
 success: RETURN {{}}
 failure: RETURN {}
```

And now to show it works:

```
>>> WRITE start
{["N"]: {"cabbage"; "farmer"; "goat"; "wolf"};
["S"]: {}}
>>> WRITE aim
{["N"]: {}; ["S"]: {"cabbage"; "farmer";
"goat"; "wolf"}}
>>> PRINT start paths.to aim
Solution 1
Move {"farmer"; "goat"}
Move {"farmer"}
Move {"cabbage"; "farmer"}
Move {"farmer"; "goat"}
Move {"farmer"; "wolf"}
```

```
Move {"farmer"}
Move {"farmer"; "goat"}
Solution 2
Move {"farmer"; "goat"}
Move {"farmer"}
Move {"farmer"; "wolf"}
Move {"farmer"; "goat"}
Move {"cabbage"; "farmer"}
Move {"farmer"}
Move {"farmer"; "goat"}
```

Solving Other Problems

Now that the programme takes most of its information from data-structures, it's interesting to try and solve a different problem with the same programme.

Consider this one: you have two jugs of different capacities, say *j* litres and *k* litres. You are allowed to empty either jug, fill either jug, or pour one into the other until the one is empty, or the other is full. The problem is, what series of actions are necessary to end up with the jugs containing *m* and *n* litres?

Right, let's call the two jugs A and B, and represent the state of the two jugs as a programming of their contents. For instance, {["A"]: 8; ["B"]: 5} shows that A contains 8 litres and B 5. We can represent the set of allowable actions (the target *allowable*) as a list of actions, where each action is a compound giving the type of action, and the name of the jug. For instance ("Fill", "A").

```
>>> PUT {} IN allowable
>>> FOR action IN {"Fill"; "Empty"; "Pour"}:
      FOR jug IN "AB":
            INSERT (action, jug) IN allowable
```

(The action ("Pour", "A") means pour A into B.)

Now, although strictly speaking, the actions possible from a given situation depend on whether the jugs are empty or full, and so on, it actually doesn't matter, because if you fill an already full jug, or empty an already empty one, you get the same situation, and the programme ensures that situations don't get repeated, so we don't have to worry. Therefore, *possible.from* is very simple:

```
HOW TO RETURN possible.from position:
  SHARE allowable
  RETURN allowable
```

There are also no illegal states:

```
>>> PUT {} IN illegal
```

Finally, we have to provide an *altered.for* for the new representations. To be able to carry out the actions like Fill we have to know the capacities of the jugs:

```
>>> PUT {} IN full
>>> PUT 8 IN full["A"]
>>> PUT 5 IN full["B"]
```

The only unobvious case is pouring: the amount that you pour is either the contents of the whole jug, or as much as will fit, whichever is less:

```
HOW TO RETURN amount altered.for actions:
  SHARE full
FOR action, jug IN actions:
  SELECT:
    action = "Empty": PUT 0 IN amount[jug]
    action = "Fill": PUT full[jug] IN
  amount[jug]
    action = "Pour":
      PUT min {amount[jug]; full[other]-
    amount[other]} IN x
      PUT amount[other] + x IN amount[other]
      PUT amount[jug] - x IN amount[jug]
  RETURN amount
 other:
  RETURN opposite jug
```

Obviously, opposite "A" gives "B", and vice-versa. Now to try it (the output format of PRINT has also been changed):

```
>>> PUT {}, {} IN start, aim
>>> PUT 0, 0 IN start["A"], start["B"]
>>> PUT 4, 0 IN aim["A"], aim["B]
>>> PRINT start paths.to aim
Solution 1
```

```
Fill A, Pour A, Empty B, Pour A, Fill A, Pour
A, Empty B, Pour A,
Empty B, Pour A, Fill A, Pour A, Fill A,
Empty A, Pour B, Fill B,
Pour B, Empty A, Pour B, Fill B, Pour B, Fill
B, Pour B, Empty A,
Pour B
...
Solution 26
Fill B, Pour B, Fill B, Pour B, Empty A, Pour
B, Fill B, Pour B,
Fill B, Pour B, Empty A, Pour B
```

Exercise

Finally, as an exercise, consider what needs to be changed in order to solve the Towers of Hanoi problem. If you just use the restriction that a disk may not be placed on a smaller disk, it gives 12 solutions for moving just two disks from one pile to another! Here's the longest (the first line means "move piece 1 from rod a to rod c"):

```
Move (1, "a", "c")
Move (1, "c", "b")
Move (2, "a", "c")
Move (1, "b", "c")
Move (1, "c", "a")
Move (2, "c", "b")
Move (1, "a", "c")
Move (1, "c", "b")
```

If you add the restriction that the same piece should not be moved twice in succession, you get two solutions:

```
Solution 1
Move (1, "a", "b")
Move (2, "a", "c")
Move (1, "b", "a")
Move (2, "c", "b")
Move (1, "a", "b")
Solution 2
Move (1, "a", "c")
```

```
Move (2, "a", "b")
Move (1, "c", "b")
```

Approximate Numbers

There are two kinds of numbers in ABC: exact and approximate. Exact numbers are held internally as a fraction of two (unbounded-length) integers, reduced to their lowest common multiple. You can retuen the two numerator and denominator of these fractions with the operators */ and /*. You can convert exact numbers to approximate ones with the operator ~ and vice versa with round, floor and ceiling.

Exact numbers are the result of computations where the result can be computed exactly: addition, subtraction, multiplication, division, and some exponentiations. However, some operations, such as taking the square root, can't deliver an exact result in general, and deliver an approximate number instead.

Of course, some exact numbers (like 4), have exact square roots, but if you want exact results in these cases you have to write your own function to calculate them, something like:

```
HOW TO RETURN xroot x:
    IF exact x:
        PUT root */x, root /*x IN a, b
        PUT (round a)/(round b) IN r
        IF r*r = x: RETURN r
RETURN root x
```

For approximate numbers, the ABC implementations use the hardware representation of floating-point, and this is the only place where ABC programmes can deliver different results on different machines (apart from the workings of the random generator): some machines have greater floating-point accuracy than others.

Machines hold floating-point numbers as an encoding of a pair of numbers *(f, e)*, where *f*, the fraction, has a fixed number of digits to some base *b*.

Such a pair then represents the number $f \times b^e$. To find out how much accuracy your machine has, you can use the following command (adapted from a routine by Malcolm (reference 1)) to find the base and number of significant digits used on your machine:

```
HOW TO PRINT ACCURACY:
    PRINT BASE
    PRINT FRACTION
PRINT BASE:
    PUT ~2, ~2, ~0 IN a, b, base
    WHILE a+1-a-1 = ~0: PUT a+a IN a
    WHILE base = ~0: PUT a+b-a, b+b IN base,b
    WRITE "Base =", base /
PRINT FRACTION:
    PUT 1, base IN sig, b
    WHILE b+1-b-1 = ~0: PUT sig+1, b*base IN
    sig, b
    WRITE "Significant digits =", sig /
    WRITE "This is about `decimal` decimal
  digits"/
decimal:
    RETURN 1 round (sig/(base log 10))
```

It works by first looking for a whole number that doesn't produce a different number when you add 1 to it. For instance, suppose the representation we are examining has 4 digits to base 10. Then you can add 1 to all 4 digit numbers, but not to 5 digit numbers, so it will try in turn 2, 4, 8, 16, 32, 64, 128, 256, 512, 1024, 2048, 4096, and 8192. Finally it will try 16384, which is only representable as 1638×10^{1}, which is 16380.

The routine then searches for a number that can be added to it which does produce a different number. Exactly which number it finds depends on whether the machine rounds the last digit of a calculation, or just chops excess digits off. So it tries to add 2, 4, and 8.

If the machine rounds then 16380 + 8 = 16388, which rounded to 4 places is 16390. However, if the machine chops, then 16388 chopped is 16380, so then it tries to add 16, which gives 16396, and chopped this gives 16390, so in either case we get the same result from the two types of machine. Now subtracting these two values, 16390 - 16380, gives the base used, in this case 10.

Having found the base, the routine then goes on to find the number of significant digits by repeatedly multiplying by the base until again 1 cannot be added. In our case, it will try 1, 10, 100, 1000, and finally 10000 to which 1 cannot be added. From the number of times that the multiplication is done, the number of significant digits can be deduced.

Here is an example of its output, for a VAX:

```
>>> PRINT ACCURACY
Base = 2
Significant digits = 56
This is about 16.9 decimal digits
```

The Consequences of Approximate Numbers

The advantage of using approximate numbers in ABC is that for large numbers they are generally faster to calculate than the equivalent exact numbers. The big disadvantage is of course that your results are only approximately correct. But how approximate is that?

To give an example, consider the value 1/((sqrt x) - (sqrt (x–1))). This is the same as (sqrt x) + (sqrt (x–1)) (you just multiply all through by ((sqrt x) + (sqrt (x–1)))/ ((sqrt x) + (sqrt (x–1)))).

However, if you calculate these using approximate numbers, you will get different results.

For instance:

```
HOW TO COMPARE VALUES FOR x:
    PUT root x, root (x-1) IN r, r1
    PUT 1/(r-r1), r+r1 IN u, v
    WRITE "1/((root x)-(root (x-1))=", u /
    WRITE "(root x)+(root (x-1))= ", v /
    WRITE "Difference =", u-v /
>>> COMPARE VALUES FOR 10**12
1/((root x)-(root (x-1)))= 2000042.97959778
(root x)+(root (x-1))= 1999999.9999995
Difference = 42.9795982764044
>>> COMPARE VALUES FOR 10**15
1/((root x)-(root (x-1)))= 63161283.7647059
(root x)+(root (x-1))= 63245553.2033676
```

```
Difference = -84269.4386616889
```

This is on a machine with nearly 17 decimal digits of accuracy, and yet the two results differ already in the third digit in the second example! The explanation for this is that if you subtract two very close numbers, you lose a lot of accuracy. Try doing it for $x = 256$ with 4 digits of accuracy: root 256 = 16.00, and root 255 = 15.97. Subtracting these two gives 0.03, leaving only one digit of accuracy where before you had four. The inverse of this is 33.33, while the sum of the two is 31.97, a very different value (and as close as you can get to the real value with 4 digits).

So the question arises, in a given programme, how can you tell how close a result is to the *real* answer? The rest of this article presents a package to help answer this question.

Range Arithmetic

This package simulates approximate arithmetic, and keeps for each arithmetic value an upper and lower bound on its real value. For instance, using 4 digits, *pi* lies between 3.141 and 3.142.

Then for each operation, it calculates the upper and lower bounds of the result. For instance, when adding two values (l , u) and (l' ,u'), the result is (rounded.down($l + l'$), rounded.up($u + u'$)). For *pi* + *pi*, this would give (6.282, 6.284). In ABC:

```
HOW TO RETURN a plus b:
    PUT a, b IN (la, ua), (lb, ub)
    RETURN down (la + lb), up (ua + ub)
```

or shorter yet:

```
HOW TO RETURN (la, ua) plus (lb, ub)
    RETURN down (la + lb), up (ua + ub)
```

Since we want to simulate approximate arithmetic using a fixed number of digits of accuracy, the functions up and down take a number and remove excess digits, rounding either up or down.

The contents of the shared location accuracy specify how many digits of **accuracy** *we are interested in:*

```
HOW TO RETURN up x:
    SHARE accuracy
```

```
IF x=0: RETURN 0
PUT 0, 10**accuracy IN shift, limit
WHILE abs x < limit: PUT x*10, shift - 1
IN x, shift
WHILE abs x > limit: PUT x/10, shift + 1
IN x, shift
RETURN (ceiling x) * 10**shift
```

This takes a number like 3.14159265, and multiplies or divides it so that its integral part has accuracy digits, also calculating the number of digits it has been shifted. So for accuracy = 4, × ends up as 3141.59265, with shift = -3. It then applies ceiling, which gives 3142, and multiplies this by 10^{-3} to shift it back to give 3.142. The function to round down is the same, except it uses floor instead of ceiling.

```
>>> PUT 4 IN accuracy
>>> WRITE down pi, up pi
3.141 3.142
>>> WRITE down 123, up 123
123 123
>>> WRITE down 12345, up 12345
12340 12350
```

Because exact arithmetic is being used, any value for accuracy can be used. Calculating to 100 places will only take more time.

Subtraction is similar to addition:

```
HOW TO RETURN (la, ua) minus (lb, ub):
    RETURN down (la-ub), up (ua-lb)
```

Multiplication is slightly harder, mainly because of problems caused when multiplying values whose upper and lower bounds have different signs.

Here we take the easy way out, and calculate all possible values and identify the maximum and minimum:

```
HOW TO RETURN (la, ua) times (lb, ub):
    RETURN minmax {la*lb; la*ub; ua*lb; ua*ub}
```

where minmax returns the minimum and maximum values from a list:

HOW TO RETURN minmax list: **RETURN** down min list, up max list.

We can do the same for division, but additionally we have to check for division by zero:

```
HOW TO RETURN (la, ua) over (lb, ub):
   CHECK NOT (lb <= 0 <= ub) \Division by zero
   RETURN minmax {la/lb; la/ub; ua/lb; ua/ub}
```

To use the package, a method is needed for converting an ABC number like pi into a range:

HOW TO RETURN range v: **RETURN** down v, up v

Just to show it works:

```
>>> WRITE range pi
3.141 3.142
>>> WRITE range 123
123 123
>>> WRITE range 12345
12340 12350
```

Also useful is a way of printing ranges more visibly as ranges:

```
 HOW TO RETURN bounds (l, u): RETURN
"[`l`:`u`] "
  >>> WRITE bounds range pi
  [3.141:3.142]
  >>> WRITE bounds range 123
  [123:123]
```

Now finally to define a function for square root. This uses the Newton-Raphson method, which repeatedly calculates for argument *a*, r = half ({ a ÷ r } + r), until two consecutive *r*'s are sufficiently close:

```
HOW TO RETURN sq.root (l, u):
    RETURN down sq.root' l, up sq.root' u
HOW TO RETURN sq.root' f:
    IF f=0: RETURN 0
PUT f, (f+1)/2 IN r, r'
    WHILE converging: PUT r', (f/r' + r')/ 2
IN r, r'
    RETURN r
converging:
    REPORT down r <> down r'
```

The definition of closeness is whether the two approximations differ only in digits outside the accuracy we interested in.

```
>>> WRITE bounds sq.root range 256
[16:16.01]
>>> WRITE bounds sq.root range 2
[1.414:1.415]
```

(Actually **sq.root'** can be speeded up by adding at the beginning

```
SHARE accuracy
PUT accuracy+1 IN accuracy
```

and replacing **(f/r' + r')/ 2** by **up((f/r' + r')/ 2)**. In that way, intermediate calculations don't get calculated with too great an accuracy.)

Now, finally back to our original problem:

```
>>> PUT range 1 IN one
>>> PUT sq.root range 256 IN r256
>>> PUT sq.root range 255 IN r255
>>> WRITE bounds (r256 plus r255)
[31.96:31.98]
>>> WRITE bounds (one over (r256 minus r255))
[20:33.34]
```

This makes it quite clear which of the two results is more accurate. This last result is both shocking and sobering. But if you work it out, root 256 is [16:16.01] and root 255 is [15.96:15.97].

The difference of these two is [0.03:0.05], so obviously the inverse is [20:33.34].

Even if we use ***range 16*** *instead of* ***r256****, we still get a wide range*:

```
WRITE bounds (range 16) minus r255)
[25:33.34]
```

OBJECT-ORIENTATION

Many languages claim to be Object-Oriented. While the exact definition of the term is highly variable depending upon who you ask, there are several qualities that most will agree an Object-Oriented language should have:

- Encapsulation/Information Hiding.
- Inheritance.
- Polymorphism/Dynamic Binding.

- All pre-defined types are Objects.
- All operations performed by sending messages to Objects.
- All user-defined types are Objects.

For the purposes of this discussion, a language is considered to be a "pure" Object-Oriented languages if it satisfies all of these qualities. A "hybrid" language may support some of these qualities, but not all.

In particular, many languages support the first three qualities, but not the final three. C++ is considered to be a multi-paradigm language, of which one paradigm it supports is Object-Orientation. Thus, C++ is not (nor does it contend to be) a pure Object-Oriented language. Python is often heralded as an Object-Oriented language, but its support for Object-Orientation seems to have been tacked on. Some operations are implemented as methods, while others are implemented as global functions.

Also, the need for an explicit "self" parameter for methods is awkward. Some complain about Python's lack of "private" or "hidden" attributes, which goes against the Encapsulation/ Information Hiding principle, while others feel that Python's "privateness is by convention" approach offers all of the practical benefits as language-enforced encapsulation without the hassle. The Ruby language, on the other hand, was created in part as a reaction to Python.

STATIC VS. DYNAMIC TYPING

The debate between static and dynamic typing has raged in Object-Oriented circles for many years with no clear conclusion. Proponents of dynamic typing contend that it is more flexible and allows for increased productivity. Those who prefer static typing argue that it enforces safer, more reliable code, and increases efficiency of the resulting product.

It is futile to attempt to settle this debate here except to say that a statically-typed language requires a very well-defined type system in order to remain as flexible as its dynamically-typed counterparts. Without the presence of genericity (templates, to use the C++ patois) and multiple type inheritance (not necessarily the same as multiple implementation inheritance), a static type system may severely inhibit the flexibility of a language. In addition, the presence of "casts" in a language can undermine the ability of the compiler to enforce type constraints.

A dynamic type system doesn't require variables to be declared as a specific type. Any variable can contain any value or object. Smalltalk and Ruby are two pure Object-Oriented languages that use dynamic typing. In many cases this can make the software more flexible and amenable to change.

However, care must be taken that variables hold the expected kind of object. Typically, if a variable contains an object of a different type than a user of the object expects, some sort of "message not understood" error is raised at run-time. Users of dynamically-typed languages claim that this type of error is infrequent in practice.

Statically-typed languages require that all variables are declared with a specific type. The compiler will then ensure that at any given time the variable contains only an object compatible with that type. (We say "compatible with that type" rather than "exactly that type" since the inheritance relationship enables subtyping, in which a class that inherits from another class is said to have an IS-A relationship with the class from which it inherits, meaning that instances of the inheriting class can be considered to be of a compatible type with instances of the inherited class.)

By enforcing the type constraint on objects contained or referred to by the variable, the compiler can ensure a "message not understood" error can never occur at run-time. On the other hand, a static type system can hinder evolution of software in some circumstances. For example, if a method takes an object as a parameter, changing the type of the object requires changing the signature of the method so that it is compatible with the new type of the object being passed.

If this same object is passed to many such methods, all of them must be updated accordingly, which could potentially be an arduous task. One must remember, though, that this ripple effect could occur even a dynamically-typed language.

If the type of the object is not what it was originally expected to be, it may not understand the messages being sent to it. Perhaps even worse is that it could understand the message but interpret it in a way not compatible with the semantics of the calling method. A statically-typed language can flag these errors at compilation-time, pointing out the precise locations of potential errors. A user of a dynamically-typed language must rely on extensive testing to ensure that all improper uses of the object are tracked down.

Eiffel is a statically-typed language that manages to remain nearly as flexible as its dynamic counterparts. Eiffel's generic classes and unprecedentedly flexible inheritance model allow it to achieve the safety and reliability of a static type system while still remaining nearly as flexible as a dynamic type system, all without requiring (nor allowing) the use of type casts. C++ also offers generic classes (known as "templates" in the C++ parlance), as well as multiple inheritance. Unfortunately, the presence of type casts and implicit type conversions can sometimes undermine the work of the compiler by allowing type errors to go undetected until run-time. Java is seriously hindered by a lack of generic classes.

This is alleviated to a degree by Java's singly-rooted type hierarchy (i.e. every class descends directly or indirectly from from the class Object), but this scheme leaves much to be desired in terms of type-safety. Forthcoming versions of Java will address this shortcoming when generic classes are introduced in Java 1.5 or later.

Java also allows type casting, but some rudimentary type checks can be made by the compiler, making casts in Java somewhat safer than in C++ and other languages.

GENERIC CLASSES

Generic classes, and more generally parametric type facilities, refer to the ability to parameterize a class with specific data types. A common example is a stack class that is parameterized by the type of elements it contains. This allows the stack to simultaneously be compile-time type safe and yet generic enough to handle any type of elements.

The primary benefit of parameterized types is that it allows statically typed languages to retain their compile-time type safety yet remain nearly as flexible as dynamically typed languages. Eiffel in particular uses generics extensively as a mechanism for type safe generic containers and algorithms. C++ templates are even more flexible, having many uses apart from simple generic containers, but also much more complex.

As already mentioned in the previous section, Java's lack of generic classes is a severe hole in the Java type system. When one considers that most living objects in a programme are stored in container classes, and that containers in Java are untyped due to lack of generics, it is questionable whether Java's type system provides any benefit over the more flexible dynamic counterparts. See also this article by Dave Thomas for a discussion of Java's type system in regards to its lack of generics.

Dynamically typed languages do not need parameterized types in order to support generic programming. Types are checked at run-time and thus dynamically typed languages support generic programming inherently.

INHERITANCE

Inheritance is the ability for a class or object to be defined as an extension or specialization of another class or object. Most object-oriented languages support class-based inheritance, while others such as SELF and JavaScript support object-based inheritance. A few languages, notably Python and Ruby, support both class- and object-based inheritance, in which a class can inherit from another class and individual objects can be extended at run time with the capabilities of other objects. For the remainder of this discussion, we'll be dealing primarily with class-based inheritance since it is by far the most common model.

Although commonly thought of as simple subtyping mechanism, there are actually many different uses of inheritance. In his landmark book *Object-Oriented Software Construction,* Bertrand Meyer identified and classified as many as 17 different forms of inheritance. Even so, most languages provide only a few syntactic constructs for inheritance which are general enough to allow inheritance to be used in many different ways.

The most important distinction that can be made between various languages' support for inheritance is whether it supports single or multiple inheritance. Multiple inheritance is the ability for a class to inherit from more than one super (or base) class. For example, an application object called Persistent Shape might inherit from both Graphical Object and Persistent Object in order to be used as both a graphical object that can be displayed on the screen as well as a persistent object that can be stored in a database.

Multiple inheritance would appear to be an essential feature for a language to support for cases such as the above when two or more distinct hierarchies must be merged into one application domain. However, there are other issues to consider before making such an assertion.

First, we must consider that multiple inheritance introduces some complications into a programming language supporting it. Issues such as name clashes and ambiguities introduced in the object model must be resolved by the language in order for multiple inheritance and this leads to additional complexity in the language. Eiffel is known for its carefully and thoroughly well-designed support for multiple inheritance, which features feature renaming and fine-grained control over the manner in which multiply-inherited features are selected and applied to the inheriting class. The mechanisms C++ provides for multiple inheritance are more complicated and less flexible leading many people to (mistakenly) believe that multiple inheritance is inherently ill-conceived and complex.

Next, we must distinguish between implementation inheritance and interface/subtype inheritance. Subtype inheritance (also known loosely as interface inheritance) is the most common form of inheritance, in which a subclass is considered to be a subtype of its super class, commonly referred to as an IS-A relationship. What this means is that the language considers an object to conform to the type of its class *or any of its super classes.* For example, a Circle IS-A Shape, so anywhere a Shape is used in a programme, a Circle may be used as well. This conformance notion is only applicable to statically typed languages since it is a feature used by the compiler to determine type correctness.

Implementation inheritance is the ability for a class to inherit part or all of its implementation from another class. For example, a Stack class that is implemented using an array might inherit from an Array class in order to define the Stack in terms of the Array. In this way, the Stack class could use any features from the Array to support its own implementation.

With pure implementation inheritance, the fact that the Stack inherits its implementation from Array would not be visible to code using the Stack; the inheritance would be strictly an implementation matter. C++ supports this notion directly with "private inheritance", in which methods from the base class are made private in the derived class.

Recent versions of Eiffel also support this form of pure implementation inheritance using what is known as non-conforming inheritance. Most languages, on the other hand, do not support pure implementation inheritance so a class that inherits from another class is always considered to be a subtype of its super class(es).

Returning to the issue of multiple inheritance, we can see that a language's support for multiple inheritance is not a boolean condition; a language can support one or more different forms of multiple inheritance in the same way it can support different forms of single inheritance (e.g. implementation and subtype inheritance).

We've already seen that C++ and Eiffel independently support pure implementation inheritance as well as subtype inheritance. Both of these languages also support multiple inheritance in both forms. Java, while it does not support *pure* implementation inheritance, provides two separate inheritance mechanisms. The extends keyword is used for a combination of implementation and subtype inheritance while the implements keyword is used for pure subtype (interface) inheritance. Subtype inheritance is less important in dynamic languages since type conformance is not generally an issue, so multiple implementation inheritance is preferred over multiple subtype inheritance (although most languages still consider any class inheriting from another to be a subtype). Smalltalk supports only a single notion of inheritance: single inheritance of both interface and implementation. This means that a class may only inherit from one other class and it inherits both implementation and interface.

Python similarly supports one form of inheritance (both implementation and subtype) but allows multiple inheritance and is thus more flexible in this regard than Smalltalk. Ruby lies somewhere in between the two approaches by allowing a class to inherit from only one class but also allowing a class to "mix in" the implementation of an arbitrary number of modules.

This model is a slightly restricted version of the model provided by Python, but the restrictions can be overcome by Ruby's ability to support a prototype-based approach using object-based inheritance. Visual Basic has no support for inheritance of any form, although support for single inheritance is slated for the **VB .NET** release.

FEATURE RENAMING

Feature renaming is the ability for a class or object to rename one of its features (a term we'll use to collectively refer to attributes and methods) that it inherited from a super class.

There are two important ways in which this can be put to use:

- Provide a feature with a more natural name for its new context
- Resolve naming ambiguities when a name is inherited from multiple inheritance paths

As an example of the first use, consider again a stack implemented by inheriting from an array. The array might provide an operation called remove_last to remove the last element of the array. In the stack, this operation is more appropriately named pop. Eiffel and Ruby both provide support for feature renaming. Ruby provides an alias method that allows you to alias any arbitrary method. Eiffel also provides support for feature renaming, although it is slightly more limited than in Ruby because you can only rename a feature in an inheritance clause.

METHOD OVERLOADING

Method overloading (also referred to as parametric polymorphism) is the ability for a class, module, or other scope to have two or more methods with the same name. Calls to these methods are disambiguated by the number and/or type of arguments passed to the method at the call site. For example, a class may have multiple print methods, one for each type of thing to be printed. The alternative to overloading in this scenario is to have a different name for each print method, such asprint_string and print_integer.

Java and C++ both support method overloading in a similar fashion. Complexities in the mechanism to disambiguate calls to overloaded methods have lead some language designers to avoid overloading in their languages. None of the other languages under consideration support method overloading. Default argument values provide a subset of the behaviour for which method overloading is used, and some languages such as Ruby and Python have chosen this route instead.

OPERATOR OVERLOADING

Operator overloading (a hotly debated topic) is the ability for a programmer to define an operator (such as +, or *) for user-defined types. This allows the operator to be used in infix, prefix, or postfix form, rather than the standard functional form. For example, a user-defined Matrix type might provide a * infix operator to perform matrix multiplication with the familiar notation: matrix1 * matrix2 .

Some (correctly) consider operator overloading to be mere syntactic "sugar" rather than an essential feature, while others (also correctly) point to the need for such syntactic sugar in numerical and other applications. Both points are valid, but it is clear that, when used appropriately, operator overloading can lead to much more readable programmes. When abused, it can lead to cryptic, obfuscated code. Consider that in the presence of operator overloading, it may not be clear whether a given operator is built in to the language or defined by the user.

For any language that supports operator overloading, two things are necessary to alleviate such obfuscation:

- All operations must be messages to objects, and thus all operators are always method calls.
- Operators must have an equivalent functional form, so that using the operator as a method call will behave precisely the same as using it in infix, prefix, or postfix form.

This second point is subtle. It means that given any operator, it must be possible to invoke that operator in functional form. For example, the following two expressions should be equivalent: 1 + 2 and 1.+(2). This ensures that no implicit behaviour is taking place that may not be immediately obvious from examining the source text.

Of the languages under consideration, Eiffel, Ruby, C++, and Python support operator overloading. Eiffel and Ruby also support the two criteria listed above for safer use of operator overloading.

Python supports the "equivalent functional form" criterion, but not the "all operations are messages to objects" criterion. C++ does not support either notion. Eiffel's mechanism is particularly flexible in that users may define arbitrary operators, rather than being limited to redefining a set of predefined operators.

HIGHER ORDER FUNCTIONS

Higher order functions are, in the simplest sense, functions that can be treated as if they were data objects. In other words, they can be bound to variables (including the ability to be stored in collections), they can be passed to other functions as parameters, and they can be returned as the result of other functions. Due to this ability, higher order functions may be viewed as a form of deferred execution, wherein a function may be defined in one context, passed to another context, and then later invoked by the second context. This is different from standard functions in that higher order functions represent anonymous lambda functions, so that the invoking context need not know the name of the function being invoked.

Lexical closures (also known as static closures, or simply closures) take this one step further by bundling up the lexical (static) scope surrounding the function with the function itself, so that the function carries its surrounding environment around with it wherever it may be used. This means that the closure can access local variables or parameters, or attributes of the object in which it is defined, and will continue to have access to them even if it is passed to another module outside of its scope.

Among the languages we're considering, Smalltalk and Ruby have supported both higher order functions and lexical closures from the beginning in the form of blocks. A block is an anonymous function that may be treated as any other data object, and is also a lexical closure. Eiffel has recently added support for higher order functions using the "agent" mechanism. The inline variant of Eiffel agents forms a lexical closure. Python, which has long supported higher order functions in the form of lambda expressions, has recently added support for closures using its improved support for nested static scopes.

While neither Java nor C++ support higher order functions directly, both provide mechanisms for mimicking their behaviour. Java's anonymous classes allow a function to be bundled with an object that can be treated much as a higher order function can. It can be bound to variables, passed to other functions as an argument, and can be returned as the result of a function.

However, the function itself is named and thus cannot be treated in a generic fashion as true higher order functions can. C++ similarly provides partial support for higher order functions using function objects (or "functors"), and add the further benefit that the function call operator may be overloaded so that functors may be treated generically. Neither

C++ nor Java, however, provide any support for lexical closures. Visual Basic provides no support for either higher order functions or lexical closures, nor is there any apparent mechanism for providing similar behaviour.

GARBAGE COLLECTION

Garbage collection is a mechanism allowing a language implementation to free memory of unused objects on behalf of the programmer, thus relieving the burden on the programmer to do so. The alternative is for the programmer to explicitly free any memory that is no longer needed. There are several strategies for garbage collection that exist in various language implementations.

Reference counting is the simplest scheme and involves the language keeping track of how many references there are to a particular object in memory, and deleting that object when that reference count becomes zero.

This scheme, although it is simple and deterministic, is not without its drawbacks, the most important being its inability to handle cycles. Cycles occur when two objects reference each other, and thus there reference counts will never become zero even if neither object is referenced by any other part of the programme. This is the scheme that is utilized by Python and Visual Basic, although in the case of Python an extra step is taken to ensure that cycles are handled appropriately.

"Mark and sweep" garbage collection is another scheme that overcomes this limitation. A mark and sweep garbage collector works in a two phase process, not surprisingly known as the mark phase and the sweep phase. The mark phase works by first starting at the "root" objects (objects on the stack, global objects, etc.), marking them as live, and recursively marking any objects referenced from them.

These marked objects are the set of live objects in programme, and any objects that were not marked in this phase are unreferenced and therefore candidates for collection. In the sweep phase, any objects in memory that were not marked as live by the mark phase are deleted from memory.

The primary drawback of mark and sweep collection is that it is non-deterministic, meaning that objects are deleted at an unspecified time during the execution of the programme. This is the most common form of garbage collection, and the one that is supported by most implementations of Eiffel, Smalltalk, Ruby, and Java. Generational garbage collection works in a similar fashion to mark and sweep garbage collection, except it capitalizes on the statistical probability that objects that have been alive the longest tend to stay alive longer than objects that were newly created.

Thus a generational garbage collector will divide objects into "generations" based upon how long they've been alive. This division can be used to reduce the time spent in the mark and sweep phases because the oldest generation of objects will not need to be collected as frequently. Generational garbage collectors are not as common as the other forms but may be found in some implementations of Eiffel, Smalltalk, Ruby, and Java. C++ does not provide any sort of garbage collection, the reasons for which are discussed at length in Bjarne Stroustrup's *The Design and Evolution of* C++.

It is possible, however, with some effort to layer reference counting garbage collection onto C++ using smart pointers. In addition there exist garbage collectors that can be integrated into C++ programmes, though their use has not caught on to any great degree within the C++ community.

UNIFORM ACCESS

The Uniform Access Principle, as published in Bertrand Meyer's Object-Oriented Software Construction, states that "All services offered by a module should be available through a uniform notation, which does not betray whether they are implemented through storage or through computation."

It is described further with "Although it may at first appear just to address a notational issue, the Uniform Access principle is in fact a design rule which influences many aspects of object-oriented design and the supporting notation. It follows from the Continuity criterion; you may also view it as a special case of Information Hiding." Say that bar is a feature of a class named Foo. For languages that do not support the Uniform Access Principle, the notation used to access bar differs depending on whether it is an attribute (storage) or a function (computation). For example, in Java you would use foo.bar if it were an attribute, but you would use foo.bar() if it were a function.

Having this notational difference means that users of Foo are exposed to unnecessary implementation details and are tightly coupled to Foo. If bar is changed from attribute to method (or vice versa), then any users of Foo must also be changed.

The Uniform Access Principle seeks to eliminate this needless coupling. A language supporting the Uniform Access Principle does not exhibit any notational differences between accessing a feature regardless of whether it is an attribute or a function. Thus, in our earlier example, access to bar would always be in the form of foo.bar, regardless of how bar is implemented. This makes clients of Foo more resilient to change.

Among our languages, only Eiffel and Ruby directly support the Uniform Access Principle, although Smalltalk renders the distinction moot by not allowing any access to attributes from clients.

CLASS VARIABLES/METHODS

Class variables and methods are owned by a class, and not any particular instance of a class. This means that for however many instances of a class exist at any given point in time, only one copy of each class variable/method exists and is shared by every instance of the class.

Smalltalk and Ruby support the most advanced notion of class variables and methods, due to their use of meta-classes and the fact that even classes are objects in these languages. Java and C++ provide "static" members which are effectively the same thing, yet more limited since they cannot be inherited. Python, surprisingly, does not support class methods or variables, but its advanced notion of a module allows workarounds for this limitation. Eiffel also does not provide direct support for class variables or methods, but it does provide similar, but limited, functionality in the form of "once" functions. Once functions are evaluated once only, and subsequent uses use a cached result.

REFLECTION

Reflection is the ability for a programme to determine various pieces of information about an object at run-time. This includes the ability to determine the type of the object, its inheritance structure, and the methods it contains, including the number and types of parameters and return types. It might also include the ability for determining the names and types of attributes of the object.

Most object-oriented languages support some form of reflection. Smalltalk, Ruby, and Python in particular have very powerful and flexible reflection mechanisms. Java also supports reflection, but not in as flexible and dynamic fashion as the others.

C++ does not support reflection as we've defined it here, but it does supported a limited form of run-time type information that allows a programme to determine the type of an object at run-time.

Eiffel also has support for a limited form of reflection, although it is much improved in the most recent versions of Eiffel, including the ability to determine the features contained in an object.

ACCESS CONTROL

Access control refers to the ability for a modules implementation to remain hidden behind its public interface. Access control is closely related to the encapsulation/ information hiding principle of object-oriented languages. For example, a class Person may have methods such as name and email, that return the person's name and e-mail address respectively.

How these methods work is an implementation detail that should not be available to users of the Person class. These methods may, for example, connect to a database to retrieve the values. The database connection code that is used to do this is not relevant to client code and should not be exposed. Language-enforced access control allows us to enforce this.

Most object-oriented languages provide at least two levels of access control: public and protected. Protected features are not available outside of the class in which they are contained, except for subclasses. This is the scheme supported by Smalltalk, in which all methods are public and all attributes are protected.

There are no protected methods in Smalltalk, so Smalltalk programmers resort to the convention of placing methods that should be protected into a "private protocol" of the class. See this discussion for the benefits and drawbacks of this approach. Visual Basic also supports these two levels of access control, although since there is no inheritance in Visual Basic, protected features are effectively private to the class in which they are declared.

Some languages, notably Java and C++, provide a third level of access control known as "private". Private features are not available outside of the class in which they are declared, even for subclasses. Note, however, that this means that objects of a particular class can access the private features of other objects of that same class.

Ruby also provides these three levels of access control, but they work slightly differently. Private in Ruby means that the feature cannot be accessed through a receiver, meaning that the feature will be available to subclasses, but not other instances of the same class. Java provides a fourth level of, known as "package private" access control which allows other classes in the same package to access such features.

Eiffel provides the most powerful and flexible access control scheme of any of these languages with what is known as "selective export". All features of an Eiffel class are by default public. However, any feature in an Eiffel class may specify an export clause which lists explicitly what other classes may access that feature.

The special class **NONE** may be used to indicate that *no* other class may access that feature. This includes attributes, but even public attributes are read only so an attribute can never be written to directly in Eiffel. In order to better support the Open-Closed principle. all features of a class are always available to subclasses in Eiffel, so there is no notion of private as there is in Java and C++. Python, curiously, does not provide any enforced access control.

Instead, it provides a mechanism of name mangling: any feature that begins with underscores will have its name mangled by the Python interpreter. Although this does not prevent client code from using such features, it is a clear indicator that the feature is not intended for use outside the class and convention dictates that these features are "use at your own risk".

DESIGN BY CONTRACT

Design by Contract is another idea set forth by Bertrand Meyer and discussed at length in *Object Oriented Software Construction* as well as the Eiffel Home Page.

In short, Design by Contract (DBC) is the ability to incorporate important aspects of a specification into the software that is implementing it.

The most important features of DBC are:

- *Pre-conditions*: Which are conditions that must be true before a method is invoked
- *Post-conditions*: Which are conditions guaranteed to be true after the invocation of a method
- *Invariants*: Which are conditions guaranteed to be true at any stable point during the lifetime of an object

There is much more to DBC than these simple facilities, including the manner in which pre-conditions, post-conditions, and invariants are inherited in compliance with the Liskov Substitution Principle. However, at least these facilities must be present to support the central notions of DBC.

As Bertrand Meyer, the original pioneer of DBC, is also the creator of Eiffel, it is no surprise that Eiffel has full support for DBC. Eiffel stands as the model for a robust DBC implementation in an object-oriented language. It is to this date still the only language with full support for DBC. Libraries exist, however for several languages, including Ruby and Java, that provide the same basic facilities.

MULTITHREADING

Multithreading is the ability for a single process to process two or more tasks concurrently. (We say concurrently rather than simultaneously because, in the absence of multiple processors, the tasks cannot run simultaneously but rather are interleaved in very small time slices and thus exhibit the appearance and semantics of concurrent execution.) The use of multithreading is becoming increasingly more common as operating system support for threads has become near ubiquitous.

Among the languages under discussion, nearly all support multithreading either directly within the language or through libraries. Ruby is somewhat unique in that its threading capabilities are built in to the interpreter itself, rather than wrappers around the operating system threading operations. This has the disadvantage that any operating system calls will block the entire interpreter, but has the advantage of being completely portable even to systems that do not support multithreading, such as **MS-DOS.**

REGULAR EXPRESSIONS

Regular expressions are pattern matching constructs capable of recognizing the class of languages known as regular languages. They are frequently used for text processing systems as well as for general applications that must use pattern recognition for other purposes.

Libraries with regular expression support exist for nearly every language, but ever since the advent of Perl it has become increasingly important for a language to support regular expressions natively.

This allows tighter integration with the rest of the language and allows more convenient syntax for use of regular expressions. Perl was the model for this kind of built-in support and Ruby, a close descendant of Perl, continues the tradition. Python, and recently Java, have included regular expression libraries as part of the standard base library distributed with the language implementation.

POINTER ARITHMETIC

Pointer arithmetic is the ability for a language to directly manipulate memory addresses and their contents. While, due to the inherent unsafety of direct memory manipulation, this ability is not often considered appropriate for high-level languages, it is essential for low-level systems applications. Thus, while object-oriented languages strive to remain at a fairly high level of abstraction, to be suitable for systems programming a language must provide such features or relegate such low-level tasks to a language with which it can interact.

Most object-oriented languages have foregone support of pointer arithmetic in favour of providing integration with C. This allows low-level routines to be implemented in C while the majority of the application is written in the higher level language.

C++ on the other hand provides direct support for pointer arithmetic, both for compatibility with C and to allow C++ to be used for systems programming without the need to drop down to a lower level language. This is the source both of C++'s great flexibility as well as much of its complexity.

LANGUAGE INTEGRATION

For various reasons, including integration with existing systems, the need to interact with low level modules, or for sheer speed, it is important for a high level language (particularly interpreted languages) to be able to integrate seamlessly with other languages.

Nearly every language to come along since C was first introduced provides such integration with C. This allows high level languages to remain free of the low level constructs that make C great for systems programming, but add much complexity. All of the languages under discussion integrate tightly with C, except for Visual Basic, which can only do so through **DCOM**. Eiffel and Ruby provide particularly easy-to-use interfaces to C as well as callbacks to the language runtime. Python, Perl, Java, and Smalltalk provide similar interfaces, though they aren't quite as easy to use. C++, naturally, integrates quite transparently with C.

BUILT-IN SECURITY

Built-in security refers to a language implementation's ability to determine whether or not a piece of code comes from a "trusted" source (such as the user's hard disk), limiting the permissions of the code if it does not. For example, Java applets are considered untrusted, and thus they are limited in the actions they can perform when executed from a user's browser. They may not, for example, read or write from or to the user's hard disk, and they may not open a network connection to anywhere but the originating host.

Several languages, including Java, Ruby, and Perl, provide this ability "out of the box". Most languages defer this protection to the user's operating environment.

CAPERS JONES LANGUAGE LEVEL

The Capers Jones Language Level is a study that attempts to identify the number of source lines of code is necessary in a given language to implement a single function point. The higher the language level, the fewer lines of code it takes to implement a function point, and thus presumably is an indicator of the productivity levels achievable using the language.

Chapter 3

Way of Programme

BEGINNING

The goal of this book is to teach you to think like a computer scientist. This way of thinking combines some of the best features of mathematics, engineering, and natural science. Like mathematicians, computer scientists use formal languages to denote ideas (specifically computations). Like engineers, they design things, assembling components into systems and evaluating tradeoffs among alternatives. Like scientists, they observe the behaviour of complex systems, form hypotheses, and test predictions.

The single most important skill for a computer scientist is problem solving. Problem solving means the ability to formulate problems, think creatively about solutions, and express a solution clearly and accurately. As it turns out, the process of learning to programme is an excellent opportunity to practice problem-solving skills. That's why this chapter is called, "The way of the programme." On one level, you will be learning to programme, a useful skill by itself. On another level, you will use programming as a means to an end. As we go along, that end will become clearer.

PYTHON PROGRAMMING LANGUAGE

The programming language you will be learning is Python. Python is an example of a high-level language; other high-level languages you might have heard of are C, C++, Perl, and Java. As you might infer from the name "high-level language," there are also low-level languages, sometimes referred to as "machine languages" or "assembly languages." Loosely speaking, computers can only execute programmes written in low-level languages. Thus, programmes written in a high-level language have to be processed before they can run. This extra processing takes some time, which is a small disadvantage of high-level languages.

But the advantages are enormous. First, it is much easier to programme in a high-level language. Programmes written in a high-level language take less time to write, they are shorter and easier to read, and they are more likely to be correct. Second, high-level languages are portable, meaning that they can run on different kinds of computers with few or no modifications.

Low-level programmes can run on only one kind of computer and have to be rewritten to run on another. Due to these advantages, almost all programmes are written in high-level languages. Low-level languages are used only for a few specialized applications. Two kinds of programmes process high-level languages into low-level languages:interpreters and compilers. An interpreter reads a high-level programme and executes it, meaning that it does what the programme says. It processes the programme a little at a time, alternately reading lines and performing computations.

A compiler reads the programme and translates it completely before the programme starts running. In this case, the high-level programme is called the source code, and the translated programme is called the object code or the executable. Once a programme is compiled, you can execute it repeatedly without further translation.

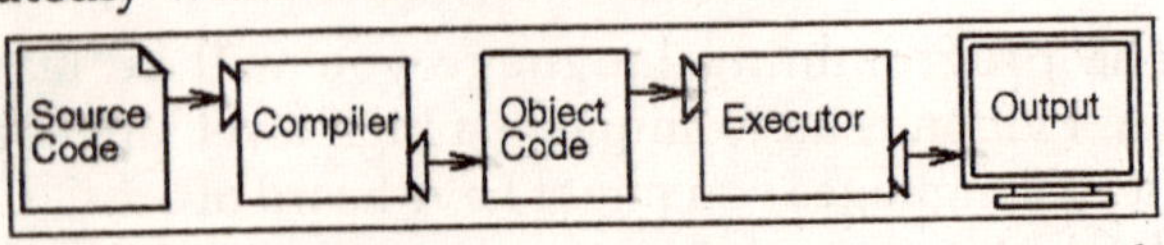

Python is considered an interpreted language because Python programmes are executed by an interpreter. There are two ways to use the interpreter: command-line mode and script mode.

In command-line mode, you type Python programmes and the interpreter prints the result:

```
$ python
Python 2.4.1 (#1, Apr 29 2005, 00:28:56)
Type "help", "copyright", "credits" or
"license" for more information.
>>> print 1 + 1
2
```

The first line of this example is the command that starts the Python interpreter. The next two lines are messages from the interpreter. The third line starts with >>>, which is the prompt the interpreter uses to indicate that it is ready. We typed print 1 + 1, and the interpreter replied 2. Alternatively, you can write a programme in a file and use the interpreter to execute the contents of the file. Such a file is called a script.

For example, we used a text editor to create a file named latoya.py *with the following contents*:

```
print 1 + 1
```

By convention, files that contain Python programmes have names that end with .py.

To execute the programme, we have to tell the interpreter the name of the script:

```
$ python latoya.py
2
```

In other development environments, the details of executing programmes may differ. Also, most programmes are more interesting than this one. Most of the examples in this book are executed on the command line. Working on the command line is convenient for programme development and testing, because you can type programmes and execute them immediately. Once you have a working programme, you should store it in a script so you can execute or modify it in the future.

DEFINITION OF A PROGRAMME

A programme is a sequence of instructions that specifies how to perform a computation. The computation might be something mathematical, such as solving a system of equations or finding the roots of a polynomial, but it can also be a symbolic computation, such as searching and replacing text in a document or (strangely enough) compiling a programme.

The details look different in different languages, but a few basic instructions appear in just about every language:

- *Input*: Get data from the keyboard, a file, or some other device.
- *Output*: Display data on the screen or send data to a file or other device.
- *Math*: Perform basic mathematical operations like addition and multiplication.
- *Conditional execution*: Check for certain conditions and execute the appropriate sequence of statements.
- *Repetition*: Perform some action repeatedly, usually with some variation.

Believe it or not, that's pretty much all there is to it. Every programme you've ever used, no matter how complicated, is made up of instructions that look more or less like these. Thus, we can describe programming as the process of breaking a large, complex task into smaller and smaller subtasks until the subtasks are simple enough to be performed with one of these basic instructions. That may be a little vague, but we will come back to this topic later when we talk aboutalgorithms.

WHAT IS DEBUGGING?

Programming is a complex process, and because it is done by human beings, it often leads to errors. For whimsical reasons, programming errors are called bugs and the process of tracking them down and correcting them is called debugging. Three kinds of errors can occur in a programme: syntax errors, runtime errors, and semantic errors. It is useful to distinguish between them in order to track them down more quickly.

Syntax Errors

Python can only execute a programme if the programme is syntactically correct; otherwise, the process fails and returns an error message. Syntax refers to the structure of a programme and the rules about that structure. For example, in English, a sentence must begin with a capital letter and end with a period.

This sentence contains a syntax error. So does this one. For most readers, a few syntax errors are not a significant problem, which is why we can read the poetry of e. e. cummings without spewing error messages.

Python is not so forgiving. If there is a single syntax error anywhere in your programme, Python will print an error message and quit, and you will not be able to run your programme.

During the first few weeks of your programming career, you will probably spend a lot of time tracking down syntax errors. As you gain experience, though, you will make fewer errors and find them faster.

Runtime Errors

The second type of error is a runtime error, so called because the error does not appear until you run the programme. These errors are also called exceptions because they usually indicate that something exceptional (and bad) has happened. Runtime errors are rare in the simple programmes you will see in the first few chapters, so it might be a while before you encounter one.

Semantic Errors

The third type of error is the semantic error. If there is a semantic error in your programme, it will run successfully, in the sense that the computer will not generate any error messages, but it will not do the right thing. It will do something else. Specifically, it will do what you told it to do.

The problem is that the programme you wrote is not the programme you wanted to write. The meaning of the programme (its semantics) is wrong. Identifying semantic errors can be tricky because it requires you to work backward by looking at the output of the programme and trying to figure out what it is doing.

Experimental Debugging

One of the most important skills you will acquire is debugging. Although it can be frustrating, debugging is one of the most intellectually rich, challenging, and interesting parts of programming. In some ways, debugging is like detective work. You are confronted with clues, and you have to infer the processes and events that led to the results you see. Debugging is also like an experimental science.

Once you have an idea what is going wrong, you modify your programme and try again. If your hypothesis was correct, then you can predict the result of the modification, and you take a step closer to a working programme. If your hypothesis was wrong, you have to come up with a new one. As Sherlock Holmes pointed out, "When you have eliminated the impossible, whatever remains, however improbable, must be the truth." (A. Conan Doyle, *The Sign of Four*)

For some people, programming and debugging are the same thing. That is, programming is the process of gradually debugging a programme until it does what you want. The idea is that you should start with a programme that does *something* and make small modifications, debugging them as you go, so that you always have a working programme.

For example, Linux is an operating system that contains thousands of lines of code, but it started out as a simple programme Linus Torvalds used to explore the Intel 80386 chip. According to Larry Greenfield, "One of Linus's earlier projects was a programme that would switch between printing AAAA and BBBB.

FORMAL AND NATURAL LANGUAGES

Natural languages are the languages that people speak, such as English, Spanish, and French. They were not designed by people (although people try to impose some order on them); they evolved naturally. Formal languages are languages that are designed by people for specific applications. For example, the notation that mathematicians use is a formal language that is particularly good at denoting relationships among numbers and symbols. Chemists use a formal language to represent the chemical structure of molecules. And most importantly: Programming languages are formal languages that have been designed to express computations. Formal languages tend to have strict rules about syntax. For example, 3+3=6 is a syntactically correct mathematical statement, but 3=+6$ is not. H_2O is a syntactically correct chemical name, but $_2Zz$ is not.

Syntax rules come in two flavors, pertaining to tokens and structure. Tokens are the basic elements of the language, such as words, numbers, and chemical elements. One of the problems with 3=+6$ is that $ is not a legal token in mathematics (at least as far as we know). Similarly, $_2Zz$ is not legal because there is no element with the abbreviation Zz.

The second type of syntax error pertains to the structure of a statement that is, the way the tokens are arranged. The statement 3=+6$ is structurally illegal because you can't place a plus sign immediately after an equal sign. Similarly, molecular formulas have to have subscripts after the element name, not before.

As an exercise, create what appears to be a well-structured English sentence with unrecognizable tokens in it. Then write another sentence with all valid tokens but with invalid structure. When you read a sentence in English or a statement in a formal language, you have to figure out what the structure of the sentence is (although in a natural language you do this subconsciously). This process is called parsing.

For example, when you hear the sentence, "The other shoe fell," you understand that "the other shoe" is the subject and "fell" is the predicate. Once you have parsed a sentence, you can figure out what it means, or the semantics of the sentence. Assuming that you know what a shoe is and what it means to fall, you will understand the general implication of this sentence. Although formal and natural languages have many features in common tokens, structure, syntax, and semantics there are many differences:

Ambiguity

Natural languages are full of ambiguity, which people deal with by using contextual clues and other information.

Formal languages are designed to be nearly or completely unambiguous, which means that any statement has exactly one meaning, regardless of context.

Redundancy

In order to make up for ambiguity and reduce misunderstandings, natural languages employ lots of redundancy. As a result, they are often verbose. Formal languages are less redundant and more concise.

Literalness

Natural languages aie full of idiom and metaphor. If I say, "The other shoe fell," there is probably no shoe and nothing falling. Formal languages mean exactly what they say. People who grow up speaking a natural language everyone often have a hard time adjusting to formal languages. In some ways, the difference between formal and natural language is like the difference between poetry and prose, but more so:

Poetry

Words are used for their sounds as well as for their meaning, and the whole poem together creates an effect or emotional response. Ambiguity is not only common but often deliberate.

Prose

The literal meaning of words is more important, and the structure contributes more meaning. Prose is more amenable to analysis than poetry but still often ambiguous.

Programmes

The meaning of a computer programme is unambiguous and literal, and can be understood entirely by analysis of the tokens and structure. Here are some suggestions for reading programmes (and other formal languages). First, remember that formal languages are much more dense than natural languages, so it takes longer to read them. Also, the structure is very important, so it is usually not a good idea to read from top to bottom, left to right. Instead, learn to parse the programme in your head, identifying the tokens and interpreting the structure. Finally, the details matter. Little things like spelling errors and bad punctuation, which you can get away with in natural languages, can make a big difference in a formal language.

The First Programme

Traditionally, the first programme written in a new language is called "Hello, World!" because all it does is display the words, "Hello, World!" In Python, it looks like this:

```
print "Hello, World!"
```

This is an example of a print statement, which doesn't actually print anything on paper. It displays a value on the screen. In this case, the result is the words

```
Hello, World!
```

The quotation marks in the programme mark the beginning and end of the value; they don't appear in the result. Some people judge the quality of a programming language by the simplicity of the "Hello, World!" programme. By this standard, Python does about as well as possible.

GLOSSARY

- *Problem solving*: The process of formulating a problem, finding a solution, and expressing the solution.
- *High-level language*: A programming language like Python that is designed to be easy for humans to read and write.
- *low-level language*: A programming language that is designed to be easy for a computer to execute; also called "machine language" or "assembly language."
- *Portability*: A property of a programme that can run on more than one kind of computer.
- *Interpret*: To execute a programme in a high-level language by translating it one line at a time.
- *Compile*: To translate a programme written in a high-level language into a low-level language all at once, in preparation for later execution.

- *Source code*: A programme in a high-level language before being compiled.
- *Object code*: The output of the compiler after it translates the programme.
- *Executable*: Another name for object code that is ready to be executed.
- *Script*: A programme stored in a file (usually one that will be interpreted).
- *Programme*: A set of instructions that specifies a computation.
- *Algorithm*: A general process for solving a category of problems.
- *Bug*: An error in a programme.
- *Debugging*: The process of finding and removing any of the three kinds of programming errors.
- *Syntax*: The structure of a programme.
- *Syntax error*: An error in a programme that makes it impossible to parse (and therefore impossible to interpret).
- *Runtime error*: An error that does not occur until the programme has started to execute but that prevents the programme from continuing.
- *Exception*: Another name for a runtime error.
- *Semantic error*: An error in a programme that makes it do something other than what the programmer intended.
- *Semantics*: The meaning of a programme.
- *Natural language*: Any one of the languages that people speak that evolved naturally.
- *Formal language*: Any one of the languages that people have designed for specific purposes, such as representing mathematical ideas or computer programmes; all programming languages are formal languages.
- *Token*: One of the basic elements of the syntactic structure of a programme, analogous to a word in a natural language.
- *Parse*: To examine a programme and analyse the syntactic structure.

- *Print statement*: An instruction that causes the Python interpreter to display a value on the screen.
- *Warning*: the **HTML** version of this document is generated from Latex and may contain translation errors. In particular, some mathematical expressions are not translated correctly.

VARIABLES, EXPRESSIONS AND STATEMENTS

VALUES AND TYPES

A value is one of the fundamental things like a letter or a number that a programme manipulates. The values we have seen so far are 2 (the result when we added 1 + 1), and 'Hello, World!'.

These values belong to different types: 2 is an integer, and 'Hello, World!' is astring, so-called because it contains a "string" of letters.

You (and the interpreter) can identify strings because they are enclosed in quotation marks.

The print statement also works for integers:

```
print 4
4
```

If you are not sure what type a value has, the interpreter can tell you.

```
type('Hello, World!')
type 'str'>
type(17)
type 'int'>
```

Not surprisingly, strings belong to the type str and integers belong to the type int.

Less obviously, numbers with a decimal point belong to a type called float, because these numbers are represented in a format called floating-point.

```
type(3.2)
type 'float'>
```

What about values like '17' and '3.2'? They look like numbers, but they are in quotation marks like strings.

```
type('17')
```

```
type 'str'>
type('3.2')
type 'str'>
```

They're strings: When you type a large integer, you might be tempted to use commas between groups of three digits, as in 1,000,000.

This is not a legal integer in Python, but it is a legal expression:

```
print 1,000,000
1 0 0
```

Well, that's not what we expected at all! Python interprets 1,000,000 as a comma-separated list of three integers, which it prints consecutively.

This is the first example we have seen of a semantic error: the code runs without producing an error message, but it doesn't do the "right" thing.

VARIABLES

One of the most powerful features of a programming language is the ability to manipulate variables. A variable is a name that refers to a value.

The assignment statement creates new variables and gives them values:

```
message = "What's up, Doc?"
n = 17
pi = 3.14159
```

This example makes three assignments. The first assigns the string "What's up, Doc?" to a new variable named message. The second gives the integer 17 to n, and the third gives the floating-point number 3.14159 to pi.

Notice that the first statement uses double quotes to enclose the string. In general, single and double quotes do the same thing, but if the string contains a single quote (or an apostrophe, which is the same character), you have to use double quotes to enclose it.

A common way to represent variables on paper is to write the name with an arrow pointing to the variable's value. This kind of figure is called a state diagrambecause it shows what state each of the variables is in (think of it as the variable's state of mind). This diagram shows the result of the assignment statements:

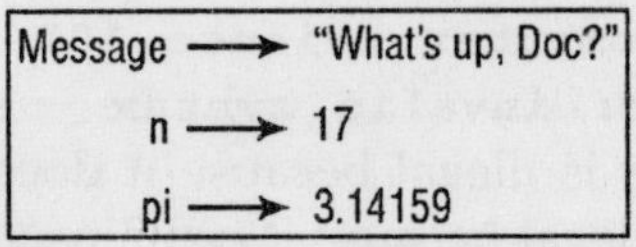

The print statement also works with variables.

```
print message
What's up, Doc?
print n
7
print pi
3.14159
```

In each case the result is the value of the variable. Variables also have types; again, we can ask the interpreter what they are.

```
type(message)
type 'str'>
type(n)
type 'int'>
type(pi)
type 'float'>
```

The type of a variable is the type of the value it refers to.

VARIABLE NAMES AND KEYWORDS

Programmers generally choose names for their variables that are meaningful they document what the variable is used for. Variable names can be arbitrarily long. They can contain both letters and numbers, but they have to begin with a letter. Although it is legal to use uppercase letters, by convention we don't. If you do, remember that case matters. Bruce and bruce are different variables.

The underscore character (_) can appear in a name. It is often used in names with multiple words, such as my_name or price_of_tea_in_china.

If you give a variable an illegal name, you get a syntax error:

```
76trombones = 'big parade'
SyntaxError: invalid syntax
```

```
more$ = 1000000
SyntaxError: invalid syntax
class = 'Computer Science 101'
SyntaxError: invalid syntax
```

76trombones is illegal because it does not begin with a letter. more$ is illegal because it contains an illegal character, the dollar sign. But what's wrong with class?

It turns out that class is one of the Python keywords. Keywords define the language's rules and structure, and they cannot be used as variable names.

Python has twenty-nine keywords:

and	def	exec	if	not	return
assert	del	finally	import	or	try
break	elif	for	in	pass	while
class	else	from	is	print	yield
continue	except	global	lambda	raise	

If the interpreter complains about one of your variable names and you don't know.

STATEMENTS

A statement is an instruction that the Python interpreter can execute. We have seen two kinds of statements: print and assignment.

When you type a statement on the command line, Python executes it and displays the result, if there is one. The result of a print statement is a value.

Assignment statements don't produce a result. A script usually contains a sequence of statements. If there is more than one statement, the results appear one at a time as the statements execute.

For example, the script

```
print 1
x = 2
print x
```

produces the output

```
1
2
```

Again, the assignment statement produces no output.

EVALUATING EXPRESSIONS

An expression is a combination of values, variables, and operators. If you type an expression on the command line, the interpreter evaluates it and displays the result:

```
1 + 1
2
```

Although expressions contain values, variables, and operators, not every expression contains all of these elements. A value all by itself is considered an expression, and so is a variable.

```
17
17
>>> x
2
```

Confusingly, evaluating an expression is not quite the same thing as printing a value.

```
message = 'Hello, World!'
message
'Hello, World!'
print message
Hello, World!
```

When the Python interpreter displays the value of an expression, it uses the same format you would use to enter a value. In the case of strings, that means that it includes the quotation marks. But if you use a print statement, Python displays the contents of the string without the quotation marks. In a script, an expression all by itself is a legal statement, but it doesn't do anything.

```
17
3.2
'Hello, World!'
1 + 1
```

The script produces no output at all. How would you change the script to display the values of these four expressions?

OPERATORS AND OPERANDS

Operators are special symbols that represent computations like addition and multiplication. The values the operator uses are called operands.

The following are all legal Python expressions whose meaning is more or less clear:

```
20+32 hour-1 hour*60+minute minute/60 5**2
(5+9)*(15-7)
```

The symbols +, –, and /, and the use of parenthesis for grouping, mean in Python what they mean in mathematics. The asterisk (*) is the symbol for multiplication, and ** is the symbol for exponentiation.

When a variable name appears in the place of an operand, it is replaced with its value before the operation is performed.

Addition, subtraction, multiplication, and exponentiation all do what you expect, but you might be surprised by division.

The following operation has an unexpected result:

```
minute = 59
minute/60
0
```

The value of minute is 59, and in conventional arithmetic 59 divided by 60 is 0.98333, not 0. The reason for the discrepancy is that Python is performinginteger division.

When both of the operands are integers, the result must also be an integer, and by convention, integer division always rounds *down,* even in cases like this where the next integer is very close.

A possible solution to this problem is to calculate a percentage rather than a fraction:

```
minute*100/60
98
```

Again the result is rounded down, but at least now the answer is approximately correct. Another alternative is to use floating-point division, which we get to inChapter 3.

ORDER OF OPERATIONS

When more than one operator appears in an expression, the order of evaluation depends on the rules of precedence. Python follows the same precedence rules for its mathematical operators that mathematics does.

The acronym PEMDAS is a useful way to remember the order of operations:

- Parentheses have the highest precedence and can be used to force an expression to evaluate in the order you want. Since expressions in parentheses are evaluated first, 2 * (3–1) is 4, and (1+1)**(5–2) is 8. You can also use parentheses to make an expression easier to read, as in (minute * 100)/ 60, even though it doesn't change the result.
- Exponentiation has the next highest precedence, so 2**1+1 is 3 and not 4, and 3*1**3 is 3 and not 27.
- Multiplication and Division have the same precedence, which is higher thanAddition and Subtraction, which also have the same precedence. So 2*3-1yields 5 rather than 4, and 2/3–1 is –1, not 1 (remember that in integer division, 2/3=0).
- Operators with the same precedence are evaluated from left to right. So in the expression minute*100/ 60, the multiplication happens first, yielding 5900/ 60, which in turn yields 98. If the operations had been evaluated from right to left, the result would have been 59*1, which is 59, which is wrong.

OPERATIONS ON STRINGS

In general, you cannot perform mathematical operations on strings, even if the strings look like numbers. The following are illegal (assuming that message has typestring):

```
message-1 'Hello'/123 message*'Hello' '15'+2
```

Interestingly, the + operator does work with strings, although it does not do exactly what you might expect. For strings, the + operator representsconcatenation, which means joining the two operands by linking them end-to-end. For example:

```
fruit = 'banana'
bakedGood = ' nut bread'
print fruit + bakedGood
```

The output of this programme is banana nut bread. The space before the word nut is part of the string, and is necessary to produce the space between the concatenated strings. The * operator also works on strings; it performs repetition. For example, 'Fun'*3is 'FunFunFun'. One of the operands has to be a string; the other has to be an integer.

On one hand, this interpretation of + and * makes sense by analogy with addition and multiplication. Just as 4*3 is equivalent to 4+4+4, we expect 'Fun'*3 to be the same as 'Fun'+'Fun'+'Fun', and it is. On the other hand, there is a significant way in which string concatenation and repetition are different from integer addition and multiplication. Can you think of a property that addition and multiplication have that string concatenation and repetition do not?

COMPOSITION

So far, we have looked at the elements of a programme variables, expressions, and statements in isolation, without talking about how to combine them. One of the most useful features of programming languages is their ability to take small building blocks and compose them. For example, we know how to add numbers and we know how to print; it turns out we can do both at the same time:

```
print 17 + 3
20
```

In reality, the addition has to happen before the printing, so the actions aren't actually happening at the same time. The point is that any expression involving numbers, strings, and variables can be used inside a print statement.

You've already seen an example of this:

```
print 'Number of minutes since midnight: ',
hour*60+minute
```

You can also put arbitrary expressions on the right-hand side of an assignment statement:

```
percentage = (minute * 100)/ 60
```

This ability may not seem impressive now, but you will see other examples where composition makes it possible to express complex computations neatly and concisely.

Warning: There are limits on where you can use certain expressions. For example, the left-hand side of an assignment statement has to be a *variable* name, not an expression. So, the following is illegal: minute+1 = hour.

COMMENTS

As programmes get bigger and more complicated, they get more difficult to read. Formal languages are dense, and it is often difficult to look at a piece of code and figure out what it is doing, or why.

For this reason, it is a good idea to add notes to your programmes to explain in natural language what the programme is doing.

These notes are called comments, and they are marked with the # symbol:

```
# compute the percentage of the hour that
has elapsed
percentage = (minute * 100)/ 60
```

In this case, the comment appears on a line by itself. You can also put comments at the end of a line:

```
percentage = (minute * 100)/ 60 # caution:
integer division
```

Everything from the # to the end of the line is ignored it has no effect on the programme. The message is intended for the programmer or for future programmers who might use this code. In this case, it reminds the reader about the ever-surprising behaviour of integer division.

This sort of comment is less necessary if you use the integer division operation,//. It has the same effect as the division operator * Note, but it signals that the effect is deliberate.

```
percentage = (minute * 100)// 60
```

The integer division operator is like a comment that says, "I know this is integer division, and I like it that way!"

GLOSSARY

Value: A number or string (or other thing to be named later) that can be stored in a variable or computed in an expression.

- *Type*: A set of values. The type of a value determines

how it can be used in expressions. So far, the types you have seen are integers (type int), floating-point numbers (type float), and strings (type string).

- *Floating-point*: A format for representing numbers with fractional parts.
- *Variable*: A name that refers to a value.
- *Statement*: A section of code that represents a command or action. So far, the statements you have seen are assignments and print statements.
- *Assignment*: A statement that assigns a value to a variable.
- *State diagram*: A graphical representation of a set of variables and the values to which they refer.
- *Keyword*: A reserved word that is used by the compiler to parse a programme; you cannot use keywords like if, def, and while as variable names.
- *Operator*: A special symbol that represents a simple computation like addition, multiplication, or string concatenation.
- *Operand*: One of the values on which an operator operates.
- *Expression*: A combination of variables, operators, and values that represents a single result value.
- *Evaluate*: To simplify an expression by performing the operations in order to yield a single value.
- *Integer division*: An operation that divides one integer by another and yields an integer. Integer division yields only the whole number of times that the numerator is divisible by the denominator and discards any remainder.
- Rules of precedence: The set of rules governing the order in which expressions involving multiple operators and operands are evaluated.
- *Concatenate*: To join two operands end-to-end.
- *Composition*: The ability to combine simple expressions and statements into compound statements and expressions in order to represent complex computations concisely.

- *Comment*: Information in a programme that is meant for other programmers (or anyone reading the source code) and has no effect on the execution of the programme.
- *Warning*: The HTML version of this document is generated from Latex and may contain translation errors. In particular, some mathematical expressions are not translated correctly.

FUNCTIONS

FUNCTION CALLS

You have already seen one example of a function call:

```
>>> type("32")
<type 'str'>
```

The name of the function is type, and it displays the type of a value or variable. The value or variable, which is called the argument of the function, has to be enclosed in parentheses. It is common to say that a function "takes" an argument and "returns" a result. The result is called the return value.

Instead of printing the return value, we could assign it to a variable:

```
betty = type("32")
print betty
type 'str'>
```

As another example, the id function takes a value or a variable and returns an integer that acts as a unique identifier for the value:

```
id(3)
134882108
betty = 3
id(betty)
134882108
```

Every value has an id, which is a unique number related to where it is stored in the memory of the computer. The id of a variable is the id of the value to which it refers.

TYPE CONVERSION

Python provides a collection of built-in functions that

convert values from one type to another. The int function takes any value and converts it to an integer, if possible, or complains otherwise:

```
int("32")
32
int("Hello")
ValueError: invalid literal for int(): Hello
```

int *can also convert floating-point values to integers, but remember that it truncates the fractional part:*

```
int(3.99999)
3
int(-2.3)
-2
```

The float function converts integers and strings to floating-point numbers:

```
float(32)
32.0
float("3.14159")
3.14159
```

Finally, the str function converts to type string:

```
str(32)
'32'
str(3.14149)
'3.14149'
```

It may seem odd that Python distinguishes the integer value 1 from the floating-point value 1.0. They may represent the same number, but they belong to different types. The reason is that they are represented differently inside the computer.

TYPE COERCION

Now that we can convert between types, we have another way to deal with integer division. Returning to the example from the previous chapter, suppose we want to calculate the fraction of an hour that has elapsed. The most obvious expression, minute / 60, does integer arithmetic, so the result is always 0, even at 59 minutes past the hour. One solution is to convert minute to floating-point and do floating-point division:

```
minute = 59
float(minute)/ 60
0.983333333333
```

Alternatively, we can take advantage of the rules for automatic type conversion, which is called type coercion. For the mathematical operators, if either operand is a float, the other is automatically converted to a float:

```
minute = 59
minute / 60.0
0.983333333333
```

By making the denominator a float, we force Python to do floating-point division.

MATH FUNCTIONS

In mathematics, you have probably seen functions like sin and log, and you have learned to evaluate expressions like sin(pi/2) and log(1/x). First, you evaluate the expression in parentheses (the argument). For example, pi/2 is approximately 1.571, and 1/x is 0.1 (if × happens to be 10.0).

Then, you evaluate the function itself, either by looking it up in a programming or by performing various computations. The sin of 1.571 is 1, and the log of 0.1 is –1 (assuming that log indicates the logarithm base 10).

This process can be applied repeatedly to evaluate more complicated expressions like log(1/sin(pi/2)). First, you evaluate the argument of the innermost function, then evaluate the function, and so on.

Python has a math module that provides most of the familiar mathematical functions. A module is a file that contains a collection of related functions grouped together.

Before we can use the functions from a module, we have to import them:

```
import math
```

To call one of the functions, we have to specify the name of the module and the name of the function, separated by a dot, also known as a period. This format is called dot notation.

```
decibel = math.log10 (17.0)
angle = 1.5
```

```
height = math.sin(angle)
```

The first statement sets decibel to the logarithm of 17, base 10. There is also a function called log that takes logarithm base e.

The third statement finds the sine of the value of the variable angle. sin and the other trigonometric functions (cos, tan, etc.) take arguments in radians. To convert from degrees to radians, divide by 360 and multiply by 2*pi. For example, to find the sine of 45 degrees, first calculate the angle in radians and then take the sine:

```
degrees = 45
angle = degrees * 2 * math.pi / 360.0
math.sin(angle)
0.707106781187
```

The constant pi is also part of the math module. If you know your geometry, you can check the previous result by comparing it to the square root of two divided by two:

```
math.sqrt(2)/ 2.0
0.707106781187
```

COMPOSITION

Just as with mathematical functions, Python functions can be composed, meaning that you use one expression as part of another.

For example, you can use any expression as an argument to a function:

```
x = math.cos(angle + math.pi/2)
```

This statement takes the value of **pi**, divides it by 2, and adds the result to the value of **angle**. The sum is then passed as an argument to the **cos** function.

You can also take the result of one function and pass it as an argument to another:

```
x = math.exp(math.log(10.0))
```

This statement finds the log base **e** of 10 and then raises e to that power. The result gets assigned to **x**.

ADDING NEW FUNCTIONS

So far, we have only been using the functions that come with Python, but it is also possible to add new functions.

Creating new functions to solve your particular problems is one of the most useful things about a general-purpose programming language.

In the context of programming, a function is a named sequence of statements that performs a desired operation. This operation is specified in a function definition. The functions we have been using so far have been defined for us, and these definitions have been hidden. This is a good thing, because it allows us to use the functions without worrying about the details of their definitions.

The syntax for a function definition is:

```
def NAME( LIST OF PARAMETERS ):
    STATEMENTS
```

You can make up any names you want for the functions you create, except that you can't use a name that is a Python keyword. The list of parameters specifies what information, if any, you have to provide in order to use the new function.

There can be any number of statements inside the function, but they have to be indented from the left margin. In the examples in this book, we will use an indentation of two spaces.

The first couple of functions we are going to write have no parameters, so the syntax looks like this:

```
def newLine():
print
```

This function is named newLine. The empty parentheses indicate that it has no parameters. It contains only a single statement, which outputs a newline character. (That's what happens when you use a print command without any arguments.)

The syntax for calling the new function is the same as the syntax for built-in functions:

```
print "First Line."
newLine()
print "Second Line."
```

The output of this programme is:

```
First line.
Second line.
```

Notice the extra space between the two lines. What if we wanted more space between the lines? We could call the same function repeatedly:

```
print "First Line."
newLine()
newLine()
newLine()
print "Second Line."
```

Or we could write a new function named ***threeLines*** *that prints three new lines*:

```
def threeLines():
newLine()
newLine()
newLine()
print "First Line."
threeLines()
print "Second Line."
```

This function contains three statements, all of which are indented by two spaces. Since the next statement is not indented, Python knows that it is not part of the function.

You should notice a few things about this programme:

- You can call the same procedure repeatedly. In fact, it is quite common and useful to do so.
- You can have one function call another function; in this case threeLines callsnewLine.

So far, it may not be clear why it is worth the trouble to create all of these new functions.

Actually, there are a lot of reasons, but this example demonstrates two:

- Creating a new function gives you an opportunity to name a group of statements. Functions can simplify a programme by hiding a complex computation behind a single command and by using English words in place of arcane code.
- Creating a new function can make a programme smaller by eliminating repetitive code. For example, a short way to print nine consecutive new lines is to call threeLines three times.

As an exercise, write a function called nineLines that usesthreeLines to print nine blank lines. How would you print twenty-seven new lines?

DEFINITIONS AND USE

Pulling together the code fragments from Section 3.6, the whole programme looks like this:

```
def newLine():
  print
def threeLines():
  newLine()
  newLine()
  newLine()
print "First Line."
threeLines()
print "Second Line."
```

This programme contains two function definitions: newLine and threeLines. Function definitions get executed just like other statements, but the effect is to create the new function. The statements inside the function do not get executed until the function is called, and the function definition generates no output. As you might expect, you have to create a function before you can execute it. In other words, the function definition has to be executed before the first time it is called.

As an exercise, move the last three lines of this programme to the top, so the function calls appear before the definitions. Run the programme and see what error message you get. As another exercise, start with the working version of the programme and move the definition of newLine after the definition of threeLines. What happens when you run this programme?

FLOW OF EXECUTION

In order to ensure that a function is defined before its first use, you have to know the order in which statements are executed, which is called the flow of execution. Execution always begins at the first statement of the programme. Statements are executed one at a time, in order from top to bottom. Function definitions do not alter the flow of execution of the programme, but remember that statements inside the function are not executed until the function is called.

Although it is not common, you can define one function inside another. In this case, the inner definition isn't executed until the outer function is called. Function calls are like a detour in the flow of execution. Instead of going to the next statement, the flow jumps to the first line of the called function, executes all the statements there, and then comes back to pick up where it left off. That sounds simple enough, until you remember that one function can call another.

While in the middle of one function, the programme might have to execute the statements in another function. But while executing that new function, the programme might have to execute yet another function! Fortunately, Python is adept at keeping track of where it is, so each time a function completes, the programme picks up where it left off in the function that called it.

When it gets to the end of the programme, it terminates. What's the moral of this sordid tale? When you read a programme, don't read from top to bottom. Instead, follow the flow of execution.

PARAMETERS AND ARGUMENTS

Some of the built-in functions you have used require arguments, the values that control how the function does its job. For example, if you want to find the sine of a number, you have to indicate what the number is.

Thus, sin takes a numeric value as an argument. Some functions take more than one argument. For example, pow takes two arguments, the base and the exponent. Inside the function, the values that are passed get assigned to variables called parameters.

Here is an example of a user-defined function that has a parameter:

```
def printTwice(bruce):
print bruce, bruce
```

This function takes a single argument and assigns it to a parameter named bruce. The value of the parameter (at this point we have no idea what it will be) is printed twice, followed by a newline. The name bruce was chosen to suggest that the name you give a parameter is up to you, but in general, you want to choose something more illustrative than *bruce*.

The function printTwice *works for any type that can be printed*:

```
>>> printTwice('Spam')
Spam Spam
printTwice(5)
5 5
printTwice(3.14159)
3.14159 3.14159
```

In the first function call, the argument is a string. In the second, it's an integer. In the third, it's a float.

The same rules of composition that apply to built-in functions also apply to user-defined functions, so we can use any kind of expression as an argument forprintTwice:

```
printTwice('Spam'*4)
SpamSpamSpamSpam SpamSpamSpamSpam
printTwice(math.cos(math.pi))
-1.0 -1.0
```

As usual, the expression is evaluated before the function is run, so printTwice prints

SpamSpamSpamSpam SpamSpamSpamSpam instead of 'Spam'*4 'Spam'*4. As an exercise, write a call to printTwice that does print 'Spam'*4'Spam'*4.

We can also use a variable as an argument:

```
michael = 'Eric, the half a bee.'
printTwice(michael)
Eric, the half a bee. Eric, the half a bee.
```

Notice something very important here. The name of the variable we pass as an argument (michael) has nothing to do with the name of the parameter (bruce). It doesn't matter what the value was called back home (in the caller); here inprintTwice, we call everybody bruce.

VARIABLES AND PARAMETERS ARE LOCAL

When you create a local variable inside a function, it only exists inside the function, and you cannot use it outside.

For example:

```
def catTwice(part1, part2):
cat = part1 + part2
printTwice(cat)
```

This function takes two arguments, concatenates them, and then prints the result twice. We can call the function with two strings:

```
chant1 = "Pie Jesu domine, "
chant2 = "Dona eis requiem."
catTwice(chant1, chant2)
Pie Jesu domine, Dona eis requiem. Pie Jesu
domine, Dona eis requiem.
```

When **catTwice** *terminates, the variable* **cat** *is destroyed. If we try to print it, we get an error:*

```
print cat
NameError: cat
```

Parameters are also local. For example, outside the function printTwice, there is no such thing as bruce. If you try to use it, Python will complain.

STACK DIAGRAMS

To keep track of which variables can be used where, it is sometimes useful to draw a stack diagram. Like state diagrams, stack diagrams show the value of each variable, but they also show the function to which each variable belongs. Each function is represented by a frame. A frame is a box with the name of a function beside it and the parameters and variables of the function inside it.

The stack diagram for the previous example looks like this:

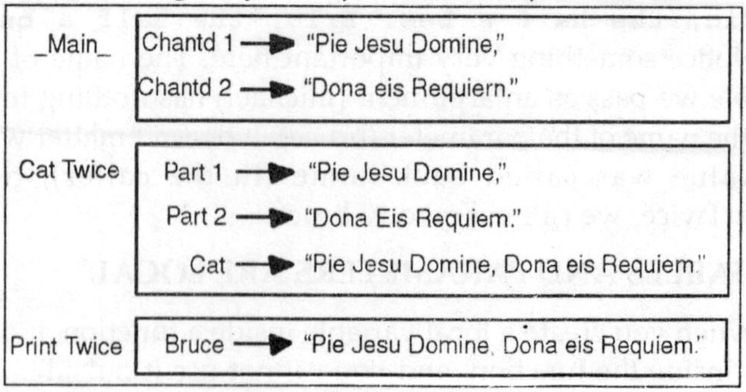

The order of the stack shows the flow of execution. printTwice was called bycatTwice, and catTwice was called by __main__, which is a special name for the topmost function. When you create a variable outside of any function, it belongs to__main__.

Each parameter refers to the same value as its corresponding argument. So, part1has the same value as chant1, part2 has the same value as chant2, and bruce has the same value as cat.

If an error occurs during a function call, Python prints the name of the function, and the name of the function that called it, and the name of the function that called*that*, all the way back to __main__.

For example, if we try to access cat from within ***printTwice****, we get a* **NameError**:

```
Traceback (innermost last):
  File "test.py", line 13, in __main__
    catTwice(chant1, chant2)
  File "test.py", line 5, in catTwice
    printTwice(cat)
  File "test.py", line 9, in printTwice
    print cat
NameError: cat
```

This list of functions is called a traceback. It tells you what programme file the error occurred in, and what line, and what functions were executing at the time. It also shows the line of code that caused the error. Notice the similarity between the traceback and the stack diagram. It's not a coincidence.

FUNCTIONS WITH RESULTS

You might have noticed by now that some of the functions we are using, such as the math functions, yield results. Other functions, like newLine, perform an action but don't return a value.

That raises some questions:

- What happens if you call a function and you don't do anything with the result (i.e., you don't assign it to a variable or use it as part of a larger expression)?

- What happens if you use a function without a result as part of an expression, such as newLine() + 7?
- Can you write functions that yield results, or are you stuck with simple function like newLine and printTwice?

The answer to the last question is that you can write functions that yield results, As an exercise, answer the other two questions by trying them out. When you have a question about what is legal or illegal in Python, a good way to find out is to ask the interpreter.

GLOSSARY

- *Function call*: A statement that executes a function. It consists of the name of the function followed by a list of arguments enclosed in parentheses.
- *Argument*: A value provided to a function when the function is called. This value is assigned to the corresponding parameter in the function.
- *Return value*: The result of a function. If a function call is used as an expression, the return value is the value of the expression.
- *Type conversion*: An explicit statement that takes a value of one type and computes a corresponding value of another type.
- *Type coercion*: A type conversion that happens automatically according to Python's coercion rules.
- *Module*: A file that contains a collection of related functions and classes.
- *Dot notation*: The syntax for calling a function in another module, specifying the module name followed by a dot (period) and the function name.
- *Function*: A named sequence of statements that performs some useful operation. Functions may or may not take arguments and may or may not produce a result.
- *Function definition*: A statement that creates a new function, specifying its name, parameters, and the statements it executes.

- *Flow of execution*: The order in which statements are executed during a programme run.
- *Parameter*: A name used inside a function to refer to the value passed as an argument.
- *Local variable*: A variable defined inside a function. A local variable can only be used inside its function.
- *Stack diagram*: A graphical representation of a stack of functions, their variables, and the values to which they refer.
- *Frame*: A box in a stack diagram that represents a function call. It contains the local variables and parameters of the function.
- *Traceback*: A list of the functions that are executing, printed when a runtime error occurs.

CONDITIONALS AND RECURSION

THE MODULUS OPERATOR

The modulus operator works on integers (and integer expressions) and yields the remainder when the first operand is divided by the second. In Python, the modulus operator is a per cent sign (%).

The syntax is the same as for other operators:

```
quotient = 7 / 3
print quotient
2
remainder = 7 % 3
>>> print remainder
1
```

So 7 divided by 3 is 2 with 1 left over.

The modulus operator turns out to be surprisingly useful. For example, you can check whether one number is divisible by another if × % y is zero, then **x** is divisible by y. Also, you can extract the right-most digit or digits from a number. For example, × % 10 yields the right-most digit of × (in base 10). Similarly × % 100 yields the last two digits.

BOOLEAN EXPRESSIONS

A boolean expression is an expression that is either true

or false. One way to write a boolean expression is to use the operator ==, which compares two values and produces a boolean value:

```
5 == 5
True
5 == 6
False
```

In the first statement, the two operands are equal, so the value of the expression isTrue; in the second statement, 5 is not equal to 6, so we get False. True and Falseare special values that are built into Python.

The == operator is one of the comparison operators; the others are:

```
x != y     #  x is not equal to y
x > y      #  x is greater than y
x < y      #  x is less than y
x => y     #  x is greater than or equal to y
x <= y     #  x is less than or equal to y
```

Although these operations are probably familiar to you, the Python symbols are different from the mathematical symbols. A common error is to use a single equal sign (=) instead of a double equal sign (==). Remember that = is an assignment operator and == is a comparison operator. Also, there is no such thing as => or <=.

LOGICAL OPERATORS

There are three logical operators: and, or, and not. The semantics (meaning) of these operators is similar to their meaning in English. For exámple, x > 0 and x < 10 is true only if **x** is greater than 0 *and* less than 10. n%2 == 0 or n%3 == 0 is true if *either* of the conditions is true, that is, if the number is divisible by 2 *or* 3.

Finally, the not operator negates a boolean expression, so not(x > y) is true if (x > y) is false, that is, if x is less than or equal to y. Strictly speaking, the operands of the logical operators should be boolean expressions, but Python is not very strict. Any nonzero number is interpreted as "true."

```
x = 5
x and 1
```

```
1
y = 0
y and 1
0
```

In general, this sort of thing is not considered good style. If you want to compare a value to zero, you should do it explicitly.

CONDITIONAL EXECUTION

In order to write useful programmes, we almost always need the ability to check conditions and change the behaviour of the programme accordingly. Conditional statements give us this ability. The simplest form is the if statement:

```
if x > 0:
  print "x is positive"
```

The boolean expression after the **if** statement is called the condition. If it is true, then the indented statement gets executed. If not, nothing happens.

*Like other compound statements, the **if** statement is made up of a header and a block of statements*:

```
HEADER:
  FIRST STATEMENT
  ...
  LAST STATEMENT
```

The header begins on a new line and ends with a colon (:). The indented statements that follow are called a block. The first unindented statement marks the end of the block. A statement block inside a compound statement is called thebody of the statement. There is no limit on the number of statements that can appear in the body of an if statement, but there has to be at least one. Occasionally, it is useful to have a body with no statements (usually as a place keeper for code you haven't written yet). In that case, you can use the pass statement, which does nothing.

ALTERNATIVE EXECUTION

A second form of the if statement is alternative execution, in which there are two possibilities and the condition determines which one gets executed. The syntax looks like this:

```
if x%2 == 0:
    print x, "is even"
else:
    print x, "is odd"
```

If the remainder when x is divided by 2 is 0, then we know that x is even, and the programme displays a message to that effect. If the condition is false, the second set of statements is executed. Since the condition must be true or false, exactly one of the alternatives will be executed. The alternatives are called branches, because they are branches in the flow of execution.

As an aside, if you need to check the parity (evenness or oddness) of numbers often, you might "wrap" this code in a function:

```
def printParity(x):
    if x%2 == 0:
        print x, "is even"
    else:
        print x, "is odd"
```

For any value of x, printParity displays an appropriate message. When you call it, you can provide any integer expression as an argument.

```
>>> printParity(17)
17 is odd
>>> y = 17
>>> printParity(y+1)
18 is even
```

CHAINED CONDITIONALS

Sometimes there are more than two possibilities and we need more than two branches.

One way to express a computation like that is a chained conditional:

```
if x < y:
    print x, "is less than", y
elif x > y:
    print x, "is greater than", y
else:
    print x, "and", y, "are equal"
```

elif is an abbreviation of "else if." Again, exactly one branch will be executed. There is no limit of the number of elif statements, but the last branch has to be anelse statement:

```
if choice == 'A':
  functionA()
elif choice == 'B':
  functionB()
elif choice == 'C':
  functionC()
else:
  print "Invalid choice."
```

Each condition is checked in order. If the first is false, the next is checked, and so on. If one of them is true, the corresponding branch executes, and the statement ends. Even if more than one condition is true, only the first true branch executes. As an exercise, wrap these examples in functions called compare(x, y) and dispatch(choice).

NESTED CONDITIONALS

One conditional can also be nested within another. We could have written the trichotomy example as follows:

```
if x == y:
  print x, "and", y, "are equal"
else:
  if x < y:
print x, "is less than", y
  else:
    print x, "is greater than", y
```

The outer conditional contains two branches. The first branch contains a simple output statement. The second branch contains another if statement, which has two branches of its own. Those two branches are both output statements, although they could have been conditional statements as well.

Although the indentation of the statements makes the structure apparent, nested conditionals become difficult to read very quickly. In general, it is a good idea to avoid them when you can. Logical operators often provide a way to simplify nested conditional statements.

For example, we can rewrite the following code using a single conditional:

```
if 0 < x:
  if x < 10:
    print "x is a positive single digit."
```

The print statement is executed only if we make it past both the conditionals, so we can use the and operator:

```
if 0 < x and x < 10:
    print "x is a positive single digit."
```

These kinds of conditions are common, so Python provides an alternative syntax that is similar to mathematical notation:

```
if 0 < x < 10:
  print "x is a positive single digit."
```

This condition is semantically the same as the compound boolean expression and the nested conditional.

THE RETURN STATEMENT

The return statement allows you to terminate the execution of a function before you reach the end.

One reason to use it is if you detect an error condition:

```
import math
def printLogarithm(x):
    if x ⇐ 0:
        print "Positive numbers only, please."
        return
  result = math.log(x)
  print "The log of x is", result
```

The function printLogarithm has a parameter named x. The first thing it does is check whether x is less than or equal to 0, in which case it displays an error message and then uses return to exit the function. The flow of execution immediately returns to the caller, and the remaining lines of the function are not executed. Remember that to use a function from the math module, you have to import it.

RECURSION

We mentioned that it is legal for one function to call another, and you have seen several examples of that. We neglected to mention that it is also legal for a function to call itself. It may not be obvious why that is a good thing, but it turns out to be one of the most magical and interesting things a programme can do.

For example, look at the following function:

```
def countdown(n):
  if n == 0:
print "Blastoff!"
  else:
  print n
  countdown(n-1)
```

countdown expects the parameter, n, to be a positive integer. If n is 0, it outputs the word, "Blastoff!" Otherwise, it outputs n and then calls a function named countdown-itself passing n-1 as an argument.

What happens if we call this function like this:

```
>>> countdown(3)
```

The execution of countdown begins with n=3, and since n is not 0, it outputs the value 3, and then calls itself...

The execution of countdown begins with n=2, and since n is not 0, it outputs the value 2, and then calls itself...

The execution of countdown begins with n=1, and since nis not 0, it outputs the value 1, and then calls itself...

The execution of countdown begins withn=0, and since n is 0, it outputs the word, "Blastoff!" and then returns.

The countdown that got n=1 returns.

The countdown that got n=2 returns.

The countdown that got n=3 returns.

And then you're back in __main__ (what a trip). So, the total output looks like this:

```
3
2
1
Blastoff!
```

As a second example, look again at the functions newLine and threeLines:

```
def newline():
  print
```

```
def threeLines():
  newLine()
  newLine()
  newLine()
```

Although these work, they would not be much help if we wanted to output 2 newlines, or 106.

A better alternative would be this:

```
def nLines(n):
  if n > 0:
     print
     nLines(n-1)
```

This programme is similar to countdown; as long as n is greater than 0, it outputs one newline and then calls itself to output n-1 additional newlines. Thus, the total number of newlines is 1 + (n – 1) which, if you do your algebra right, comes out ton. The process of a function calling itself is recursion, and such functions are said to be recursive.

STACK DIAGRAMS FOR RECURSIVE FUNCTIONS

Every time a function gets called, Python creates a new function frame, which contains the function's local variables and parameters. For a recursive function, there might be more than one frame on the stack at the same time.

This figure shows a stack diagram for countdown called with n = 3:

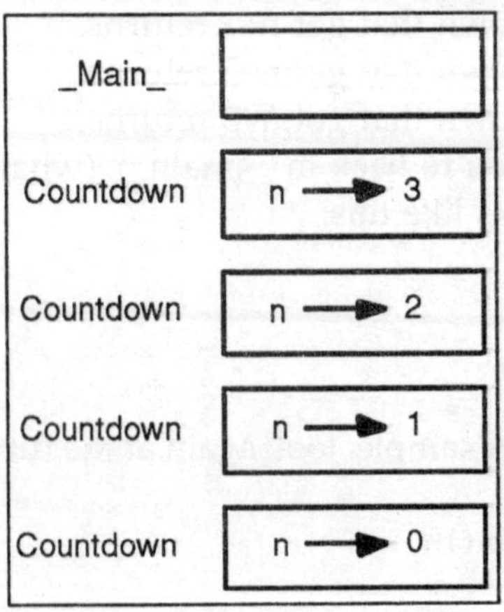

As usual, the top of the stack is the frame for __main__. It is empty because we did not create any variables in __main__ or pass any arguments to it.

The four countdown frames have different values for the parameter n. The bottom of the stack, where n=0, is called the base case. It does not make a recursive call, so there are no more frames. As an exercise, draw a stack diagram for nLines called with n=4.

INFINITE RECURSION

If a recursion never reaches a base case, it goes on making recursive calls forever, and the programme never terminates. This is known as infinite recursion, and it is generally not considered a good idea. Here is a minimal programme with an infinite recursion:

```
def recurse():
    recurse()
```

In most programming environments, a programme with infinite recursion does not really run forever.

Python reports an error message when the maximum recursion depth is reached:

```
File "<stdin>", line 2, in recurse
(98 repetitions omitted)
File "<stdin>", line 2, in recurse
RuntimeError: Maximum recursion depth exceeded
```

This traceback is a little bigger than the one we saw in the previous chapter. When the error occurs, there are 100 recurse frames on the stack!

As an exercise, write a function with infinite recursion and run it in the Python interpreter.

KEYBOARD INPUT

The programmes we have written so far are a bit rude in the sense that they accept no input from the user. They just do the same thing every time.

Python provides built-in functions that get input from the keyboard. The simplest is called raw_input. When this function is called, the programme stops and waits for the user to type something. When the user presses Return or the Enter key, the programme resumes and raw_input returns what the user typed as a string:

```
input = raw_input ()
What are you waiting for?
print input
What are you waiting for?
```

Before calling **raw_input**, it is a good idea to print a message telling the user what to input. This message is called a prompt.

We can supply a prompt as an argument to **raw_input**:

```
name = raw_input ("What...is your name?
")
What...is your name? Arthur, King of the
Britons!
>>> print name
Arthur, King of the Britons!
```

If we expect the response to be an integer, we can use the input function:

```
prompt = "What...is the airspeed velocity of
an unladen
swallow?\n"
speed = input(prompt)
```

The sequence \n at the end of the string represents a newline, so the user's input appears below the prompt.

If the user types a string of digits, it is converted to an integer and assigned tospeed.

Unfortunately, if the user types a character that is not a digit, the programme crashes:

```
speed = input (prompt)
What...is the airspeed velocity of an unladen
swallow?
What do you mean, an African or a European
swallow?
SyntaxError: invalid syntax
```

To avoid this kind of error, it is generally a good idea to use raw_input to get a string and then use conversion functions to convert to other types.

GLOSSARY

- *Modulus operator*: An operator, denoted with a per cent sign (%), that works on integers and yields the remainder when one number is divided by another.
- *Boolean expression*: An expression that is either true or false.
- *Comparison operator*: One of the operators that compares two values: ==, !=, >, <, Þ, and Ü.
- *Logical operator*: One of the operators that combines boolean expressions: and, or, and not.
- *Conditional statement*: A statement that controls the flow of execution depending on some condition.
- *Condition*: The boolean expression in a conditional statement that determines which branch is executed.
- *Compound statement*: A statement that consists of a header and a body. The header ends with a colon (:). The body is indented relative to the header.
- *Block*: A group of consecutive statements with the same indentation.
- *Body*: The block in a compound statement that follows the header.
- *Nesting*: One programme structure within another, such as a conditional statement inside a branch of another conditional statement.
- *Recursion*: The process of calling the function that is currently executing.
- *Base case*: A branch of the conditional statement in a recursive function that does not result in a recursive call.
- *Infinite recursion*: A function that calls itself recursively without ever reaching the base case. Eventually, an infinite recursion causes a runtime error.
- *Prompt*: A visual cue that tells the user to input data.
- *Warning*: The **HTML** version of this document is generated from Latex and may contain translation errors. In particular, some mathematical expressions are not translated correctly.

FRUITFUL FUNCTIONS

RETURN VALUES

Some of the built-in functions we have used, such as the math functions, have produced results. Calling the function generates a new value, which we usually assign to a variable or use as part of an expression.

```
e = math.exp(1.0)
height = radius * math.sin(angle)
```

But so far, none of the functions we have written has returned a value. In this chapter, we are going to write functions that return values, which we will call fruitful functions, for want of a better name.

The first example is area, which returns the area of a circle with the given radius:

```
import math
def area(radius):
  temp = math.pi * radius**2
  return temp
```

We have seen the **return** statement before, but in a fruitful function the returnstatement includes a return value. This statement means: "Return immediately from this function and use the following expression as a return value."

The expression provided can be arbitrarily complicated, so we could have written this function more concisely:

```
def area(radius):
    return math.pi * radius**2
```

On the other hand, temporary variables like **temp** often make debugging easier.

Sometimes it is useful to have multiple return statements, one in each branch of a conditional:

```
def absoluteValue(x):
    if x < 0:
        return -x
else:
  return x
```

Since these return statements are in an alternative conditional, only one will be executed. As soon as one is executed, the function terminates without executing any subsequent statements. Code that appears after a return statement, or any other place the flow of execution can never reach, is called dead code. In a fruitful function, it is a good idea to ensure that every possible path through the programme hits a return statement.

For example:

```
def absoluteValue(x):
  if x < 0:
     return -x
  elif x > 0:
    return x
```

This programme is not correct because if x happens to be 0, neither condition is true, and the function ends without hitting a return statement. In this case, the return value is a special value called None:

```
print absoluteValue(0)
None
```

As an exercise, write a compare function that returns1 if x > y, 0 if x == y, and -1 if x < y.

PROGRAMME DEVELOPMENT

At this point, you should be able to look at complete functions and tell what they do. Also, if you have been doing the exercises, you have written some small functions. As you write larger functions, you might start to have more difficulty, especially with runtime and semantic errors.

To deal with increasingly complex programmes, we are going to suggest a technique called incremental development. The goal of incremental development is to avoid long debugging sessions by adding and testing only a small amount of code at a time. As an example, suppose you want to find the distance between two points, given by the coordinates (x_1, y_1) and (x_2, y_2).

By the Pythagorean theorem, the distance is:

$$\text{Distance} = \sqrt{(x_2 - x_1)^2 + (y_2 - y_1)^2}$$

The first step is to consider what a distance function

should look like in Python. In other words, what are the inputs (parameters) and what is the output (return value)?

In this case, the two points are the inputs, which we can represent using four parameters. The return value is the distance, which is a floating-point value.

Already we can write an outline of the function:

```
def distance(x1, y1, x2, y2):
  return 0.0
```

Obviously, this version of the function doesn't compute distances; it always returns zero. But it is syntactically correct, and it will run, which means that we can test it before we make it more complicated.

To test the new function, we call it with sample values:

```
distance(1, 2, 4, 6)
0.0
```

We chose these values so that the horizontal distance equals 3 and the vertical distance equals 4; that way, the result is 5 (the hypotenuse of a 3–4–5 triangle). When testing a function, it is useful to know the right answer.

At this point we have confirmed that the function is syntactically correct, and we can start adding lines of code. After each incremental change, we test the function again. If an error occurs at any point, we know where it must be in the last line we added.

A logical first step in the computation is to find the differences $x_2 - x_1$ and $y_2 - y_1$. We will store those values in temporary variables named dx and dy and print them.

```
def distance(x1, y1, x2, y2):
  dx = x2 - x1
  dy = y2 - y1
  print "dx is", dx
  print "dy is", dy
  return 0.0
```

If the function is working, the outputs should be 3 and 4. If so, we know that the function is getting the right arguments and performing the first computation correctly. If not, there are only a few lines to check.

Next we compute the sum of squares of dx *and* dy:

```
def distance(x1, y1, x2, y2):
  dx = x2 - x1
  dy = y2 - y1
  dsquared = dx**2 + dy**2
  print "dsquared is: ", dsquared
  return 0.0
```

Notice that we removed the print statements we wrote in the previous step. Code like that is called scaffolding because it is helpful for building the programme but is not part of the final product. Again, we would run the programme at this stage and check the output (which should be 25).

Finally, if we have imported the math module, we can use the sqrt *function to compute and return the result*:

```
def distance(x1, y1, x2, y2):
  dx = x2 - x1
  dy = y2 - y1
  dsquared = dx**2 + dy**2
  result = math.sqrt(dsquared)
  return result
```

If that works correctly, you are done. Otherwise, you might want to print the value of result before the return statement. When you start out, you should add only a line or two of code at a time. As you gain more experience, you might find yourself writing and debugging bigger chunks. Either way, the incremental development process can save you a lot of debugging time.

The key aspects of the process are:

- Start with a working programme and make small incremental changes. At any point, if there is an error, you will know exactly where it is.
- Use temporary variables to hold intermediate values so you can output and check them.
- Once the programme is working, you might want to remove some of the scaffolding or consolidate multiple statements into compound expressions, but only if it does not make the programme difficult to read.

As an exercise, use incremental development to write a function called hypotenuse that returns the length of the hypotenuse of a right triangle given the lengths of the two legs as arguments. Record each stage of the incremental development process as you go.

COMPOSITION

As you should expect by now, you can call one function from within another. This ability is called composition. As an example, we'll write a function that takes two points, the centre of the circle and a point on the perimeter, and computes the area of the circle.

Assume that the centre point is stored in the variables xc and yc, and the perimeter point is in xp and yp. The first step is to find the radius of the circle, which is the distance between the two points.

Fortunately, there is a function, distance, that does that:

```
radius = distance(xc, yc, xp, yp)
```

The second step is to find the area of a circle with that radius and return it:

```
result = area(radius)
return result
```

Wrapping that up in a function, we get:

```
def area2(xc, yc, xp, yp):
    radius = distance(xc, yc, xp, yp)
    result = area(radius)
    return result
```

We called this function area2 to distinguish it from the area function defined earlier. There can only be one function with a given name within a given module. The temporary variables radius and result are useful for development and debugging, but once the programme is working, we can make it more concise by composing the function calls:

```
def area2(xc, yc, xp, yp):
return area(distance(xc, yc, xp, yp))
```

As an exercise, write a function slope(x1, y1, x2, y2) that returns the slope of the line through the points (x1, y1) and (x2, y2). Then use this function in a function called intercept(x1, y1, x2, y2) that returns the y-intercept of the line through the points(x1, y1) and (x2, y2).

BOOLEAN FUNCTIONS

Functions can return boolean values, which is often convenient for hiding complicated tests inside functions.

For example:

```
def isDivisible(x, y):
  if x % y == 0:
    return True
else:
  return False
```

The name of this function is isDivisible. It is common to give boolean functions names that sound like yes/no questions. isDivisible returns either True or False to indicate whether the x is or is not divisible by y. We can make the function more concise by taking advantage of the fact that the condition of the if statement is itself a boolean expression.

We can return it directly, avoiding the if statement altogether:

```
def isDivisible(x, y):
    return x % y == 0
```

This session shows the new function in action:

```
is Divisible(6, 4)
False
is Divisible(6, 3)
True
```

Boolean functions are often used in conditional statements:

```
if isDivisible(x, y):
    print "x is divisible by y"
else:
    print "x is not divisible by y"
```

It might be tempting to write something like:

```
if isDivisible(x, y) == True:
```

But the extra comparison is unnecessary. As an exercise, write a function isBetween(x, y, z) that returnsTrue if y le x le z or False otherwise.

MORE RECURSION

So far, you have only learned a small subset of Python, but you might be interested to know that this subset is a *complete* programming language, which means that anything that can be computed can be expressed in this language. Any programme ever written could be rewritten using only the language features you have learned so far (actually, you would need a few commands to control devices like the keyboard, mouse, disks, etc., but that's all).

Proving that claim is a nontrivial exercise first accomplished by Alan Turing, one of the first computer scientists (some would argue that he was a mathematician, but a lot of early computer scientists started as mathematicians). Accordingly, it is known as the Turing Thesis. If you take a course on the Theory of Computation, you will have a chance to see the proof.

To give you an idea of what you can do with the tools you have learned so far, we'll evaluate a few recursively defined mathematical functions. A recursive definition is similar to a circular definition, in the sense that the definition contains a reference to the thing being defined. A truly circular definition is not very useful: *Frabjuous*: An adjective used to describe something that is frabjuous. If you saw that definition in the dictionary, you might be annoyed. On the other hand, if you looked up the definition of the mathematical function factorial, you might get something like this:

```
0! = 1
n! = n (n-1)!
```

This definition says that the factorial of 0 is 1, and the factorial of any other value,n, is n multiplied by the factorial of n-1. So 3! is 3 times 2!, which is 2 times 1!, which is 1 times 0!. Putting it all together, 3! equals 3 times 2 times 1 times 1, which is 6. If you can write a recursive definition of something, you can usually write a Python programme to evaluate it. The first step is to decide what the parameters are for this function.

With little effort, you should conclude that factorial has a single parameter:

```
def factorial(n):
```

If the argument happens to be 0, all we have to do is return 1:

```
def factorial(n):
  if n == 0:
    return 1
```

Otherwise, and this is the interesting part, we have to make a recursive call to find the factorial of n-1 and then multiply it by n:

```
def factorial(n):
  if n == 0:
    return 1
else:
  recurse = factorial(n-1)
  result = n * recurse
  return result
```

The flow of execution for this programme is similar to the flow of countdown.

If we call factorial with the value 3:

Since 3 is not 0, we take the second branch and calculate the factorial of n-1...

Since 2 is not 0, we take the second branch and calculate the factorial of n-1...

Since 1 is not 0, we take the second branch and calculate the factorial of n-1...

Since 0 *is* 0, we take the first branch and return 1 without making any more recursive calls.

The return value (1) is multiplied by n, which is 1, and the result is returned.

The return value (1) is multiplied by n, which is 2, and the result is returned.

The return value (2) is multiplied by n, which is 3, and the result, 6, becomes the return value of the function call that started the whole process.

Here is what the stack diagram looks like for this sequence of function calls:

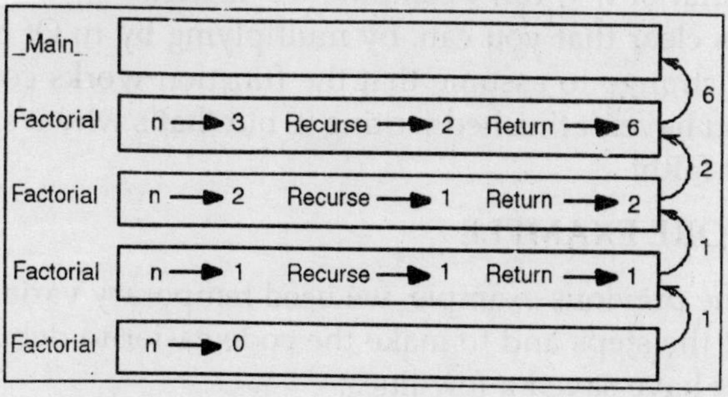

The return values are shown being passed back up the stack. In each frame, the return value is the value of result, which is the product of n and recurse. Notice that in the last frame, the local variables recurse and result do not exist, because the branch that creates them did not execute.

LEAP OF FAITH

Following the flow of execution is one way to read programmes, but it can quickly become labyrinthine. An alternative is what we call the "leap of faith." When you come to a function call, instead of following the flow of execution, you *assume*that the function works correctly and returns the appropriate value.

In fact, you are already practicing this leap of faith when you use built-in functions. When you call math.cos or math.exp, you don't examine the implementations of those functions. You just assume that they work because the people who wrote the built-in functions were good programmers.

The same is true when you call one of your own functions. For example, we wrote a function called isDivisible that determines whether one number is divisible by another. Once we have convinced ourselves that this function is correct by testing and examining the code we can use the function without looking at the code again.

The same is true of recursive programmes. When you get to the recursive call, instead of following the flow of execution, you should assume that the recursive call works (yields the correct result) and then ask yourself, "Assuming that I can find the factorial of n-1, can I compute the factorial of n?" In this case, it is clear that you can, by multiplying by n. Of course, it's a bit strange to assume that the function works correctly when you haven't finished writing it, but that's why it's called a leap of faith!

ONE MORE EXAMPLE

In the previous example, we used temporary variables to spell out the steps and to make the code easier to debug, but we could have saved a few lines:

```
def factorial(n):
    if n == 0:
      return 1
  else:
    return n * factorial(n-1)
```

From now on, we will tend to use the more concise form, but we recommend that you use the more explicit version while you are developing code. When you have it working, you can tighten it up if you are feeling inspired.

After factorial, the most common example of a recursively defined mathematical function is fibonacci, which has the following definition:

```
fibonacci(0)  = 1
fibonacci(1)  = 1
fibonacci(n)  = fibonacci(n 1)  + fibonacci(n-
2);
```

Translated into Python, it looks like this:

```
def fibonacci (n):
  if n == 0 or n == 1:
      return 1
  else:
    return fibonacci(n-1)  + fibonacci(n-2)
```

If you try to follow the flow of execution here, even for fairly small values of n, your head explodes. But according to the leap of faith, if you assume that the two recursive calls work correctly, then it is clear that you get the right result by adding them together.

CHECKING TYPES

What happens if we call factorial and give it 1.5 as an argument?

```
  factorial (1.5)
  RuntimeError: Maximum recursion depth
exceeded
```

It looks like an infinite recursion. But how can that be? There is a base case when n == 0. The problem is that the values of n *miss* the base case. In the first recursive call, the value of n is 0.5. In the next, it is –0.5. From there, it gets smaller and smaller, but it will never be 0. We have two choices. We can try to generalize the factorial function to work with floating-point numbers, or we can make factorial check the type of its argument. The first option is called the gamma function and it's a little beyond the scope of this book. So we'll go for the second.

We can use the built-in function isinstance to verify the type of the argument.

While we're at it, we also make sure the argument is positive:

```
def factorial (n):
  if not isinstance(n, int):
      print "Factorial is only defined for
    integers."
      return -1
elif n < 0:
    print "Factorial is only defined for
  positive integers."
      return -1
    elif n == 0:
      return 1
    else:
      return n * factorial(n-1)
```

Now we have three base cases. The first catches nonintegers. The second catches negative integers. In both cases, the programme prints an error message and returns a special value, –1, to indicate that something went wrong:

```
factorial ("fred")
Factorial is only defined for integers.
-1
factorial (-2)
Factorial is only defined for positive
integers.
-1
```

If we get past both checks, then we know that n is a positive integer, and we can prove that the recursion terminates.

This programme demonstrates a pattern sometimes called a guardian. The first two conditionals act as guardians, protecting the code that follows from values that might cause an error. The guardians make it possible to prove the correctness of the code.

GLOSSARY

- *Fruitful function*: A function that yields a return value.
- *Return value*: The value provided as the result of a function call.
- *Temporary variable*: A variable used to store an intermediate value in a complex calculation.
- *Dead code*: Part of a programme that can never be executed, often because it appears after a return statement.
- *None*: A special Python value returned by functions that have no return statement, or a return statement without an argument.
- *Incremental development*: A programme development plan intended to avoid debugging by adding and testing only a small amount of code at a time.
- *Scaffolding*: Code that is used during programme development but is not part of the final version.
- *Guardian*: A condition that checks for and handles circumstances that might cause an error.

ITERATION

MULTIPLE ASSIGNMENT

As you may have discovered, it is legal to make more than one assignment to the same variable. A new assignment makes an existing variable refer to a new value (and stop referring to the old value).

```
bruce = 5
print bruce,
bruce = 7
print bruce
```

The output of this programme is 5 7, because the first time bruce is printed, his value is 5, and the second time, his value is 7. The comma at the end of the first printstatement suppresses the newline after the output, which is why both outputs appear on the same line.

Here is what multiple assignment looks like in a state diagram:

With multiple assignment it is especially important to distinguish between an assignment operation and a statement of equality. Because Python uses the equal sign (=) for assignment, it is tempting to interpret a statement like a = b as a statement of equality. It is not!

First, equality is commutative and assignment is not. For example, in mathematics, if a = 7 then 7 = a. But in Python, the statement a = 7 is legal and 7 = a is not.

Furthermore, in mathematics, a statement of equality is always true. If a = b now, then a will always equal b.

In Python, an assignment statement can make two variables equal, but they don't have to stay that way:

```
a = 5
b = a   # a and b are now equal
a = 3   # a and b are no longer equal
```

The third line changes the value of a but does not change the value of b, so they are no longer equal. (In some programming languages, a different symbol is used for assignment, such as ← or :=, to avoid confusion.)

Although multiple assignment is frequently helpful, you should use it with caution. If the values of variables change frequently, it can make the code difficult to read and debug.

THE WHILE STATEMENT

Computers are often used to automate repetitive tasks. Repeating identical or similar tasks without making errors is something that computers do well and people do poorly.

We have seen two programmes, nLines and countdown, that use recursion to perform repetition, which is also called iteration. Because iteration is so common, Python provides several language features to make it easier. The first feature we are going to look at is the while statement.

Here is what countdown looks like with a while statement:

```
def countdown(n):
  while n > 0:
    print n
    n = n-1
print "Blastoff!"
```

Since we removed the recursive call, this function is not recursive. You can almost read the while statement as if it were English. It means, "While n is greater than 0, continue displaying the value of n and then reducing the value of nby. When you get to 0, display the word Blastoff!"

More formally, here is the flow of execution for a while statement:

- Evaluate the condition, yielding 0 or 1.
- If the condition is false (0), exit the while statement and continue execution at the next statement.
- If the condition is true (1), execute each of the statements in the body and then go back to step 1.

The body consists of all of the statements below the header with the same indentation. This type of flow is called a loop because the third step loops back around to the top. Notice that if the condition is false the first time through the loop, the statements inside the loop are never executed.

The body of the loop should change the value of one or more variables so that eventually the condition becomes false and the loop terminates. Otherwise the loop will repeat forever, which is called an infinite loop. An endless source of amusement for computer scientists is the observation that the directions on shampoo, "Lather, rinse, repeat," are an infinite loop.

In the case of countdown, we can prove that the loop terminates because we know that the value of n is finite, and we can see that the value of n gets smaller each time through the loop, so eventually we have to get to 0.

In other cases, it is not so easy to tell:

```
def sequence(n):
  while n != 1:
    print n,
```

```
    if n%2 == 0:      # n is even
      n = n/2
    else:             # n is odd
      n = n*3+1
```

The condition for this loop is n != 1, so the loop will continue until n is 1, which will make the condition false.

Each time through the loop, the programme outputs the value of n and then checks whether it is even or odd. If it is even, the value of n is divided by 2. If it is odd, the value is replaced by n*3+1. For example, if the starting value (the argument passed to sequence) is 3, the resulting sequence is 3, 10, 5, 16, 8, 4, 2, 1.

Since n sometimes increases and sometimes decreases, there is no obvious proof that n will ever reach 1, or that the programme terminates. For some particular values of n, we can prove termination. For example, if the starting value is a power of two, then the value of n will be even each time through the loop until it reaches 1. The previous example ends with such a sequence, starting with 16.

Particular values aside, the interesting question is whether we can prove that this programme terminates for *all positive values* of n. So far, no one has been able to prove it *or* disprove it! As an exercise, rewrite the function nLines from Section 4.9using iteration instead of recursion.

TABLES

One of the things loops are good for is generating tabular data. Before computers were readily available, people had to calculate logarithms, sines and cosines, and other mathematical functions by hand. To make that easier, mathematics books contained long tables listing the values of these functions. Creating the tables was slow and boring, and they tended to be full of errors.

When computers appeared on the scene, one of the initial reactions was, "This is great! We can use the computers to generate the tables, so there will be no errors." That turned out to be true (mostly) but shortsighted. Soon thereafter, computers and calculators were so pervasive that the tables became obsolete. Well, almost. For some operations, computers use tables of values to get an approximate answer and then perform computations to improve the approximation. In some cases, there have been errors in the underlying tables, most famously in the programming the Intel Pentium used to perform floating-point division.

Although a log programming is not as useful as it once was, it still makes a good example of iteration. The following programme outputs a sequence of values in the left column and their logarithms in the right column:

```
x = 1.0
while x < 10.0:
  print x, '\t', math.log(x)
  x = x + 1.0
```

The string '\t' represents a tab character.

As characters and strings are displayed on the screen, an invisible marker called the cursor keeps track of where the next character will go. After a printstatement, the cursor normally goes to the beginning of the next line. The tab character shifts the cursor to the right until it reaches one of the tab stops.

Tabs are useful for making columns of text line up, as in the output of the previous programme:

```
1.0    0.0
2.0    0.69314718056
3.0    1.09861228867
4.0    1.38629436112
5.0    1.60943791243
6.0    1.79175946923
7.0    1.94591014906
8.0    2.07944154168
9.0    2.19722457734
```

If these values seem odd, remember that the log function uses base e. Since powers of two are so important in computer science, we often want to find logarithms with respect to base 2. To do that, we can use the following formula:

$$\log_2 x = \frac{\log_e x}{\log_e 2}$$

Changing the output statement to:

```
print x, '\t', math.log(x)/math.log(2.0)
```

yields:

```
1.0    0.0
2.0    1.0
3.0    1.58496250072
4.0    2.0
5.0    2.32192809489
6.0    2.58496250072
7.0    2.80735492206
8.0    3.0 9.0 3.16992500144
```

We can see that 1, 2, 4, and 8 are powers of two because their logarithms base 2 are round numbers. If we wanted to find the logarithms of other powers of two, we could modify the programme like this:

```
x = 1.0
while x < 100.0:
    print x, '\t', math.log(x)/math.log(2.0)
    x = x * 2.0
```

Now instead of adding something to x each time through the loop, which yields an arithmetic sequence, we multiply x by something, yielding a geometric sequence.

The result is:

```
1.0     0.0
2.0     1.0
4.0     2.0
8.0     3.0
16.0    4.0
32.0    5.0
64.0    6.0
```

Because of the tab characters between the columns, the position of the second column does not depend on the number of digits in the first column. Logarithm tables may not be useful any more, but for computer scientists, knowing the powers of two is! *As an exercise, modify this programme so that it outputs the powers of two up to 65,536 (that's 2^{16}). Print it out and memorize it.* The backslash character in '\t' indicates the beginning of an escape sequence. Escape sequences are used to represent invisible characters like tabs and newlines. The sequence \n represents a newline. An escape sequence can appear anywhere in a string; in the example, the tab escape sequence is the only thing in the string. How do you think you represent a backslash in a string? As an exercise, write a single string that

```
    produces
              this
                      output.
```

TWO-DIMENSIONAL TABLES

A two-dimensional programming is a programming where you read the value at the intersection of a row and a column. A multiplication programming is a good example. Let's say you want to print a multiplication programming for the values from 1 to 6.

A good way to start is to write a loop that prints the multiples of 2, all on one line:

```
i = 1
while i <= 6:
  print 2*i, '  ',
  i = i + 1
print
```

The first line initializes a variable named i, which acts as a counter or loop variable. As the loop executes, the value of i increases from 1 to 6. When i is 7, the loop terminates. Each time through the loop, it displays the value of **2*i**, followed by three spaces. Again, the comma in the print statement suppresses the newline. After the loop completes, the second print statement starts a new line.

The output of the programme is:

```
2    4    6    8    10    12
```

So far, so good. The next step is to encapsulate and generalize.

ENCAPSULATION AND GENERALIZATION

Encapsulation is the process of wrapping a piece of code in a function, allowing you to take advantage of all the things functions are good. Generalization means taking something specific, such as printing the multiples of 2, and making it more general, such as printing the multiples of any integer.

This function encapsulates the previous loop and generalizes it to print multiples ofn:

```
def printMultiples(n):
  i = 1
  while i <= 6:
    print n*i, '\t',
    i = i + 1
  print
```

To encapsulate, all we had to do was add the first line, which declares the name of the function and the parameter list. To generalize, all we had to do was replace the value 2 with the parameter n.

If we call this function with the argument 2, we get the same output as before. With the argument 3, the output is:

```
3     6     9     12     15     18
```

With the argument 4, the output is:

```
4     8     12     16     20     24
```

By now you can probably guess how to print a multiplication programming by callingprintMultiples repeatedly with different arguments.

In fact, we can use another loop:

```
i = 1
while i <= 6:
  printMultiples(i)
  i = i + 1
```

Notice how similar this loop is to the one inside printMultiples. All we did was replace the print statement with a function call.

Table. The Output of This Programme is a Multiplication.

1	2	3	4	5	6
2	4	6	8	10	12
3	6	9	12	15	18
4	8	12	16	20	24
5	10	15	20	25	30
6	12	18	24	30	36

MORE ENCAPSULATION

To demonstrate encapsulation again, let's take the code from the end and wrap it up in a function:

```
def printMultTable():
i = 1
  while i Ü 6:
    printMultiples(i)
    i = i + 1
```

This process is a common development plan. We develop code by writing lines of code outside any function, or typing them in to the interpreter. When we get the code working, we extract it and wrap it up in a function.

This development plan is particularly useful if you don't know, when you start writing, how to divide the programme into functions. This approach lets you design as you go along.

LOCAL VARIABLES

You might be wondering how we can use the same variable, i, in bothprintMultiples and printMultTable. Doesn't it cause problems when one of the functions changes the value of the variable?

The answer is no, because the i in printMultiples and the i in printMultTable are*not* the same variable. Variables created inside a function definition are local; you can't access a local variable from outside its "home" function. That means you are free to have multiple variables with the same name as long as they are not in the same function.

The stack diagram for this programme shows that the two variables named i are not the same variable. They can refer to different values, and changing one does not affect the other.

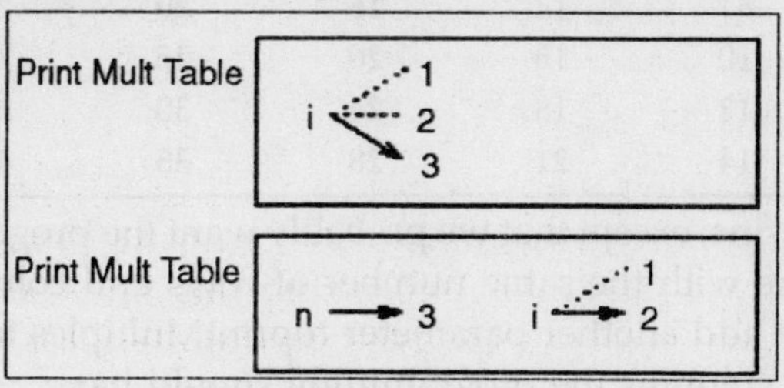

The value of i in print MultTable goes from 1 to 6. In the diagram it happens to be 3. The next time through the loop it will be 4. Each time through the loop,print MultTable calls print Multiples with the current value of i as an argument. That value gets assigned to the parameter n. Inside print Multiples, the value of i goes from 1 to 6. In the diagram, it happens to be 2. Changing this variable has no effect on the value of i in print MultTable.

It is common and perfectly legal to have different local variables with the same name. In particular, names like i and j are used frequently as loop variables. If you avoid using them in one function just because you used them somewhere else, you will probably make the programme harder to read.

MORE GENERALIZATION

As another example of generalization, imagine you wanted a programme that would print a multiplication programming of any size, not just the six-by-six table.

You could add a parameter to **printMultTable**:

```
def printMultTable(high):
  i = 1
  while i Ü high:
    printMultiples(i)
    i = i + 1
```

We replaced the value 6 with the parameter high. *If we call* printMultTable *with the argument 7, it displays:*

1	2	3	4	5	6
2	4	6	8	10	12
3	6	9	12	15	18
4	8	12	16	20	24
5	10	15	20	25	30
6	12	18	24	30	36
7	14	21	28	35	42

This is fine, except that we probably want the programming to be square with the same number of rows and columns. To do that, we add another parameter toprintMultiples to specify how many columns the programming should have.

Just to be annoying, we call this parameter high, demonstrating that different functions can have parameters with the same name (just like local variables).

Here's the whole programme:

```
def printMultiples(n, high):
  i = 1
  while i Ü high:
    print n*i, '\t',
    i = i + 1
  print
def printMultTable(high):
  i = 1
  while i ⇐ high:
    printMultiples(i, high)
    i = i + 1
```

Notice that when we added a new parameter, we had to change the first line of the function and we also had to change the place where the function is called in printMultTable.

Table. As Expected, this Programme Generates a Square Seven-by-seven.

1	2	3	4	5	6	7
2	4	6	8	10	12	14
3	6	9	12	15	18	21
4	8	12	16	20	24	28
5	10	15	20	25	30	35
6	12	18	24	30	36	42
7	14	21	28	35	42	49

When you generalize a function appropriately, you often get a programme with capabilities you didn't plan. For example, you might notice that, because ab = ba, all the entries in the table appear twice. You could save ink by printing only half the table. To do that, you only have to change one line of printMultTable. Change

```
printMultiples(i, high)
```

to

```
printMultiples(i, i)
```

and you get

1						
2	4					
3	6	9				
4	8	12	16			
5	10	15	20	25		
6	12	18	24	30	36	
7	14	21	28	35	42	49

As an exercise, trace the execution of this version ofprint MultTable and figure out how it works.

A few times now, we have mentioned "all the things functions are good for." By now, you might be wondering what exactly those things are. Here are some of them:

- Giving a name to a sequence of statements makes your programme easier to read and debug.
- Dividing a long programme into functions allows you to separate parts of the programme, debug them in isolation, and then compose them into a whole.
- Functions facilitate both recursion and iteration.
- Well-designed functions are often useful for many programmes. Once you write and debug one, you can reuse it.

GLOSSARY

- *Multiple assignment*: Making more than one assignment to the same variable during the execution of a programme.
- *Iteration*: Repeated execution of a set of statements using either a recursive function call or a loop.
- *Loop*: A statement or group of statements that execute repeatedly until a terminating condition is satisfied.
- *Infinite loop*: A loop in which the terminating condition is never satisfied.
- *Body*: The statements inside a loop.
- *Loop variable*: A variable used as part of the terminating condition of a loop.
- *Tab*: A special character that causes the cursor to move to the next tab stop on the current line.

- *Newline*: A special character that causes the cursor to move to the beginning of the next line.
- *Cursor*: An invisible marker that keeps track of where the next character will be printed.
- *Escape sequence*: An escape character (\) followed by one or more printable characters used to designate a nonprintable character.
- *Encapsulate*: To divide a large complex programme into components (like functions) and isolate the components from each other (by using local variables, for example).
- *Generalize*: To replace something unnecessarily specific (like a constant value) with something appropriately general (like a variable or parameter). Generalization makes code more versatile, more likely to be reused, and sometimes even easier to write.
- *Development plan*: A process for developing a programme. In this chapter, we demonstrated a style of development based on developing code to do simple, specific things and then encapsulating and generalizing.

Chapter 4

Introduction to C Language

C- LANGUAGE

C is a relatively small language, but one which wears well. C's small, unambitious feature set is a real advantage: there's less to learn; there isn't excess baggage in the way when you don't need it. It can also be a disadvantage: since it doesn't do everything for you, there's a lot you have to do yourself. C is sometimes referred to as a "high-level assembly language." Some people think that's an insult, but it's actually a deliberate and significant aspect of the language.

If you have programmed in assembly language, you'll probably find C very natural and comfortable (although if you continue to focus too heavily on machine-level details, you'll probably end up with unnecessarily nonportable programmes). If you haven't programmed in assembly language, you may be frustrated by C's lack of certain higher-level features.

In either case, you should understand why C was designed this way: so that seemingly-simple constructions expressed in C would not expand to arbitrarily expensive (in time or space) machine language constructions when compiled. If you write a C programme simply and succinctly, it is likely to result in a succinct, efficient machine language executable.

If you find that the executable programme resulting from a C programme is not efficient, it's probably because of something silly you did, not because of something the compiler did behind ycur back which you have no control over. In any case, there's no point in complaining about C's low-level flavor: C is what it is. A programming language is a tool, and no tool can perform every task unaided.

If you're building a house, and I'm teaching you how to use a hammer, and you ask how to assemble rafters and trusses into gables, that's a legitimate question, but the answer has fallen out of the realm of "How do I use a hammer?" and into "How do I build a house?".

In the same way, we'll see that C does not have built-in features to perform every function that we might ever need to do while programming. As mentioned above, C imposes relatively few built-in ways of doing things on the programmer.

Some common tasks, such as manipulating strings, allocating memory, and doing input/output (I/O), are performed by calling on library functions. Other tasks which you might want to do, such as creating or listing directories, or interacting with a mouse, or displaying windows or other user-interface elements, or doing colour graphics, are not defined by the C language at all.

You can do these things from a C programme, of course, but you will be calling on services which are peculiar to your programming environment (compiler, processor, and operating system) and which are not defined by the C standard. Since this course is about portable C programming, it will also be steering clear of facilities not provided in all C environments.

Another aspect of C that's worth mentioning here is that it is, to put it bluntly, a bit dangerous. C does not, in general, try hard to protect a programmer from mistakes. If you write a piece of code which will (through some oversight of yours) do something wildly different from what you intended it to do, up to and including deleting your data or trashing your disk, and if it is possible for the compiler to compile it, it generally will.

You won't get warnings of the form "Do you really mean to...?" or "Are you sure you really want to...?". C is often compared to a sharp knife: it can do a surgically precise job on some exacting task you have in mind, but it can also do a surgically precise job of cutting off your finger. It's up to you to use it carefully.

This aspect of C is very widely criticized; it is also used (justifiably) to argue that C is not a good teaching language. C aficionados love this aspect of C because it means that C does not try to protect them from themselves: when they know what they're doing, even if it's risky or obscure, they can do it. Students of C hate this aspect of C because it often seems as if the language is some kind of a conspiracy specifically designed to lead them into booby traps.

This is another aspect of the language which it's fairly pointless to complain about. If you take care and pay attention, you can avoid many of the pitfalls. These notes will point out many of the obvious (and not so obvious) trouble spots.

EXAMPLES

FIRST EXAMPLE

The best way to learn programming is to dive right in and start writing real programmes. This way, concepts which would otherwise seem abstract make sense, and the positive feedback you get from getting even a small programme to work gives you a great incentive to improve it or write the next one.

Diving in with "real" programmes right away has another advantage, if only pragmatic: if you're using a conventional compiler, you can't run a fragment of a programme and see what it does; nothing will run until you have a complete (if tiny or trivial) programme. You can't learn everything you'd need to write a complete programme all at once, so you'll have to take some things "on faith" and parrot them in your first programmes before you begin to understand them.

(You can't learn to programme just one expression or statement at a time any more than you can learn to speak a foreign language one word at a time. If all you know is a handful of words, you can't actually *say* anything: you also need to know something about the language's word order and grammar and sentence structure and declension of articles and verbs.) Besides the occasional necessity to take things on faith, there is a more serious potential drawback of this "dive in and programme" approach: it's a small step from learning-by-doing to learning-by-trial-and-error, and when you learn programming by trial-and-error, you can very easily learn many errors.

When you're not sure whether something will work, or you're not even sure what you could use that might work, and you try something, and it does work, you do *not* have any guarantee that what you tried worked for the right reason. You might just have "learned" something that works only by accident or only on your compiler, and it may be very hard to un-learn it later, when it stops working.

Therefore, whenever you're not sure of something, be very careful before you go off and try it "just to see if it will work." Of course, you can never be absolutely sure that something is going to work before you try it, otherwise we'd never have to try things. But you should have an expectation that something is going to work before you try it, and if you can't predict how to do something or whether something would work and find yourself having to determine it experimentally, make a note in your mind that whatever you've just learned (based on the outcome of the experiment) is suspect.

The first example programme is the first example programme in any language: print or display a simple string, and exit. Here is "hello, world" programme:

```
#include <stdio.h>
main()
{
  printf("Hello, world!\n");
  return 0;
}
```

If you have a C compiler, the first thing to do is figure out how to type this programme in and compile it and run it and see where its output went.The first line is practically boilerplate; it will appear in almost all programmes we write. It asks that some definitions having to do with the "Standard

I/O Library" be included in our programme; these definitions are needed if we are to call the library function printf correctly. The second line says that we are defining a function named main.

Most of the time, we can name our functions anything we want, but the function name main is special: it is the function that will be "called" first when our programme starts running. The empty pair of parentheses indicates that our main function accepts no*arguments*, that is, there isn't any information which needs to be passed in when the function is called.

The braces { and } surround a list of statements in C. Here, they surround the list of statements making up the function main.

The line

```
printf("Hello, world!\n");
```

is the first statement in the programme. It asks that the function printf be called; printf is a library function which prints formatted output. The parentheses surroundprintf's argument list: the information which is handed to it which it should act on. The semicolon at the end of the line terminates the statement.

(printf's name reflects the fact that C was first developed when Teletypes and other printing terminals were still in widespread use. Today, of course, video displays are far more common. printf's "prints" to the *standard output*, that is, to the default location for programme output to go.

Nowadays, that's almost always a video screen or a window on that screen. If you do have a printer, you'll typically have to do something extra to get a programme to print to it.)

printf's first (and, in this case, only) argument is the string which it should print. The string, enclosed in double quotes "", consists of the words "Hello, world!" followed by a special sequence: \n. In strings, any two-character sequence beginning with the backslash \ represents a single special character.

The sequence \nrepresents the "new line" character, which prints a carriage return or line feed or whatever it takes to end one line of output and move down to the next. (This programme only prints one line of output, but it's still important to terminate it.)

The second line in the main function is

```
return 0;
```

In general, a function may return a value to its caller, and main is no exception. When main returns (that is, reaches its end and stops functioning), the programme is at its end, and the return value from main tells the operating system (or whatever invoked the programme that main is the main function of) whether it succeeded or not. By convention, a return value of 0 indicates success.

This programme may look so absolutely trivial that it seems as if it's not even worth typing it in and trying to run it, but doing so may be a big (and is certainly a vital) first hurdle. On an unfamiliar computer, it can be arbitrarily difficult to figure out how to enter a text file containing programme source, or how to compile and link it, or how to invoke it, or what happened after (if?) it ran.

The most experienced C programmers immediately go back to this one, simple programme whenever they're trying out a new system or a new way of entering or building programmes or a new way of printing output from within programmes. As Kernighan and Ritchie say, everything else is comparatively easy.

How *you* compile and run this (or any) programme is a function of the compiler and operating system you're using. The first step is to type it in, exactly as shown; this may involve using a text editor to create a file containing the programme text. You'll have to give the file a name, and all C compilers require that files containing C source end with the extension .c. So you might place the programme text in a file called hello.c. The second step is to compile the programme.

(Strictly speaking, compilation consists of two steps, compilation proper followed by linking, but we can overlook this distinction at first, especially because the compiler often takes care of initiating the linking step automatically.) On many Unix systems, the command to compile a C programme from a source file hello.c is

```
cc -o hello hello.c
```

You would type this command at the Unix shell prompt, and it requests that the cc (C compiler) programme be run, placing its output (i.e. the new executable programme it creates) in the file hello, and taking its input (i.e. the source code to be compiled) from the file hello.c.

The third step is to run (execute, invoke) the newly-built hello programme. Again on a Unix system, this is done simply by typing the program's name:

```
hello
```

Depending on how your system is set up (in particular, on whether the current directory is searched for executables, based on the PATH variable), you may have to type

```
./hello
```

to indicate that the hello programme is in the current directory (as opposed to some "bin" directory full of executable programmes, elsewhere).

You may also have your choice of C compilers. On many Unix machines, the cc command is an older compiler which does not recognize modern, ANSI Standard C syntax. An old compiler will accept the simple programmes we'll be starting with, but it will not accept most of our later programmes.

If you find yourself getting baffling compilation errors on programmes which you've typed in exactly as they're shown, it probably indicates that you're using an older compiler. On many machines, another compiler called acc or gcc is available, and you'll want to use it, instead. (Both acc and gcc are typically invoked the same as cc; that is, the above cc command would instead be typed, say, gcc -o hello hello.c .) (One final caveat about Unix systems: don't name your test programmes test, because there's already a standard command called test, and you and the command interpreter will get badly confused if you try to replace the system's test command with your own, not least because your own almost certainly does something completely different.)

Under MS-DOS, the compilation procedure is quite similar. The name of the command you type will depend on your compiler (e.g. cl for the Microsoft C compiler,tc or bcc for

Borland's Turbo C, etc.). You may have to manually perform the second, linking step, perhaps with a command named link or tlink. The executable file which the compiler/linker creates will have a name ending in .exe (or perhaps .com), but you can still invoke it by typing the base name (e.g. hello). See your compiler documentation for complete details; one of the manuals should contain a demonstration of how to enter, compile, and run a small programme that prints some simple output, just as we're trying to describe here. In an integrated or "visual" progamming environment, such as those on the Macintosh or under various versions of Microsoft Windows, the steps you take to enter, compile, and run a programme are somewhat different (and, theoretically, simpler). Typically, there is a way to open a new source window, type source code into it, give it a file name, and add it to the programme (or "project") you're building. If necessary, there will be a way to specify what other source files (or "modules") make up the programme. Then, there's a button or menu selection which compiles and runs the programme, all from within the programming environment. (There will also be a way to create a standalone executable file which you can run from outside the environment.)

In a PC-compatible environment, you may have to choose between creating DOS programmes or Windows programmes. (If you have troubles pertaining to the printf function, try specifying a target environment of MS-DOS. Supposedly, some compilers which are targeted at Windows environments won't let you call printf, because until you call some fancier functions to request that a window be created, there's no window for printf to print to.) Again, check the introductory or tutorial manual that came with the programming package; it should walk you through the steps necessary to get your first programme running.

SECOND EXAMPLE

Our second example is of little more practical use than the first, but it introduces a few more programming language elements:

```
#include <stdio.h>
/* print a few numbers, to illustrate a simple
loop */
main()
{
  int i;
  for(i = 0; i < 10; i = i + 1)
  printf("i is %d\n", i);
  return 0;
}
```

As before, the line #include <stdio.h> is boilerplate which is necessary since we're calling the printf function, and main() and the pair of braces {} indicate and delineate the function named main we're (again) writing.

The first new line is the line

/* print a few numbers, to illustrate a simple loop */ which is a *comment*. Anything between the characters /* and */ is ignored by the compiler, but may be useful to a person trying to read and understand the programme. You can add comments anywhere you want to in the programme, to document what the programme is, what it does, who wrote it, how it works, what the various functions are for and how *they* work, what the various variables are for, etc.

The second new line, down within the function main, is

```
int i;
```

which *declares* that our function will use a variable named i. The variable's type is int, which is a plain integer.

Next, we set up a *loop*:

```
for(i = 0; i < 10; i = i + 1)
```

The keyword for indicates that we are setting up a "for loop." A for loop is controlled by three expressions, enclosed in parentheses and separated by semicolons. These expressions say that, in this case, the loop starts by setting i to 0, that it continues as long as i is less than 10, and that after each iteration of the loop, i should be incremented by 1 (that is, have 1 added to its value).

Finally, we have a call to the printf function, as before, but with several differences. First, the call to printf is within the *body* of the for loop. This means that control flow does not pass once through the printf call, but instead that the call is performed as many times as are dictated by the for loop. In this case, printfwill be called several times: once when i is 0, once when i is 1, once when i is 2, and so on until i is 9, for a total of 10 times.

A second difference in the printf call is that the string to be printed, "i is %d", contains a per cent sign. Whenever printf sees a per cent sign, it indicates thatprintf is not supposed to print the exact text of the string, but is instead supposed to read another one of its arguments to decide what to print. The letter after the per cent sign tells it what type of argument to expect and how to print it. In this case, the letter d indicates that printf is to expect an int, and to print it in decimal. Finally, we see that printf is in fact being called with another argument, for a total of two, separated by commas. The second argument is the variable i, which is in fact an int, as required by %d. The effect of all of this is that each time it is called, printf will print a line containing the current value of the variable i:

```
i is 0
i is 1
i is 2
...
```

After several trips through the loop, i will eventually equal 9. After that trip through the loop, the third control expression i = i + 1 will increment its value to 10. The condition i < 10 is no longer true, so no more trips through the loop are taken. Instead, control flow jumps down to the statement following the for loop, which is the return statement. The main function returns, and the programme is finished.

PROGRAMME STRUCTURE

We'll have more to say later about programme structure, but for now let's observe a few basics. A programme consists of one or more functions; it may also contain global variables. (Our two example programmes so far have contained one function apiece, and no global variables.) At the top of a source file are typically a few boilerplate lines such as #include <stdio.h>, followed by the definitions (i.e. code) for the functions. (It's also possible to split up the several functions making up a larger programme into several source files, as we'll see in a later chapter.)

Each function is further composed of *declarations* and *statements*, in that order. When a sequence of statements should act as one (for example, when they should all serve together as the body of a loop) they can be enclosed in braces (just as for the outer body of the entire function). The simplest kind of statement is an *expression statement*, which is an expression (presumably performing some useful operation) followed by a semicolon. Expressions are further composed of *operators*, *objects*(variables), and *constants*.

C source code consists of several *lexical elements*. Some are words, such as for, return, main, and i, which are either *keywords* of the language (for, return) or *identifiers* (names) we've chosen for our own functions and variables (main, i). There are *constants* such as 1 and 10 which introduce new values into the programme.

There are *operators* such as =, +, and >, which manipulate variables and values. There are other punctuation characters (often called *delimiters*), such as parentheses and squiggly braces {}, which indicate how the other elements of the programme are grouped. Finally, all of the preceding elements can be separated by*whitespace*: spaces, tabs, and the "carriage returns" between lines.

The source code for a C programme is, for the most part, "free form." This means that the compiler does not care how the code is arranged: how it is broken into lines, how the lines are indented, or whether whitespace is used between things like variable names and other punctuation. (Lines like #include <stdio.h> are an exception; they must appear alone on their own lines, generally unbroken.

Only lines beginning with # are affected by this rule; we'll see other examples later.) You can use whitespace, indentation, and appropriate line breaks to make your programmes more readable for yourself and other people (even though the compiler doesn't care). You can place explanatory *comments* anywhere in your programme—any text between the characters /* and */ is ignored by the compiler. (In fact, the compiler pretends that all it saw was whitespace.) Though comments are ignored by the compiler, well-chosen comments can make a programme *much* easier to read.

The usage of whitespace is our first *style* issue. It's typical to leave a blank line between different parts of the programme, to leave a space on either side of operators such as + and =, and to *indent* the bodies of loops and other control flow constructs.

Typically, we arrange the indentation so that the subsidiary statements controlled by a loop statement (the "loop body," such as the printf call in our second example programme) are all aligned with each other and placed one tab stop (or some consistent number of spaces) to the right of the controlling statement.

This indentation (like all whitespace) is not required by the compiler, but it makes programs*much* easier to read. (However, it can also be misleading, if used incorrectly or in the face of inadvertent mistakes. The compiler will decide what "the body of the loop" is based on its own rules, not the indentation, so if the indentation does not match the compiler's interpretation, confusion is inevitable.)

To drive home the point that the compiler doesn't care about indentation, line breaks, or other whitespace, here are a few (extreme) examples: The fragments

```
for(i = 0; i < 10; i = i + 1)
printf("%d\n", i);
`and
for(i = 0; i < 10; i = i + 1) printf("%d\n",
i);
and
for(i=0;i<10;i=i+1)printf("%d\n",i);
and
for(i = 0; i < 10; i = i + 1)
printf("%d\n", i);
and
```

```
for ( i
= 0 ;
i < 10
; i =
i + 1
) printf (
"%d\n" , i
) ;
```

and

```
for
(i=0;
i<10;i=
i+1)printf
("%d\n", i);
```

are all treated exactly the same way by the compiler.

Some programmers argue forever over the best set of "rules" for indentation and other aspects of programming style, calling to mind the old philosopher's debates about the number of angels that could dance on the head of a pin. Style issues (such as how a programme is laid out) *are* important, but they're not something to be too dogmatic about, and there are also other, deeper style issues besides mere layout and typography: Although C compilers do not care about how a programme looks, proper indentation and spacing are critical in making programmes easy for people to read. We recommend writing only one statement per line, and using blanks around operators to clarify grouping. The position of braces is less important, although people hold passionate beliefs. We have chosen one of several popular styles. Pick a style that suits you, then use it consistently.

There is some value in having a reasonably standard style (or a few standard styles) for code layout. Please don't take the above advice to "pick a style that suits you" as an invitation to invent your own brand-new style. If (perhaps after you've been programming in C for a while) you have specific objections to specific facets of existing styles, you're welcome to modify them, but if you don't have any particular leanings, you're probably best off copying an existing style at first. (If you want to place your own stamp of originality on the programmes that you write, there are better avenues for your creativity than inventing a bizarre layout; you might instead try to make the logic easier to follow, or the user interface easier to use, or the code freer of bugs.)

DATA TYPES AND OPERATORS

In this we'll learn about C's basic types, how to write constants and declare variables of these types, and what the basic operators are. As Kernighan and Ritchie say, "The type of an object determines the set of values it can have and what operations can be performed on it."

This is a fairly formal, mathematical definition of what a type is, but it is traditional (and meaningful). There are several implications to remember:

- The "set of values" is finite. C's int type can not represent *all* of the integers; its float type can not represent *all* floating-point numbers.
- When you're using an object (that is, a variable) of some type, you may have to remember what values it can take on and what operations you can perform on it. For example, there are several operators which play with the binary (bit-level) representation of integers, but these operators are not meaningful for and may not be applied to floating-point operands.
- When declaring a new variable and picking a type for it, you have to keep in mind the values and operations you'll be needing.

TYPES

There are only a few basic data types in C.

The first ones we'll be encountering and using are:

- Char a character
- Int an integer, in the range -32,767 to 32,767
- Long int a larger integer (up to +-2,147,483,647)
- Float a floating-point number
- Double a floating-point number, with more precision and perhaps greater range than float

If you can look at this list of basic types and say to yourself, "Oh, how simple, there are only a few types, I won't have to worry much about choosing among them," you'll have an easy time with declarations. (Some masochists wish that the type system were more complicated so that they could specify more things about each variable, but those of us who would rather not have to specify these extra things each time are glad that we don't have to.)

The ranges listed above for types int and long int are the guaranteed minimum ranges. On some systems, either of these types (or, indeed, any C type) may be able to hold larger values, but a programme that depends on extended ranges will not be as portable. Some programmers become obsessed with knowing exactly what the sizes of data objects will be in various situations, and go on to write programmes which depend on these exact sizes. Determining or controlling the size of an object is occasionally important, but most of the time we can sidestep size issues and let the compiler do most of the worrying.

(From the ranges listed above, we can determine that type int must be at least 16 bits, and that type long int must be at least 32 bits. But neither of these sizes is exact; many systens have 32-bit ints, and some systems have 64-bit long ints.) You might wonder how the computer stores characters. The answer involves a *character set*, which is simply a mapping between some set of characters and some set of small numeric codes.

Most machines today use the **ASCII** character set, in which the letter A is represented by the code 65, the ampersand & is represented by the code 38, the digit 1 is represented by the code 49, the space character is represented by the code 32, etc. (Most of the time, of course, you have *no* need to know or even worry about these particular code values; they're automatically translated into the right shapes on the screen or printer when characters are printed out, and they're automatically generated when you type characters on the keyboard. Eventually, though, we'll appreciate, and even take some control over, exactly when these translations—from characters to their numeric codes—are performed.) Character codes are usually small—the largest code value in **ASCII** is 126, which is the ~ (tilde or circumflex) character. Characters usually fit in a byte, which is usually 8 bits. In C, type char is defined as occupying one byte, so it is usually 8 bits.

Most of the simple variables in most programmes are of types int, long int, or double. Typically, we'll use int and double for most purposes, and long int any time we need to hold integer values greater than 32,767. As we'll see, even when we're manipulating individual characters, we'll usually use an int variable, for reasons to be discussed later. Therefore, we'll rarely use individual variables of type char; although we'll use plenty of arrays of char.

CONSTANTS

A *constant* is just an immediate, absolute value found in an expression. The simplest constants are decimal integers, e.g. 0,1, 2, 123 . Occasionally it is useful to specify constants in base 8 or base 16 (octal or hexadecimal); this is done by prefixing an extra 0 (zero) for octal, or 0x for hexadecimal: the constants 100, 0144, and 0x64 all represent the same number. (If you're not using these non-decimal constants, just remember not to use any leading zeroes. If you accidentally write 0123 intending to get one hundred and twenty three, you'll get 83 instead, which is 123 base 8.)

We write constants in decimal, octal, or hexadecimal for our convenience, not the compiler's. The compiler doesn't care; it always converts everything into binary internally, anyway. (There is, however, no good way to specify constants in source code in binary.) A constant can be forced to be of type long int by suffixing it with the letter L (in upper or lower case, although upper case is strongly recommended, because a lower case l looks too much like the digit 1).

A constant that contains a decimal point or the letter e (or both) is a floating-point constant: 3.14, 10., .01, 123e4, 123.456e7 . The e indicates multiplication by a power of 10; 123.456e7 is 123.456 times 10 to the 7th, or 1,234,560,000. (Floating-point constants are of type double by default.)

We also have constants for specifying characters and strings. (Make sure you understand the difference between a character and a string: a character is exactly one character; a string is a set of zero or more characters; a string containing one character is distinct from a lone character.)

A character constant is simply a single character between single quotes:'A','.','%'. The numeric value of a character constant is, naturally enough, that character's value in the machine's character set. (In **ASCII**, for example, 'A' has the value 65.)

A *string* is represented in C as a sequence or array of characters. (We'll have more to say about arrays in general, and strings in particular, later.) A string constant is a sequence of zero or more characters enclosed in double quotes: "apple","hello, world", "this is a test".

Within character and string constants, the backslash character \ is special, and is used to represent characters not easily typed on the keyboard or for various reasons not easily typed in constants. The most common of these "character escapes" are:

```
\n a "newline" character
\b a backspace
\r a carriage return (without a line feed)
\' a single quote (e.g. in a character
constant)
\" a double quote (e.g. in a string constant)
\\ a single backslash
```

For example, "he said \"hi\"" is a string constant which contains two double quotes, and '\'' is a character constant consisting of a (single) single quote. Notice once again that the character constant 'A' is very different from the string constant "A".

DECLARATIONS

Informally, a *variable* (also called an *object*) is a place you can store a value. So that you can refer to it unambiguously, a variable needs a name. You can think of the variables in your programme as a set of boxes or cubbyholes, each with a label giving its name; you might imagine that storing a value "in" a variable consists of writing the value on a slip of paper and placing it in the cubbyhole.

A *declaration* tells the compiler the name and type of a variable you'll be using in your programme. In its simplest form, a declaration consists of the type, the name of the variable, and a terminating semicolon:

```
char c;
int i;
float f;
```

You can also declare several variables of the same type in one declaration, separating them with commas:

```
int i1, i2;
```

The placement of declarations is significant. You can't place them just anywhere (i.e. they cannot be interspersed with the other statements in your programme).

They must either be placed at the beginning of a function, or at the beginning of a brace-enclosed block of statements (which we'll learn about in the next chapter), or outside of any function. Furthermore, the placement of a declaration, as well as its storage class, controls several things about its *visibility* and *lifetime*. You may wonder *why* variables must be declared before use.

There are two reasons:

- It makes things somewhat easier on the compiler; it knows right away what kind of storage to allocate and what code to emit to store and manipulate each variable; it doesn't have to try to intuit the programmer's intentions.
- It forces a bit of useful discipline on the programmer: you cannot introduce variables willy-nilly; you must think about them enough to pick appropriate types for them. (The compiler's error messages to you, telling you that you apparently forgot to declare a variable, are as often helpful as they are a nuisance: they're helpful when they tell you that you misspelled a variable, or forgot to think about exactly how you were going to use it.)

Although there are a few places where declarations can be omitted (in which case the compiler will assume an implicit declaration), making use of these removes the advantages of reason 2 above, so I recommend always declaring everything explicitly.

Most of the time, I recommend writing one declaration per line. For the most part, the compiler doesn't care what order declarations are in. You can order the declarations alphabetically, or in the order that they're used, or to put related declarations next to each other. Collecting all variables of the same type together on one line essentially orders declarations by type, which isn't a very useful order (it's only slightly more useful than random order).

A declaration for a variable can also contain an initial value. This *initializer* consists of an equals sign and an expression, which is usually a single constant:

```
int i = 1;
int i1 = 10, i2 = 20;
```

VARIABLE NAMES

Within limits, you can give your variables and functions any names you want. These names (the formal term is "identifiers") consist of letters, numbers, and underscores. For our purposes, names must begin with a letter.

Theoretically, names can be as long as you want, but extremely long ones get tedious to type after a while, and the compiler is not required to keep track of extremely long ones perfectly. (What this means is that if you were to name a variable, say,supercalafragalisticespialidocious, the compiler might get lazy and pretend that you'd named it super calafragalisticespialidocio, such that if you later misspelled itsupercalafragalisticespialidociouz, the compiler wouldn't catch your mistake.

Nor would the compiler necessarily be able to tell the difference if for some perverse reason you *deliberately* declared a second variable namedsupercalafragalisticespialidociouz.) The capitalization of names in C is significant: the variable names variable, Variable, and **VARIABLE** (as well as silly combinations like variAble) are all distinct. A final restriction on names is that you may not use *keywords* (the words such as int and for which are part of the syntax of the language) as the names of variables or functions (or as identifiers of any kind).

ARITHMETIC OPERATORS

The basic operators for performing arithmetic are the same in many computer languages:

```
+ addition
- subtraction
* multiplication
/ division
% modulus (remainder)
```

The - operator can be used in two ways: to subtract two numbers (as in a - b), or to negate one number (as in -a + bor a + -b). When applied to integers, the division operator / discards any remainder, so 1 / 2 is 0 and 7 / 4 is 1. But when either operand is a floating-point quantity (type float or double), the division operator yields a floating-point result, with a potentially nonzero fractional part. So 1 / 2.0 is 0.5, and 7.0 / 4.0 is 1.75.

The *modulus* operator % gives you the remainder when two integers are divided: 1 % 2 is 1; 7 % 4 is 3. (The modulus operator can only be applied to integers.) An additional arithmetic operation you might be wondering about is exponentiation. Some languages have an exponentiation operator (typically ^ or **), but C doesn't. (To square or cube a number, just multiply it by itself.)

Multiplication, division, and modulus all have higher *precedence* than addition and subtraction. The term "precedence" refers to how "tightly" operators bind to their operands (that is, to the things they operate on). In mathematics, multiplication has higher precedence than addition, so 1 + 2 * 3 is 7, not 9. In other words, 1 + 2 * 3 is equivalent to1 + (2 * 3). C is the same way. All of these operators "group" from left to right, which means that when two or more of them have the same precedence and participate next to each other in an expression, the evaluation conceptually proceeds from left to right. For example, 1 - 2 - 3 is equivalent to (1 - 2) - 3 and gives -4, not +2. ("Grouping" is sometimes called *associativity*, although the term is used somewhat differently in programming than it is in mathematics. Not all C operators group from left to right; a few group from right to left.) Whenever the default precedence or associativity doesn't give you the grouping you want, you can always use explicit parentheses. For example, if you wanted to add 1 to 2 and then multiply the result by 3, you could write (1 + 2) * 3. By the way, the word "arithmetic" as used in the title of this section is an adjective, not a noun, and it's pronounced differently than the noun: the accent is on the third syllable.

ASSIGNMENT OPERATORS

The assignment operator = assigns a value to a variable. For example,

```
x = 1
```

sets x to 1, and

```
a = b
```

sets a to whatever b's value is. The expression

```
i = i + 1
```

is, as we've mentioned elsewhere, the standard programming idiom for increasing a variable's value by 1: this expression takes i's old value, adds 1 to it, and stores it back into i. (C provides several "shortcut" operators for modifying variables in this and similar ways, which we'll meet later.) We've called the = sign the "assignment operator" and referred to "assignment expressions" because, in fact, = *is* an operator just like + or -. C does not have "assignment statements"; instead, an assignment like a = b is an expression and can be used wherever any expression can appear. Since it's an expression, the assignment a = b has a value, namely, the same value that's assigned to a. This value can then be used in a larger expression; for example, we might write

```
c = a = b
```

which is equivalent to

```
c = (a = b)
```

and assigns b's value to both a and c. (The assignment operator, therefore, groups from right to left.). It's usually a matter of style whether you initialize a variable with an initializer in its declaration or with an assignment expression near where you first use it. That is, there's no particular difference between

```
int a = 10;
```

and

```
int a;
/* later... */
a = 10;
```

FUNCTION CALLS

We'll have much more to say about functions in a later chapter, but for now let's just look at how they're called.You call a function by mentioning its name followed by a pair of parentheses. If the function takes any arguments, you place the arguments between the parentheses, separated by commas. These are all function calls:

```
printf("Hello, world!\n")
printf("%d\n", i)
sqrt(144.)
getchar()
```

The arguments to a function can be arbitrary expressions. Therefore, you don't have to say things like

```
int sum = a + b + c;
printf("sum = %d\n", sum);
```

if you don't want to; you can instead collapse it to

```
printf("sum = %d\n", a + b + c);
```

Many functions return values, and when they do, you can embed calls to these functions within larger expressions:

```
c = sqrt(a * a + b * b)
x = r * cos(theta)
i = f1(f2(j))
```

The first expression squares a and b, computes the square root of the sum of the squares, and assigns the result to c. (In other words, it computes a * a + b * b, passes that number to the sqrt function, and assigns sqrt's return value toc.) The second expression passes the value of the variable theta to the cos (cosine) function, multiplies the result by r, and assigns the result to x. The third expression passes the value of the variable j to the function f2, passes the return value of f2 immediately to the function f1, and finally assigns f1's return value to the variable i.

STATEMENT AND CONTROL

Statements are the "steps" of a programme. Most statements compute and assign values or call functions, but we will eventually meet several other kinds of statements as well. By default, statements are executed in sequence, one after another. We can, however, modify that sequence by using *control flow constructs* which arrange that a statement or group of statements is executed only if some condition is true or false, or executed over and over again to form a *loop*.

(A somewhat different kind of control flow happens when we call a function: execution of the caller is suspended while the called function proceeds. My definitions of the terms *statement* and *control flow* are somewhat circular. A statement is an element within a programme which you can apply control flow to; control flow is how you specify the order in which the statements in your programme are executed. (A weaker definition of a statement might be "a part of your programme that does something," but this definition could as easily be applied to expressions or functions.)

EXPRESSION STATEMENTS

Most of the statements in a C programme are *expression statements*. An expression statement is simply an expression followed by a semicolon. The lines

```
i = 0;
i = i + 1;
```

and

```
printf("Hello, world!\n");
```

are all expression statements. (In some languages, such as Pascal, the semicolon separates statements, such that the last statement is not followed by a semicolon. In C, however, the semicolon is a statement terminator; all simple statements are followed by semicolons. The semicolon is also used for a few other things in C; we've already seen that it terminates declarations, too.)

Expression statements do all of the real work in a C programme. Whenever you need to compute new values for variables, you'll typically use expression statements (and they'll typically contain assignment operators). Whenever you want your programme to do something visible, in the real world, you'll typically call a function (as part of an expression statement).

We've already seen the most basic example: calling the function printf to print text to the screen. But anything else you might do—read or write a disk file, talk to a modem or printer, draw pictures on the screen—will also involve function calls. Expressions and expression statements can be arbitrarily complicated. They don't have to consist of exactly one simple function call, or of one simple assignment to a variable. For one thing, many functions return values, and the values they return can then be used by other parts of the expression. For example, C provides a sqrt (square root) function, which we might use to compute the hypotenuse of a right triangle like this:

```
c = sqrt(a*a + b*b);
```

To be useful, an expression statement must do something; it must have some lasting effect on the state of the programme. (Formally, a useful statement must have at least one *side effect*.) The first two sample expression statements in this section (above) assign new values to the variable i, and the third one calls printf to print something out, and these are good examples of statements that do something useful.

(To make the distinction clear, we may note that degenerate constructions such as

```
0;
i;
```

or

```
i + 1;
```

are syntactically valid statements—they consist of an expression followed by a semicolon—but in each case, they compute a value without doing anything with it, so the computed value is discarded, and the statement is useless. But if the "degenerate" statements in this paragraph don't make much sense to you, don't worry; it's because they, frankly, don't make much sense.)

It's also possible for a single expression to have multiple side effects, but it's easy for such an expression to be (a) confusing or (b) undefined. For now, we'll only be looking at expressions (and, therefore, statements) which do one well-defined thing at a time.

IF STATEMENTS

The simplest way to modify the control flow of a programme is with an if statement, which in its simplest form looks like this:

```
if(x > max)
max = x;
```

Even if you didn't know any C, it would probably be pretty obvious that what happens here is that if x is greater than max,x gets assigned to max. (We'd use code like this to keep track of the maximum value of x we'd seen—for each new x, we'd compare it to the old maximum value max, and if the new value was greater, we'd update max.)

More generally, we can say that the syntax of an if statement is:

```
if( expression )
statement
```

where *expression* is any expression and *statement* is any statement. What if you have a series of statements, all of which should be executed together or not at all depending on whether some condition is true? The answer is that you enclose them in braces:

```
if( expression )
{
  statement<sub>1</sub>
  statement<sub>2</sub>
  statement<sub>3</sub>
}
```

As a general rule, anywhere the syntax of C calls for a statement, you may write a series of statements enclosed by braces. (You do not need to, and should not, put a semicolon after the closing brace, because the series of statements enclosed by braces is not itself a simple expression statement.)

An if statement may also optionally contain a second statement, the "else clause," which is to be executed if the condition is not met.

Here is an example:

```
if(n > 0)
average = sum / n;
else {
printf("can't compute average\n");
average = 0;
}
```

The first statement or block of statements is executed if the condition *is* true, and the second statement or block of statements (following the keyword else) is executed if the condition is *not* true. In this example, we can compute a meaningful average only if n is greater than 0; otherwise, we print a message saying that we cannot compute the average. The general syntax of an if statement is therefore

```
if( expression )
statement<sub>1</sub>
else
statement<sub>2</sub>
```

(where both *statement₁* and *statement₂* may be lists of statements enclosed in braces).

It's also possible to nest one if statement inside another. (For that matter, it's in general possible to nest any kind of statement or control flow construct within another.) For example, here is a little piece of code which decides roughly which quadrant of the compass you're walking into, based on an x value which is positive if you're walking east, and a y value which is positive if you're walking north:

```
if(x > 0)
{
if(y > 0)
```

```
printf("Northeast.\n");
else printf("Southeast.\n");
}
else {
if(y > 0)
printf("Northwest.\n");
else printf("Southwest.\n");
}
```

When you have one if statement (or loop) nested inside another, it's a very good idea to use explicit braces {}, as shown, to make it clear (both to you and to the compiler) how they're nested and which else goes with which if. It's also a good idea to indent the various levels, also as shown, to make the code more readable to humans.

Why do both? You use indentation to make the code visually more readable to yourself and other humans, but the compiler doesn't pay attention to the indentation (since all whitespace is essentially equivalent and is essentially ignored). Therefore, you also have to make sure that the punctuation is right.

Here is an example of another common arrangement of if and else. Suppose we have a variable grade containing a student's numeric grade, and we want to print out the corresponding letter grade.

Here is code that would do the job:

```
if(grade >= 90)
printf("A");
else if(grade >= 80)
printf("B");
else if(grade >= 70)
printf("C");
else if(grade >= 60)
printf("D");
else printf("F");
```

What happens here is that exactly one of the five printf calls is executed, depending on which of the conditions is true. Each condition is tested in turn, and if one is true, the corresponding statement is executed, and the rest are skipped. If none of the conditions is true, we fall through to the last one, printing "F". In the cascaded if/else/if/else/... chain, each else clause is another if statement. This may be more obvious at first if we reformat the example, including every set of braces and indenting each if statement relative to the previous one:

```
   if(grade >= 90)
 {
   printf("A");
 }
   else {
   if(grade >= 80)
 {
   printf("B");
 }
   else {
   if(grade >= 70)
 {
   printf("C");
 }
   else {
   if(grade >= 60)
 {
   printf("D");
 }
     else {
     printf("F");
     }
   }
 }
}
```

By examining the code this way, it should be obvious that exactly one of the printf calls is executed, and that whenever one of the conditions is found true, the remaining conditions do not need to be checked and none of the later statements within the chain will be executed. But once you've convinced yourself of this and learned to recognize the idiom, it's generally preferable to arrange the statements as in the first example, without trying to indent each successive if statement one tabstop further out.

BOOLEAN EXPRESSIONS

An if statement like

```
if(x > max)
max = x;
```

is perhaps deceptively simple. Conceptually, we say that it checks whether the condition x > max is "true" or "false". The mechanics underlying C's conception of "true" and "false," however, deserve some explanation. We need to understand how true and false values are represented, and how they are interpreted by statements like if. As far as C is concerned, a true/false condition can be represented as an integer. (An integer can represent many values; here we care about only two values: "true" and "false." The study of mathematics involving only two values is called Boolean algebra, after George Boole, a mathematician who refined this study.) In C, "false" is represented by a value of 0 (zero), and "true" is represented by any value that is nonzero. Since there are many nonzero values (at least 65,534, for values of type int), when we have to pick a specific value for "true," we'll pick 1.

The *relational operators* such as <, <=, >, and >= are in fact operators, just like +, -, *, and /. The relational operators take two values, look at them, and "return" a value of 1 or 0 depending on whether the tested relation was true or false. The complete set of relational operators in C is:

```
< less than
<=  less than or equal
> greater than
>=  greater than or equal
==  equal
!=  not equal
```

For example, 1 < 2 is 1, 3 > 4 is 0, 5 == 5 is 1, and 6 != 6 is 0.

We've now encountered perhaps the most easy-to-stumble-on "gotcha!" in C: the equality-testing operator is ==, not a single =, which is assignment. If you accidentally write

```
if(a = 0)
```

(and you probably will at some point; everybody makes this mistake), it will *not* test whether a is zero, as you probably intended. Instead, it will *assign* 0 to a, and then perform the "true" branch of the if statement if a is *non*zero. But a will have just been assigned the value 0, so the "true" branch will never be taken! (This could drive you crazy while debugging—you wanted to do something if a was 0, and after the test, a *is* 0, whether it was supposed to be or not, but the "true" branch is nevertheless not taken.)

The relational operators work with arbitrary numbers and generate true/false values. You can also combine true/false values by using the *Boolean operators,* which take true/false values as operands and compute new true/false values. The three Boolean operators are:

```
&& and
|| or
! not (takes one operand; "unary")
```

The && ("and") operator takes two true/false values and produces a true (1) result if both operands are true (that is, if the left-hand side is true and the right-hand side is true). The || ("or") operator takes two true/false values and produces a true (1) result if either operand is true. The ! ("not") operator takes a single true/false value and negates it, turning false to true and true to false (0 to 1 and nonzero to 0).

For example, to test whether the variable i lies between 1 and 10, you might use

```
if(1 < i && i < 10)
...
```

Here we're expressing the relation "i is between 1 and 10" as "1 is less than i and i is less than 10." It's important to understand why the more obvious expression

```
if(1 < i < 10) /* WRONG */
```

would not work. The expression 1 < i < 10 is parsed by the compiler analogously to 1 + i + 10. The expression 1 + i + 10 is parsed as (1 + i) + 10 and means "add 1 to i, and then add the result to 10." Similarly, the expression 1 < i < 10 is parsed as (1 < i) < 10 and means "see if 1 is less than i, and then see if the result is less than 10." But in this case, "the result" is 1 or

0, depending on whether i is greater than 1. Since both 0 and 1 are less than 10, the expression 1 < i < 10 would *always* be true in C, regardless of the value of i!

Relational and Boolean expressions are usually used in contexts such as an if statement, where something is to be done or not done depending on some condition. In these cases what's actually checked is whether the expression representing the condition has a zero or nonzero value. As long as the expression is a relational or Boolean expression, the interpretation is just what we want. For example, when we wrote

```
if(x > max)
```

the > operator produced a 1 if x was greater than max, and a 0 otherwise. The if statement interprets 0 as false and 1 (or any nonzero value) as true. But what if the expression is not a relational or Boolean expression? As far as C is concerned, the controlling expression (of conditional statements like if) can in fact be *any* expression: it doesn't have to "look like" a Boolean expression; it doesn't have to contain relational or logical operators. All C looks at (when it's evaluating an if statement, or anywhere else where it needs a true/false value) is whether the expression evaluates to 0 or nonzero. For example, if you have a variable x, and you want to do something if x is nonzero, it's possible to write

```
if(x)
statement
```

and the statement will be executed if x is nonzero (since nonzero means "true"). This possibility (that the controlling expression of an if statement doesn't have to "look like" a Boolean expression) is both useful and potentially confusing. It's useful when you have a variable or a function that is "conceptually Boolean," that is, one that you consider to hold a true or false (actually nonzero or zero) value. For example, if you have a variableverbose which contains a nonzero value when your programme should run in verbose mode and zero when it should be quiet, you can write things like

```
if (verbose)
printf ("Starting first pass\n");
```

and this code is both legal and readable, besides which it does what you want. The standard library contains a functionisupper() which tests whether a character is an upper-case letter, so if c is a character, you might write

```
if (isupper(c))
...
```

Both of these examples (verbose and isupper()) are useful and readable.

However, you will eventually come across code like

```
if (n)
average = sum / n;
```

where n is just a number. Here, the programmer wants to compute the average only if n is nonzero (otherwise, of course, the code would divide by 0), and the code works, because, in the context of the if statement, the trivial expression n is (as always) interpreted as "true" if it is nonzero, and "false" if it is zero.

"Coding shortcuts" like these can seem cryptic, but they're also quite common, so you'll need to be able to recognize them even if you don't choose to write them in your own code. Whenever you see code like

```
if(x)
```

or

```
if(f())
```

where x or f() do not have obvious "Boolean" names, you can read them as "if x is nonzero" or "if f() returns nonzero."

WHILE LOOPS

Loops generally consist of two parts: one or more *control expressions* which (not surprisingly) control the execution of the loop, and the *body*, which is the statement or set of statements which is executed over and over. The most basic *loop* in C is the while loop. A while loop has one control expression, and executes as long as that expression is true. This example repeatedly doubles the number 2 (2, 4, 8, 16,...) and prints the resulting numbers as long as they aie less than 1000:

```
int x = 2;
while(x < 1000)
```

```
{
  printf("%d\n", x);
  x = x * 2;
}
```

(Once again, we've used braces {} to enclose the group of statements which are to be executed together as the body of the loop.)

The general syntax of a while loop is

```
while( expression )
statement
```

A while loop starts out like an if statement: if the condition expressed by the *expression* is true, the *statement* is executed. However, after executing the statement, the condition is tested again, and if it's still true, the statement is executed again. (Presumably, the condition depends on some value which is changed in the body of the loop.) As long as the condition remains true, the body of the loop is executed over and over again. (If the condition is false right at the start, the body of the loop is not executed at all.)

As another example, if you wanted to print a number of blank lines, with the variable n holding the number of blank lines to be printed, you might use code like this:

```
while(n > 0)
{
  printf("\n");
  n = n - 1;
}
```

After the loop finishes (when control "falls out" of it, due to the condition being false), n will have the value 0. You use a while loop when you have a statement or group of statements which may have to be executed a number of times to complete their task.

The controlling expression represents the condition "the loop is not done" or "there's more work to do." As long as the expression is true, the body of the loop is executed; presumably, it makes at least some progress at its task. When the expression becomes false, the task is done, and the rest of the programme (beyond the loop) can proceed. When we think about a loop in this way, we can seen an additional important property: if the expression evaluates to "false" before the very first trip through the loop, we make *zero* trips through the loop. In other words, if the task is already done (if there's no work to do) the body of the loop is not executed at all. (It's always a good idea to think about the "boundary conditions" in a piece of code, and to make sure that the code will work correctly when there is no work to do, or when there is a trivial task to do, such as sorting an array of one number. Experience has shown that bugs at boundary conditions are quite common.)

FOR LOOPS

Our second loop, which we've seen at least one example of already, is the for loop. The first one we saw was:

```
for (i = 0; i < 10; i = i + 1)
printf("i is %d\n", i);
```

More generally, the syntax of a for loop is

for(*expr₁; expr₂; expr₃*) *statement* (Here we see that the for loop has three control expressions. As always, the *statement* can be a brace-enclosed block.) Many loops are set up to cause some variable to step through a range of values, or, more generally, to set up an initial condition and then modify some value to perform each succeeding loop as long as some condition is true.

The three expressions in a for loop encapsulate these conditions: *expr₁* sets up the initial condition, *expr₂* tests whether another trip through the loop should be taken, and *expr₃* increments or updates things after each trip through the loop and prior to the next one. In our first example, we had i = 0 as*expr₁*, i < 10 as *expr₂*, i = i + 1 as *expr₃*, and the call to printf as*statement*, the body of the loop.

So the loop began by setting i to 0, proceeded as long as i was less than 10, printed outi's value during each trip through the loop, and added 1 to i between each trip through the loop. When the compiler sees a for loop, first, *expr<sub>1</ sub>* is evaluated. Then, *expr₂* is evaluated, and if it is true, the body of the loop (*statement*) is executed.

Then, *expr₃* is evaluated to go to the next step, and*expr₂* is evaluated again, to see if there *is* a next step. During the execution of a for loop, the sequence is:

```
expr<sub>1</sub>
expr<sub>2</sub>
statement
expr<sub>3</sub>
expr<sub>2</sub>
statement
expr<sub>3</sub>
...
expr<sub>2</sub>
statement
expr<sub>3</sub>
expr<sub>2</sub>
```

The first thing executed is *expr₁*. *expr₃* is evaluated after *every* trip through the loop. The last thing executed is always *expr₂*, because when *expr₂* evaluates false, the loop exits.

All three expressions of a for loop are optional. If you leave out *expr₁*, there simply is no initialization step, and the variable(s) used with the loop had better have been initialized already. If you leave out *expr₂*, there is no test, and the default for the for loop is that another trip through the loop should be taken (such that unless you break out of it some other way, the loop runs forever). If you leave out *expr₃*, there is no increment step.

The semicolons separate the three controlling expressions of a for loop. (These semicolons, by the way, have nothing to do with statement terminators.) If you leave out one or more of the expressions, the semicolons remain. Therefore, one way of writing a deliberately infinite loop in C is

```
for(;;)
...
```

It's useful to compare C's for loop to the equivalent loops in other computer languages you might know. The C loop

```
for(i = x; i <= y; i = i + z)
```

is roughly equivalent to:

```
for I = X to Y step Z(BASIC)
do 10 i=x,y,z (FORTRAN)
for i := x to y  (Pascal)
```

In C (unlike **FORTRAN**), if the test condition is false before the first trip through the loop, the loop won't be traversed at all. In C (unlike Pascal), a loop control variable (in this case, i) is guaranteed to retain its final value after the loop completes, and it is also legal to modify the control variable within the loop, if you really want to.

(When the loop terminates due to the test condition turning false, the value of the control variable after the loop will be the first value for which the condition failed, not the last value for which it succeeded.) It's also worth noting that a for loop can be used in more general ways than the simple, iterative examples we've seen so far. The "control variable" of a for loop does not have to be an integer, and it does not have to be incremented by an additive increment.

It could be "incremented" by a multiplicative factor (1, 2, 4, 8,...) if that was what you needed, or it could be a floating-point variable, or it could be another type of variable which we haven't met yet which would step, not over numeric values, but over the elements of an array or other data structure.

Strictly speaking, a for loop doesn't have to have a "control variable" at all; the three expressions can be anything, although the loop will make the most sense if they are related and together form the expected initialize, test, increment sequence.

The powers-of-two example of the previous section does fit this pattern, so we could rewrite it like this:

```
int x;
for(x = 2; x < 1000; x = x * 2)
printf("%d\n", x);
```

There is no earth-shaking or fundamental difference between the while and for loops. In fact, given the general for loop for(*expr₁*; *expr₂*; *expr₃*) *statement* you could usually rewrite it as a while loop, moving the initialize and increment expressions to statements before and within the loop:

```
expr<sub>1</sub>;
while(expr<sub>2</sub>)
{
  statement
  expr<sub>3</sub>;
}
```

Similarly, given the general while loop

```
while(expr)
statement
```

you could rewrite it as a for loop:

```
for(; expr; )
statement
```

Another contrast between the for and while loops is that although the test expression (*expr₂*) is optional in a for loop, it is required in a while loop. If you leave out the controlling expression of a while loop, the compiler will complain about a syntax error. (To write a deliberately infinite while loop, you have to supply an expression which is always nonzero. The most obvious one would simply be while(1) .)

If it's possible to rewrite a for loop as a while loop and vice versa, why do they both exist? Which one should you choose? In general, when you choose a for loop, its three expressions should all manipulate the same variable or data structure, using the initialize, test, increment pattern. If they don't manipulate the same variable or don't follow that pattern, wedging them into a for loop buys nothing and a while loop would probably be clearer. (The reason that one loop or the other can be clearer is simply that, when you see a for loop, you *expect* to see an idiomatic initialize/test/increment of a single variable, and if the for loop you're looking at doesn't end up matching that pattern, you've been momentarily misled.)

BREAK AND CONTINUE

Sometimes, due to an exceptional condition, you need to jump out of a loop early, that is, before the main controlling expression of the loop causes it to terminate normally. Other times, in an elaborate loop, you may want to jump back to the top of the loop (to test the controlling expression again, and perhaps begin a new trip through the loop) without playing out all the steps of the current loop. The break and continue statements allow you to do these two things. (They are, in fact, essentially restricted forms of goto.). To put everything we've seen in this chapter together, as well as demonstrate the use of the break statement, here is a programme for printing prime numbers between 1 and 100:

```
#include <stdio.h>
#include <math.h>
main()
{
int i, j;
printf("%d\n", 2);
for(i = 3; i <= 100; i = i + 1)
{
for(j = 2; j < i; j = j + 1)
{
if(i % j == 0)
break;
if(j > sqrt(i))
{
printf("%d\n", i);
break;
}
}
}
return 0;
}
```

The outer loop steps the variable i through the numbers from 3 to 100; the code tests to see if each number has any divisors other than 1 and itself. The trial divisor j loops from 2 up to i. j is a divisor of i if the remainder of i divided by jis 0, so the code uses C's "remainder" or "modulus" operator% to make this test.

(Remember that i % j gives the remainder when i is divided by j.) If the programme finds a divisor, it uses break to break out of the inner loop, without printing anything. But if it notices that jhas risen higher than the square root of i, without its having found any divisors, then i must not have any divisors, so i is prime, and its value is printed.

(Once we've determined that i is prime by noticing that j > sqrt(i), there's no need to try the other trial divisors, so we use a second break statement to break out of the loop in that case, too.) The simple algorithm and implementation we used here (like many simple prime number algorithms) does not work for 2, the only even prime number, so the programme "cheats" and prints out 2 no matter what, before going on to test the numbers from 3 to 100.

Many improvements to this simple programme are of course possible; you might experiment with it. (Did you notice that the "test" expression of the inner loop for(j = 2; j < i; j = j + 1) is in a sense unnecessary, because the loop always terminates early due to one of the two break statements?)

ARRAYS

So far, we've been declaring simple variables: the declaration

```
int i;
```

declares a single variable, named i, of type int. It is also possible to declare an *array* of several elements. The declaration

```
int a[10];
```

declares an array, named a, consisting of ten elements, each of type int. Simply speaking, an array is a variable that can hold more than one value. You specify which of the several values you're referring to at any given time by using a numeric*subscript*. (Arrays in programming are similar to vectors or matrices in mathematics.)

We can represent the array a above with a picture like this:

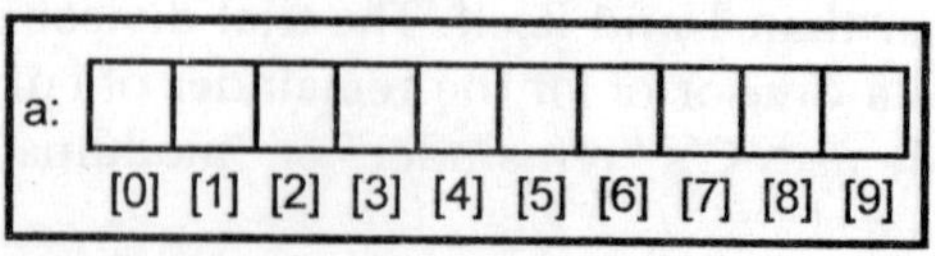

In C, arrays are *zero-based*: the ten elements of a 10-element array are numbered from 0 to 9. The subscript which specifies a single element of an array is simply an integer expression in square brackets. The first element of the array isa[0], the second element is a[1], etc. You can use these "array subscript expressions" anywhere you can use the name of a simple variable, for example:

```
a[0] = 10;
a[1] = 20;
a[2] = a[0] + a[1];
```

Notice that the subscripted array references (i.e. expressions such as a[0] and a[1]) can appear on either side of the assignment operator.

The subscript does not have to be a constant like 0 or 1; it can be any integral expression. For example, it's common to loop over all elements of an array:

```
int i;
for(i = 0; i < 10; i = i + 1)
a[i] = 0;
```

This loop sets all ten elements of the array a to 0. Arrays are a real convenience for many problems, but there is not a lot that C will do with them for you automatically. In particular, you can neither set all elements of an array at once nor assign one array to another; both of the assignments

```
a = 0; /* WRONG */
```

and

```
int b[10];
b = a; /* WRONG */
```

are illegal.

To set all of the elements of an array to some value, you must do so one by one, as in the loop example above. To copy the contents of one array to another, you must again do so one by one:

```
int b[10];
for(i = 0; i < 10; i = i + 1)
b[i] = a[i];
```

Remember that for an array declared

```
int a[10];
```

there is no element a[10]; the topmost element is a[9]. This is one reason that zero-based loops are also common in C.

Note that the for loop

```
for(i = 0; i < 10; i = i + 1)
    ...
```

does just what you want in this case: it starts at 0, the number 10 suggests (correctly) that it goes through 10 iterations, but the less-than comparison means that the last trip through the loop has i set to 9.

(The comparison i <= 9 would also work, but it would be less clear and therefore poorer style.) In the little examples so far, we've always looped over all 10 elements of the sample array a.

It's common, however, to use an array that's bigger than necessarily needed, and to use a second variable to keep track of how many elements of the array are currently in use. For example, we might have an integer variable

```
int na;  /* number of elements of a[] in use */
```

Then, when we wanted to do something with a (such as print it out), the loop would run from 0 to na, not 10 (or whatevera's size was):

```
for(i = 0; i < na; i = i + 1)
printf("%d\n", a[i]);
```

Naturally, we would have to ensure ensure that na's value was always less than or equal to the number of elements. Arrays are not limited to type int; you can have arrays of char or double or any other type.

Here is a slightly larger example of the use of arrays. Suppose we want to investigate the behaviour of rolling a pair of dice.

The total roll can be anywhere from 2 to 12, and we want to count how often each roll comes up. We will use an array to keep track of the counts: a[2] will count how many times we've rolled 2, etc.

We'll simulate the roll of a die by calling C's random number generation function, rand(). Each time you call rand(), it returns a different, pseudo-random integer.

The values that rand() returns typically span a large range, so we'll use C's*modulus* (or "remainder") operator % to produce random numbers in the range we want. The expression rand() % 6produces random numbers in the range 0 to 5, and rand() % 6 + 1 produces random numbers in the range 1 to 6.

Here is the programme:

```
#include <stdio.h>
#include <stdlib.h>
main()
{
int i;
int d1, d2;
int a[13];/* uses [2..12] */
for(i = 2; i <= 12; i = i + 1)
a[i] = 0;
for(i = 0; i < 100; i = i + 1)
{
d1 = rand() % 6 + 1;
d2 = rand() % 6 + 1;
a[d1 + d2] = a[d1 + d2] + 1;
}
for(i = 2; i <= 12; i = i + 1)
printf("%d: %d\n", i, a[i]);
return 0;
}
```

We include the header <stdlib.h> because it contains the necessary declarations for the rand() function. We declare the array of size 13 so that its highest element will be a[12]. (We're wasting a[0] and a[1]; this is no great loss.) The variables d1 and d2 contain the rolls of the two individual dice; we add them together to decide which cell of the array to increment, in the line

```
a[d1 + d2] = a[d1 + d2] + 1;
```

After 100 rolls, we print the array out. Typically (as craps players well know), we'll see mostly 7's, and relatively few 2's and 12's.

ARRAY INITIALIZATION

Although it is not possible to assign to all elements of an array at once using an assignment expression, it is possible to initialize some or all elements of an array when the array is defined.

The syntax looks like this:

```
int a[10] = {0, 1, 2, 3, 4, 5, 6, 7, 8, 9};
```

The list of values, enclosed in braces {}, separated by commas, provides the initial values for successive elements of the array. (Under older, pre-ANSI C compilers, you could not always supply initializers for "local" arrays inside functions; you could only initialize "global" arrays, those outside of any function.

Those compilers are now rare, so you shouldn't have to worry about this distinction any more. We'll talk more about local and global variables later in this chapter.)

If there are fewer initializers than elements in the array, the remaining elements are automatically initialized to 0.

For example,

```
int a[10] = {0, 1, 2, 3, 4, 5, 6};
```

would initialize a[7], a[8], and a[9] to 0. When an array definition includes an initializer, the array dimension may be omitted, and the compiler will infer the dimension from the number of initializers.

For example,

```
int b[] = {10, 11, 12, 13, 14};
```

would declare, define, and initialize an array b of 5 elements (i.e. just as if you'd typed int b[5]). Only the dimension is omitted; the brackets [] remain to indicate that b is in fact an array.

In the case of arrays of char, the initializer may be a string constant:

```
char s1[7] = "Hello,";
char s2[10] = "there,";
char s3[] = "world!";
```

As before, if the dimension is omitted, it is inferred from the size of the string initializer. (We haven't covered strings in detail yet—we'll do so in chapter—but it turns out that all strings in C are terminated by a special character with the value 0. Therefore, the array s3 will be of size 7, and the explicitly-sized s1 does need to be of size at least 7. For s2, the last 4 characters in the array will all end up being this zero-value character.)

MULTIDIMENSIONAL ARRAYS

When we said that "Arrays are not limited to type int; you can have arrays of... any other type," we meant that more literally than you might have guessed. If you have an "array of int," it means that you have an array each of whose elements is of type int.

But you can have an array each of whose elements is of type *x*, where *x* is any type you choose. In particular, you can have an array each of whose elements is another array! We can use these arrays of arrays for the same sorts of tasks as we'd use multidimensional arrays in other computer languages (or matrices in mathematics).

Naturally, we are not limited to arrays of arrays, either; we could have an array of arrays of arrays, which would act like a 3-dimensional array, etc.

The declaration of an array of arrays looks like this:

```
int a2[5][7];
```

You have to read complicated declarations like these "inside out." What this one says is that a2 is an array of 5 somethings, and that each of the somethings is an array of 7 ints. More briefly, "a2 is an array of 5 arrays of 7 ints," or, "a2 is an array of array of int." In the declaration of a2, the brackets closest to the identifier a2 tell you what a2 first and foremost is.

That's how you know it's an array of 5 arrays of size 7, not the other way around. You can think of a2 as having 5 "rows" and 7 "columns," although this interpretation is not mandatory. (You could also treat the "first" or inner subscript as "x" and the second as "y." Unless you're doing something fancy, all you have to worry about is that the subscripts when you access the array match those that you used when you declared it, as in the examples below.) To illustrate the use of multidimensional arrays, we might fill in the elements of the above array a2 using this piece of code:

```
int i, j;
```

```
for(i = 0; i < 5; i = i + 1)
{
  for(j = 0; j < 7; j = j + 1)
  a2[i][j] = 10 * i + j;
}
```

This pair of nested loops sets a[1][2] to 12, a[4][1] to 41, etc. Since the first dimension of a2 is 5, the first subscripting index variable, i, runs from 0 to 4. Similarly, the second subscript varies from 0 to 6.

We could print a2 out (in a two-dimensional way, suggesting its structure) with a similar pair of nested loops:

```
for(i = 0; i < 5; i = i + 1)
{
  for(j = 0; j < 7; j = j + 1)
  printf("%d\t", a2[i][j]);
  printf("\n");
}
```

(The character \t in the printf string is the tab character.)

Just to see more clearly what's going on, we could make the "row" and "column" subscripts explicit by printing them, too:

```
for(j = 0; j < 7; j = j + 1)
printf("\t%d:", j);
printf("\n");
for(i = 0; i < 5; i = i + 1)
{
printf("%d:", i);
for(j = 0; j < 7; j = j + 1)
printf("\t%d", a2[i][j]);
printf("\n");
}
```

This last fragment would print

```
0: 1: 2: 3: 4: 5: 6:
0: 0  1  2  3  4  5  6
1: 10 11 12 13 14 15 16
2: 20 21 22 23 24 25 26
3: 30 31 32 33 34 35 36
4: 40 41 42 43 44 45 46
```

Finally, there's no reason we have to loop over the "rows" first and the "columns" second; depending on what we wanted to do, we could interchange the two loops, like this:

```
for(j = 0; j < 7; j = j + 1)
{
 for(i = 0; i < 5; i = i + 1)
 printf("%d\t", a2[i][j]);
 printf("\n");
}
```

Notice that i is still the first subscript and it still runs from 0 to 4, and j is still the second subscript and it still runs from 0 to 6.

VISIBILITY

We haven't said so explicitly, but variables are channels of communication within a programme. You set a variable to a value at one point in a programme, and at another point (or points) you read the value out again. The two points may be in adjoining statements, or they may be in widely separated parts of the programme.

How long does a variable last? How widely separated can the setting and fetching parts of the programme be, and how long after a variable is set does it persist? Depending on the variable and how you're using it, you might want different answers to these questions.

The *visibility* of a variable determines how much of the rest of the programme can access that variable. You can arrange that a variable is visible only within one part of one function, or in one function, or in one source file, or anywhere in the programme. (We haven't really talked about source files yet; we'll be exploring them soon.)

Why would you want to limit the visibility of a variable? For maximum flexibility, wouldn't it be handy if all variables were potentially visible everywhere? As it happens, that arrangement would be *too* flexible: everywhere in the programme, you would have to keep track of the names of all the variables declared anywhere else in the programme, so that you didn't accidentally re-use one. Whenever a variable had the wrong value by mistake, you'd have to search the entire programme for the bug, because any statement in the entire programme could potentially have modified that variable.

You would constantly be stepping all over yourself by using a common variable name like i in two parts of your programme, and having one snippet of code accidentally overwrite the values being used by another part of the code. The communication would be sort of like an old party line—you'd always be accidentally interrupting other conversations, or having your conversations interrupted.

To avoid this confusion, we generally give variables the narrowest or smallest visibility they need. A variable declared within the braces {} of a function is visible only within that function; variables declared within functions are called *local variables*. If another function somewhere else declares a local variable with the same name, it's a different variable entirely, and the two don't clash with each other.

On the other hand, a variable declared outside of any function is a *global variable*, and it is potentially visible anywhere within the programme. You use global variables when you *do* want the communications path to be able to travel to any part of the programme.

When you declare a global variable, you will usually give it a longer, more descriptive name (not something generic like i) so that whenever you use it you will remember that it's the same variable everywhere. Another word for the visibility of variables is *scope*.

How long do variables last? By default, local variables (those declared within a function) have *automatic duration*: they spring into existence when the function is called, and they (and their values) disappear when the function returns. Global variables, on the other hand, have *static duration*: they last, and the values stored in them persist, for as long as the programme does. (Of course, the values can in general still be overwritten, so they don't necessarily persist forever.)

Finally, it is possible to split a function up into several source files, for easier maintenance. When several source files are combined into one programme (we'll be seeing how in the next chapter) the compiler must have a way of correlating the global variables which might be used to communicate between the several source files.

Furthermore, if a global variable is going to be useful for communication, there must be exactly one of it: you wouldn't want one function in one source file to store a value in one global variable named globalvar, and then have another function in another source file read from a*different* global variable named globalvar.

Therefore, a global variable should have exactly one *defining instance,* in one place in one source file. If the same variable is to be used anywhere else (i.e. in some other source file or files), the variable is declared in those other files with an *external declaration,* which is not a defining instance. The external declaration says, "hey, compiler, here's the name and type of a global variable I'm going to use, but don't define it here, don't allocate space for it; it's one that's defined somewhere else, and I'm just referring to it here."

If you accidentally have two distinct defining instances for a variable of the same name, the compiler (or the linker) will complain that it is "multiply defined." It is also possible to have a variable which is global in the sense that it is declared outside of any function, but private to the one source file it's defined in. Such a variable is visible to the functions in that source file but not to any functions in any other source files, even if they try to issue a matching declaration.

You get any extra control you might need over visibility and lifetime, and you distinguish between defining instances and external declarations, by using *storage classes*. A storage class is an extra keyword at the beginning of a declaration which modifies the declaration in some way. Generally, the storage class (if any) is the first word in the declaration, preceding the type name.

(Strictly speaking, this ordering has not traditionally been necessary, and you may see some code with the storage class, type name, and other parts of a declaration in an unusual order.) We said that, by default, local variables had automatic duration. To give them static duration (so that, instead of coming and going as the function is called, they persist for as long as the function does), you precede their declaration with thestatic keyword:

```
static int i;
```

By default, a declaration of a global variable (especially if it specifies an initial value) is the defining instance. To make it an external declaration, of a variable which is defined somewhere else, you precede it with the keyword extern:

```
extern int j;
```

Finally, to arrange that a global variable is visible only within its containing source file, you precede it with the statickeyword:

```
static int k;
```

Notice that the static keyword can do two different things: it adjusts the duration of a local variable from automatic to static, or it adjusts the visibility of a global variable from truly global to private-to-the-file.

To summarize, we've talked about two different attributes of a variable: visibility and duration. These are orthogonal, as shown in this table:

	duration:	
visibility:	automatic	static
local	normal local variables	static local variables
global	N/A	normal global variables

We can also distinguish between file-scope global variables and truly global variables, based on the presence or absence of the static keyword.

We can also distinguish between external declarations and defining instances of global variables, based on the presence or absence of the extern keyword.

DEFAULT INITIALIZATION

The duration of a variable (whether static or automatic) also affects its default initialization. If you do not explicitly initialize them, automatic-duration variables (that is, local, non-static ones) are not guaranteed to have any particular initial value; they will typically contain garbage. It is therefore a fairly serious error to attempt to use the value of an automatic variable which has never been initialized or assigned to: the programme will either work incorrectly, or the garbage value may just happen to be "correct" such that the programme appears to work correctly!

However, the particular value that the garbage takes on can vary depending literally on *anything*: other parts of the programme, which compiler was used, which hardware or operating system the programme is running on, the time of day, the phase of the moon.

So you hardly want to say that a programme which uses an uninitialized variable "works"; it may seem to work, but it works for the wrong reason, and it may stop working tomorrow. Static-duration variables (global and static local), on the other hand, are guaranteed to be initialized to 0 if you do not use an explicit initializer in the definition.

(Once upon a time, there was another distinction between the initialization of automatic vs. static variables: you could initialize *aggregate* objects, such as arrays, only if they had static duration. If your compiler complains when you try to initialize a local array, it's probably an old, pre-ANSI compiler. Modern, ANSI-compatible compilers remove this limitation, so it's no longer much of a concern.)

EXAMPLES

Here is an example demonstrating almost everything we've seen so far:

```
int globalvar = 1;
extern int anotherglobalvar;
static int privatevar;
f()
{
  int localvar;
  int localvar2 = 2;
  static int persistentvar;
}
```

Here we have six variables, three declared outside and three declared inside of the function f(). Globalvar is a global variable. The declaration we see is its defining instance (it happens also to include an initial value).globalvar can be used anywhere in this source file, and it could be used in other source files, too (as long as corresponding external declarations are issued in those other source files).

Anotherglobalvar is a second global variable. It is *not* defined here; the defining instance for it (and its initialization) is somewhere else. Privatevar is a "private" global variable. It can be used anywhere within this source file, but functions in other source files cannot access it, even if they try to issue external declarations for it. (If other source files try to declare a global variable called "privatevar", they'll get their own; they won't be sharing this one.) Since it has static duration and receives no explicit initialization, privatevar will be initialized to 0.

Localvar is a local variable within the function f(). It can be accessed only within the function f(). (If any other part of the programme declares a variable named "localvar", that variable will be distinct from the one we're looking at here.)localvar is conceptually "created" each time f() is called, and disappears when f() returns. Any value which was stored in localvar last time f() was running will be lost and will not be available next time f() is called. Furthermore, since it has no explicit initializer, the value of localvar will in general be garbage each time f() is called.

Localvar2 is also local, and everything that we said about localvar applies to it, except that since its declaration includes an explicit initializer, it will be initialized to 2 each time f() is called. Finally, persistentvar is again local to f(), but it *does* maintain its value between calls to f(). It has static duration but no explicit initializer, so its initial value will be 0. The defining instances and external declarations we've been looking at so far have all been of simple variables.

There are also defining instances and external declarations of functions, which we'll be looking at in the next chapter. (Also, don't worry about static variables for now if they don't make sense to you; they're a relatively sophisticated concept, which you won't need to use at first.) The term *declaration* is a general one which encompasses defining instances and external declarations; defining instances and external declarations are two different kinds of declarations. Furthermore, either kind of declaration suffices to inform the compiler of the name and type of a particular variable (or function).

If you have the defining instance of a global variable in a source file, the rest of that source file can use that variable without having to issue any external declarations. It's only in source files where the defining instance hasn't been seen that you need external declarations. You will sometimes hear a defining instance referred to simply as a "definition," and you will sometimes hear an external declaration referred to simply as a "declaration." These usages are mildly ambiguous, in that you can't tell out of context whether a "declaration" is a generic declaration (that might be a defining instance or an external declaration) or whether it's an external declaration that specifically is not a defining instance.

(Similarly, there are other constructions that can be called "definitions" in C, namely the definitions of preprocessor macros, structures, and typedefs, none of which we've met.) In these notes, we'll try to make things clear by using the unambiguous terms *defining instance* and *external declaration*. Elsewhere, you may have to look at the context to determine how the terms "definition" and "declaration" are being used.

FUNCTION BASICS

So what defines a function? It has a *name* that you call it by, and a list of zero or more *arguments* or *parameters* that you hand to it for it to act on or to direct its work; it has a *body* containing the actual instructions (statements) for carrying out the task the function is supposed to perform; and it may give you back a *return value*, of a particular type.

Here is a very simple function, which accepts one argument, multiplies it by 2, and hands that value back:

```
int multbytwo(int x)
{
  int retval;
  retval = x * 2;
```

```
    return retval;
}
```

On the first line we see the return type of the function (int), the name of the function (multbytwo), and a list of the function's arguments, enclosed in parentheses. Each argument has both a name and a type; multbytwo accepts one argument, of type int, named x. The name x is arbitrary, and is used only within the definition of multbytwo. The caller of this function only needs to know that a single argument of type int is expected; the caller does not need to know what name the function will use internally to refer to that argument. (In particular, the caller does not have to pass the value of a variable named x.)

Next we see, surrounded by the familiar braces, the body of the function itself. This function consists of one declaration (of a local variable retval) and two statements. The first statement is a conventional expression statement, which computes and assigns a value to retval, and the second statement is a return statement, which causes the function to return to its caller, and also specifies the value which the function returns to its caller.

The return statement can return the value of any expression, so we don't really need the local retval variable; the function could be collapsed to

```
int multbytwo(int x)
{
    return x * 2;
}
```

How do we call a function? We've been doing so informally since day one, but now we have a chance to call one that we've written, in full detail. Here is a tiny skeletal programme to call multby2:

```
#include <stdio.h>
extern int multbytwo(int);
int main()
{
    int i, j;
    i = 3;
```

```
    j = multbytwo(i);
    printf("%d\n", j);
    return 0;
}
```

This looks much like our other test programmes, with the exception of the new line

```
extern int multbytwo(int);
```

This is an *external function prototype declaration.* It is an external declaration, in that it declares something which is defined somewhere else. (We've already seen the defining instance of the function multbytwo, but maybe the compiler hasn't seen it yet.)

The function prototype declaration contains the three pieces of information about the function that a caller needs to know: the function's name, return type, and argument type(s). Since we don't care what name the multbytwo function will use to refer to its first argument, we don't need to mention it. (On the other hand, if a function takes several arguments, giving them names in the prototype may make it easier to remember which is which, so names may optionally be used in function prototype declarations.)

Finally, to remind us that this is an external declaration and not a defining instance, the prototype is preceded by the keyword extern. The presence of the function prototype declaration lets the compiler know that we intend to call this function, multbytwo. The information in the prototype lets the compiler generate the correct code for calling the function, and also enables the compiler to check up on our code (by making sure, for example, that we pass the correct number of arguments to each function we call).

Down in the body of main, the action of the function call should be obvious: the line

```
j = multbytwo(i);
```

calls multbytwo, passing it the value of i as its argument. When multbytwo returns, the return value is assigned to the variable j. (Notice that the value of main's local variable i will become the value of multbytwo's parameter x; this is absolutely not a problem, and is a normal sort of affair.)

This example is written out in "longhand," to make each step equivalent. The variable i isn't really needed, since we could just as well call

```
j = multbytwo(3);
```

And the variable j isn't really needed, either, since we could just as well call

```
printf("%d\n", multbytwo(3));
```

Here, the call to multbytwo is a subexpression which serves as the second argument to printf. The value returned bymultbytwo is passed immediately to printf. (Here, as in general, we see the flexibility and generality of expressions in C. An argument passed to a function may be an arbitrarily complex subexpression, and a function call is itself an expression which may be embedded as a subexpression within arbitrarily complicated surrounding expressions.)

We should say a little more about the mechanism by which an argument is passed down from a caller into a function. Formally, C is *call by value*, which means that a function receives *copies* of the values of its arguments. We can illustrate this with an example. Suppose, in our implementation of multbytwo, we had gotten rid of the unnecessary retvalvariable like this:

```
int multbytwo(int x)
{
  x = x * 2;
  return x;
}
```

We might wonder, if we wrote it this way, what would happen to the value of the variable i when we called

```
j = multbytwo(i);
```

When our implementation of multbytwo changes the value of x, does that change the value of i up in the caller? The answer is no. x receives a copy of i's value, so when we change x we don't change i.

However, there is an exception to this rule. When the argument you pass to a function is not a single variable, but is rather an array, the function does *not* receive a copy of the array, and it therefore *can* modify the array in the caller. The reason is that it might be too expensive to copy the entire array, and furthermore, it can be useful for the function to write into the caller's array, as a way of handing back more data than would fit in the function's single return value.

FUNCTION PROTOTYPES

In modern C programming, it is considered good practice to use prototype declarations for all functions that you call. As we mentioned, these prototypes help to ensure that the compiler can generate correct code for calling the functions, as well as allowing the compiler to catch certain mistakes you might make.

Strictly speaking, however, prototypes are optional. If you call a function for which the compiler has not seen a prototype, the compiler will do the best it can, assuming that you're calling the function correctly.

If prototypes are a good idea, and if we're going to get in the habit of writing function prototype declarations for functions we call that we've written (such as multbytwo), what happens for library functions such as printf? Where are their prototypes? The answer is in that boilerplate line

```
#include <stdio.h>
```

we've been including at the top of all of our programmes. stdio.h is conceptually a file full of external declarations and other information pertaining to the "Standard I/O" library functions, including printf. The #include directive (which we'll meet formally in a later chapter) arranges that all of the declarations within stdio.h are considered by the compiler, rather as if we'd typed them all in ourselves. Somewhere within these declarations is an external function prototype declaration forprintf, which satisfies the rule that there should be a prototype for each function we call.

(For other standard library functions we call, there will be other "header files" to include.) Finally, one more thing about external function prototype declarations. We've said that the distinction between external declarations and defining instances of normal variables hinges on the presence or absence of the keyword extern.

The situation is a little bit different for functions. The "defining instance" of a function is the function, including its body (that is, the brace-enclosed list of declarations and statements implementing the function). An external declaration of a function, even without the keyword extern, looks nothing like a function declaration. Therefore, the keyword extern is optional in function prototype declarations. If you wish, you can write

```
int multbytwo(int);
```

and this is just as good an external function prototype declaration as

```
extern int multbytwo(int);
```

(In the first form, without the extern, as soon as the compiler sees the semicolon, it knows it's not going to see a function body, so the declaration can't be a definition.) You may want to stay in the habit of using extern in all external declarations, including function declarations, since "extern = external declaration" is an easier rule to remember.

FUNCTION PHILOSOPHY

What makes a good function? The most important aspect of a good "building block" is that have a single, well-defined task to perform. When you find that a programme is hard to manage, it's often because it has not been designed and broken up into functions cleanly. Two obvious reasons for moving code down into a function are because:

- It appeared in the main programme several times, such that by making it a function, it can be written just once, and the several places where it used to appear can be replaced with calls to the new function.
- The main programme was getting too big, so it could be made (presumably) smaller and more manageable by lopping part of it off and making it a function.

These two reasons are important, and they represent significant benefits of well-chosen functions, but they are not sufficient to automatically identify a good function. As we've been suggesting, a good function has at least these two additional attributes:

- It does just one well-defined task, and does it well.
- Its interface to the rest of the programme is clean and narrow.

Attribute 3 is just a restatement of two things we said above. Attribute 4 says that you shouldn't have to keep track of too many things when calling a function. If you know what a function is supposed to do, and if its task is simple and well-defined, there should be just a few pieces of information you have to give it to act upon, and one or just a few pieces of information which it returns to you when it's done.

If you find yourself having to pass lots and lots of information to a function, or remember details of its internal implementation to make sure that it will work properly this time, it's often a sign that the function is not sufficiently well-defined. (A poorly-defined function may be an arbitrary chunk of code that was ripped out of a main programme that was getting too big, such that it essentially has to have access to all of that main function's local variables.)

The whole point of breaking a programme up into functions is so that you don't have to think about the entire programme at once; ideally, you can think about just one function at a time. We say that a good function is a "black box," which is supposed to suggest that the "container" it's in is opaque—callers can't see inside it (and the function inside can't see out).

When you call a function, you only have to know what it does, not how it does it. When you're *writing* a function, you only have to know what it's supposed to do, and you don't have to know why or under what circumstances its caller will be calling it. (When designing a function, we should perhaps think about the callers just enough to ensure that the function we're designing will be easy to call, and that we aren't accidentally setting things up so that callers will have to think about any internal details.)

Some functions may be hard to write (if they have a hard job to do, or if it's hard to make them do it truly well), but that difficulty should be compartmentalized along with the function itself. Once you've written a "hard" function, you should be able to sit back and relax and watch it do that hard work on call from the rest of your programme. It should be pleasant to notice (in the ideal case) how much easier the rest of the programme is to write, now that the hard work can be deferred to this workhorse function.

(In fact, if a difficult-to-write function's interface is well-defined, you may be able to get away with writing a quick-and-dirty version of the function first, so that you can begin testing the rest of the programme, and then go back later and rewrite the function to do the hard parts. As long as the function's original interface anticipated the hard parts, you won't have to rewrite the rest of the programme when you fix the function.)

If you find that difficulties pervade a programme, that the hard parts can't be buried inside black-box functions and then forgotten about; if you find that there are hard parts which involve complicated interactions among multiple functions, then the programme probably needs redesigning.

For the purposes of explanation, we've been seeming to talk so far only about "main programmes" and the functions they call and the rationale behind moving some piece of code down out of a "main programme" into a function. But in reality, there's obviously no need to restrict ourselves to a two-tier scheme. Any function we find ourself writing will often be appropriately written in terms of sub-functions, sub-sub-functions, etc. (Furthermore, the "main programme," main(), is itself just a function.)

SEPARATE COMPILATION LOGISTICS

When a programme consists of many functions, it can be convenient to split them up into several source files. Among other things, this means that when a change is made, only the source file containing the change has to be recompiled, not the whole programme.

The job of putting the pieces of a programme together and producing the final executable falls to a tool called the *linker*. (We may or may not need to invoke the linker explicitly; a compiler often invokes it automatically, as needed.) The linker looks through all of the pieces making up the programme, sorting out the external declarations and defining instances. The compiler has noted the definitions made by each source file, as well as the declarations of things used by each source file but (presumably) defined elsewhere. For each thing (global variable or function) used but not defined by one piece of the programme, the linker looks for another piece which does define that thing.

The logistics of writing a programme in several source files, and then compiling and linking all of the source files together, depend on the programming environment you're using. We'll cover two possibilities, depending on whether you're using a traditional command-line compiler or a newer integrated development environment (IDE) or other graphical user interface (GUI) compiler.

When using a command-line compiler, there are usually two main steps involved in building an executable programme from one or more source files. First, each source file is compiled, resulting in an *object file* containing the machine instructions (generated by the compiler) corresponding to just the code in that source file.

Second, the various object files are *linked*together, with each other and with *libraries* containing code for functions which you did not write (such as printf), to produce a final, executable programme.

Under Unix, the cc command can perform one or both steps. So far, we've been using extremely simple invocations of ccsuch as

```
cc -o hello hello.c
```

This invocation compiles a single source file, hello.c, links it, and places the executable in a file named hello.

Suppose we have a programme which we're trying to build from three separate source files, x.c, y.c, and z.c. We could compile all three of them, and link them together, all at once, with the command

```
cc -o myprog x.c y.c z.c
```

Alternatively, we could compile them separately: the -c option to cc tells it to compile only, but not to link. Instead of building an executable, it merely creates an object file, with a name ending in .o, for each source file compiled.

So the three commands

```
cc -c x.c
cc -c y.c
cc -c y.c
```

would compile x.c, y.c, and z.c and create object files x.o, y.o, and z.o. Then, the three object files could be linked together using

```
cc -o myprog x.o y.o z.o
```

When the cc command is given an .o file, it knows that it does not have to compile it (it's an object file, already compiled); it just sends it through to the link process.

Above we mentioned that the second, linking step also involves pulling in library functions. Normally, the functions from the Standard C library are linked in automatically. Occasionally, you must request a library manually; one common situation under Unix is that the math functions tend to be in a separate math library, which is requested by using -lm on the command line.

Since the libraries must typically be searched *after* your program's own object files are linked (so that the linker knows which library functions your programme uses), any -l option must appear *after* the names of your files on the command line. For example, to link the object file mymath.o (previously compiled with cc -c mymath.c) together with the math library, you might use

```
cc -o mymathprog mymath.o -lm
```

(The l in the -l option is the lower case ell, for library; it is *not* the digit 1.)

Everything we've said about cc also applies to most other Unix C compilers. (Many of you will be using gcc, the FSF's GNU C Compiler.) There are command-line compilers for MS-DOS systems which work similarly. For example, the Microsoft C compiler comes with a CL ("compile and link") command, which works almost the same as Unix cc. You can compile and link in one step:

```
cl hello.c
```

```
or you can compile only:
cl /c hello.c
```

creating an object file named hello.obj which you can link later. The preceding has all been about command-line compilers.

If you're using some kind of integrated development environment, such as Borland's Turbo C or the Microsoft Programmer's Workbench or Visual C or Think C or Codewarrior, most of the mechanical details are taken care of for you. Typically you define a "project," and there's a way to specify the list of files which make up your project.

I/O MODEL

The I/O model does not distinguish between the types of physical devices supporting the I/O. Each source or sink of data is treated in the same way, and is viewed as a *stream* of bytes. Since the smallest object that can be represented in C is the character, access to a file is permitted at any character boundary. Any number of characters can be read or written from a movable point, known as the *file position indicator*. The characters will be read, or written, in sequence from this point, and the position indicator moved accordingly.

The position indicator is initially set to the beginning of a file when it is opened, but can also be moved by means of positioning requests. Opening a file in append mode has an implementation defined effect on the stream's file position indicator. The overall effect is to provide sequential reads or writes unless the stream was opened in append mode, or the file position indicator is explicitly moved. There are two types of file, *text files* and *binary files*, which, within a programme, are manipulated as *text streams* and *binary* streams once they have been opened for I/O. The stdio package does not permit operations on the contents of files 'directly', but only by viewing them as streams.

TEXT STREAMS

The Standard specifies what is meant by the term *text stream*, which essentially considers a file to contain lines of text.

A line is a sequence of zero or more characters terminated by a newline character.

It is quite possible that the actual representation of lines in the external environment is different from this and there may be transformations of the data stream on the way in and out of the programme; a common requirement is to translate the '\n' line-terminator into the sequence '\r\n' on output, and do the reverse on input. Other translations may also be necessary.

Data read in from a text stream is guaranteed to compare equal to the data that was earlier written out to the file if the data consists only of complete lines of printable characters and the control characters horizontal-tab and newline, no newline character is immediately preceded by space characters and the last character is a newline.

It is guaranteed that, if the last character written to a text file is a newline, it will read back as the same. It is implementation defined whether the last line written to a text file must terminate with a newline character; this is because on some implementations text files and binary files are the same.

Some implementations may strip the leading space from lines consisting only of a space followed by a newline, or strip trailing spaces at the end of a line! An implementation must support text files with lines containing at least 254 characters, including the terminating newline. Opening a text stream in update mode may result in a binary stream in some implementations.

Writing on a text stream may cause some implementations to truncate the file at that point—any data beyond the last byte of the current write being discarded.

BINARY STREAMS

A binary stream is a sequence of characters that can be used to record a program's internal data, such as the contents of structures or arrays in binary form. Data read in from a binary stream will always compare equal to data written out earlier to the same stream, under the same implementation.

In some circumstances, an implementation-defined number of NUL characters may be appended to a binary stream.

THE STDIO.H HEADER FILE

To provide support for streams of the various kinds, a number of functions and macros exist. The <stdio.h> header file contains the various declarations necessary for the functions, together with the following macro and type declarations:

`FILE`

The type of an object used to contain stream control information. Users of stdio never need to know the contents of these objects, but simply manipulate pointers to them. It is not safe to copy these objects within the programme; sometimes their addresses may be 'magic'.

`fpos_t`

A type of object that can be used to record unique values of a stream's file position indicator.

`_IOFBF _IOLBF _IONBF`

Values used to control the buffering of a stream in conjunction with thesetvbuf function.

`BUFSIZ`

The size of the buffer used by the setbuf function. An integral constant expression whose value is at least 256.

`EOF`

A negative integral constant expression, indicating the end-of-file condition on a stream i.e. that there is no more input.

`FILENAME_MAX`

The maximum length which a filename can have, if there is a limit, or otherwise the recommended size of an array intended to hold a file name.

`FOPEN_MAX`

The minimum number of files that the implementation guarantees may be held open concurrently; at least eight are guaranteed. Note that three predefined streams exist and may need to be closed if a programme needs to open more than five files explicitly.

`L_tmpnam`

The maximum length of the string generated by tmpnam; an integral constant expression.

`SEEK_CUR SEEK_END SEEK_SET`

Integral constant expressions used to control the actions of fseek.

`TMP_MAX`

The minimum number of unique filenames generated by tmpnam; an integral constant expression with a value of at least 25.

`stdin stdout stderr`

Predefined objects of type **(FILE *)** referring to the standard input, output and error streams respectively. These streams are automatically open when a programme starts execution.

OPENING, CLOSING AND BUFFERING OF STREAMS

OPENING

A stream is connected to a file by means of the fopen, freopen or tmpfilefunctions. These functions will, if successful, return a pointer to a **FILE** object.

Three streams are available without any special action; they are normally all connected to the physical device associated with the executing programme: usually your terminal. They are referred to by the names stdin, the *standard input*, stdout, the *standard output*, and stderr, the *standard error* streams.

Normal keyboard input is from stdin, normal terminal output is to stdout, and error messages are directed to stderr. The separation of error messages from normal output messages allows the stdout stream to be connected to something other than the terminal device, and still to have error messages appear on the screen in front of you, rather than to be redirected to this file.

These files are only fully buffered if they do not refer to interactive devices. As mentioned earlier, the file position indicator may or may not be movable, depending on the underlying device. It is not possible, for example, to move the file position indicator on stdin if that is connected to a terminal, as it usually is.

All non-temporary files must have a *filename,* which is a string. The rules for what constitutes valid filenames are implementation defined. Whether a file can be simultaneously open multiple times is also implementation defined. Opening a new file may involve creating the file. Creating an existing file causes its previous contents to be discarded.

CLOSING

Files are closed by explicitly calling fclose, exit or by returning from main. Any buffered data is flushed. If a programme stops for some other reason, the status of files which it had open is undefined.

BUFFERING

There are three types of buffering:

`Unbuffered`

Minimum internal storage is used by stdio in an attempt to send or receive data as soon as possible.

`Line buffered`

Characters are processed on a line-by-line basis. This is commonly used in interactive environments, and internal buffers are flushed only when full or when a newline is processed.

`Fully buffered`

Internal buffers are only flushed when full. The buffering associated with a stream can always be flushed by using fflushexplicitly. Support for the various types of buffering is implementation defined, and can be controlled within these limits using setbuf and setvbuf.

DIRECT FILE MANIPULATION

A number of functions exist to operate on files directly.

```
#include <stdio.h>
int remove(const char *filename);
```

```
int rename(const char *old, const char *new);
char *tmpnam(char *s);
FILE *tmpfile(void);
```

remove

Causes a file to be removed. Subsequent attempts to open the file will fail, unless it is first created again. If the file is already open, the operation ofremove is implementation defined. The return value is zero for success, any other value for failure.

rename

Changes the name of the file identified by old to new. Subsequent attempts to open the original name will fail, unless another file is created with the old name. As with remove, rename returns zero for a successful operation, any other value indicating a failure. If a file with the new name exists prior to calling rename, the behaviour is implementation defined. If rename fails for any reason, the original file is unaffected.

tmpnam

Generates a string that may be used as a filename and is guaranteed to be different from any existing filename. It may be called repeatedly, each time generating a new name. The constant **TMP_MAX** is used to specify how many times tmpnam may be called before it can no longer find a unique name.**TMP_MAX** will be at least 25.

If tmpnam is called more than this number of times, its behaviour is undefined by the Standard, but many implementations offer no practical limit. If the argument s is set to **NULL**, then tmpnam uses an internal buffer to build the name, and returns a pointer to that. Subsequent calls may alter the same internal buffer. The argument may instead point to an array of at leastL_tmpnam characters, in which case the name will be filled into the supplied buffer.

Such a filename may then be created, and used as a temporary file. Since the name is generated by the function, it is unlikely to be very useful in any other context. Temporary files of this nature are not removed, except by direct calls to the remove function. They are most often used to pass temporary data between two separate programmes.

tmpfile

Creates a temporary binary file, opened for update, and returns a pointer to the stream of that file. The file will be removed when the stream is closed. If no file could be opened, tmpfile returns a null pointer.

OPENING NAMED FILES

Named files are opened by a call to the fopen function, whose declaration is this:

```
#include <stdio.h>
FILE *fopen(const char *pathname, const char
*mode);
```

The pathname argument is the name of the file to open, such as that returned fromtmpnam, or some programme-specific filename.

Files can be opened in a variety of *modes,* such as *read* mode for reading data,*write* mode for writing data, and so on. Note that if you only want to write data to a file, fopen will *create* the file if it does not already exist, or truncate it to zero length if it did exist.

The Standard list of modes is shown in Table, although implementations may permit extra modes by appending extra characters at the end of the modes.

Table. File Opening Modes

Mode	Type of file	Read	Write	Create	Truncate
	"r"	text	yes	n–	n–
	no				
	"rb"	binary	yes	n–	n–
	no				
	"r+"	text	yes	yes	n–
	no				
	"r+b"	binary	yes	yes	n–
	no				
	"rb+"	binary	yes	yes	n–
	no				
	"w"	text	n–	yes	yes
	yes				

"wb"	binary	n–	yes	yes	yes
"w+"	text	yes	yes	yes	yes
"w+b"	binary	yes	yes	yes	yes
"wb+"	binary	yes	yes	yes	yes
"a"	text	n–	yes	yes	no
"ab"	binary	n–	yes	yes	no
"a+"	text	yes	yes	yes	no
"a+b"	binary	n–	yes	yes	no
"ab+"	binary	n–	yes	yes	no

Beware that some implementations of binary files may pad the last record with **NULL** characters, so opening them with modes ab, ab+ or a+b could position the file pointer beyond the last data written.

If a file is opened in append mode, *all* writes will occur at the end of the file, regardless of attempts to move the file position indicator with fseek. The initial position fo the file position indicator will be implementation defined.

Attempts to open a file in read mode, indicated by an 'r' as the first character in the mode string, will fail if the file does not already exist or can't be read.

Files opened for update ('+' as the second or third character of mode) may be both read and written, but a read may not immediately follow a write, or a write follow a read, without an intervening call to one (or more) of fflush, fseek, fsetpos or rewind.

The only exception is that a write may immediately follow a read if **EOF** was read. It may also be possible in some implementations to omit the b in the binary modes, using the same modes for text and binary files.

Streams opened by fopen are fully buffered only if they are not connected to an interactive device; this ensures that prompts and responses are handled properly. If fopen fails to open a file, it returns a null pointer; otherwise, it returns a pointer to the object controlling the stream. The stdin, stdout and stderr objects are not necessarily modifiable and it may not be possible to use the value returned fromfopen for assignment to one of them. For this reason, freopen is provided.

FREOPEN

The freopen function is used to take an existing stream pointer and associate it with another named file:

```
#include <stdio.h>
FILE *freopen(const char *pathname,
const char *mode, FILE *stream);
```

The mode argument is the same as for fopen. The stream is closed first, and any errors from the close are ignored. On error, **NULL** is returned, otherwise the new value for stream is returned.

CLOSING FILES

An open file is closed using fclose.

```
#include <stdio.h>
int fclcse(FILE *stream);
```

Any unwritten data buffered for stream is flushed out and any unread data is thrown away. If a buffer had been automatically allocated for the stream, it is freed. The file is then closed. Zero is returned on success, **EOF** if any error occurs.

SETBUF, SETVBUF

These two functions are used to change the buffering strategy for an open stream:

```
#include <stdio.h>
int setvbuf(FILE *stream, char *buf,
int type, size_t size);
void setbuf(FILE *stream, char *buf);
```

They must be used *before* the file is either read from or written to. The typeargument defines how the stream will be buffered.

Table. Type of Buffering

Value	Effect
_IONBF	Do not buffer I/O
_IOFBF	Fully buffer I/O
_IOLBF	*Line buffer*: flush buffer when full, when newline is written or when a read is requested.

The buf argument can be a null pointer, in which case an array is automatically allocated to hold the buffered data. Otherwise, the user can provide a buffer, but should ensure that its lifetime is at least as long as that of the stream: a common mistake is to use automatic storage allocated inside a compound statement; in correct usage it is usual to obtain the storage from malloc instead. The size of the buffer is specified by the size argument.

A call of setbuf is exactly the same as a call of setvbuf with **IOFBF** for the typeargument, and **BUFSIZ** for the size argument. If buf is a null pointer, the value_**IONBF** is used for type instead. No value is returned by setbuf, setvbuf returns zero on success, non-zero if invalid values are provided for type or size, or the request cannot be complied with.

FFLUSH

```
#include <stdio.h>
int fflush(FILE *stream);
```

If stream refers to a file opened for output or update, any unwritten data is 'written' out. Exactly what that means is a function of the host environment and C cannot guarantee, for example, that data immediately reaches the surface of a disk which might be supporting the file. If the stream is associated with a file opened for input or update, any preceding ungetc operation is forgotten.

The most recent operation on the stream must have been an output operation; if not, the behaviour is undefined. A call of fflush with an argument of zero flushes every output or update stream. Care is taken to avoid those streams that have not had an output as their last operation, thus avoiding the undefined behaviour mentioned above. **EOF** is returned if an error occurs, otherwise zero.

PRINTF

printf's name comes from print formatted. It generates output under the control of a *format string* (its first argument) which consists of literal characters to be printed and also special character sequences—*format specifiers*—which request that other arguments be fetched, formatted, and inserted into the string. Our very first programme was nothing more than a call to printf, printing a constant string:

```
printf("Hello, world!\n");
```

Our second programme also featured a call to printf:

```
printf("i is %d\n", i);
```

In that case, whenever printf "printed" the string "i is %d", it did not print it verbatim; it replaced the two characters%d with the value of the variable i.

There are quite a number of format specifiers for printf. Here are the basic ones :

```
%d  print an int argument in decimal
%ld print a long int argument in decimal
%c  print a character
%s  print a string
%f  print a float or double argument
%e  same as %f, but use exponential notation
%g  use %e or %f, whichever is better
%-  print an int argument in octal (base 8)
%x  print an int argument in hexadecimal (base
16)
%%  print a single %
```

It is also possible to specify the width and precision of numbers and strings as they are inserted (somewhat like **FORTRAN** format statements); we'll present those details in a later chapter. (Very briefly, for those who are curious: a notation like %3d means to print an int in a field at least 3 spaces wide; a notation like %5.2f means to print a float ordouble in a field at least 5 spaces wide, with two places to the right of the decimal.)

To illustrate with a few more examples: the call

```
printf("%c %d %f %e %s %d%%\n", '1', 2, 3.14,
56000000., "eight", 9);
```

would print

```
1 2 3.140000 5.600000e+07 eight 9%
```

The call

```
printf("%d %o %x\n", 100, 100, 100);
```

would print

```
100 144 64
```

Successive calls to printf just build up the output a piece at a time, so the calls

```
printf("Hello, ");
printf("world!\n");
```

would also print Hello, world! (on one line of output).

Earlier we learned that C represents characters internally as small integers corresponding to the characters' values in the machine's character set (typically **ASCII**). This means that there isn't really much difference between a character and an integer in C; most of the difference is in whether we choose to interpret an integer as an integer or a character. printf is one place where we get to make that choice: %d prints an integer value as a string of digits representing its decimal value, while %c prints the character corresponding to a character set value. So the lines

```
char c = 'A';
int i = 97;
printf("c = %c, i = %d\n", c, i);
```

would print c as the character A and i as the number 97. But if, on the other hand, we called

```
printf("c = %d, i = %c\n", c, i);
```

we'd see the decimal value (printed by %d) of the character 'A', followed by the character (whatever it is) which happens to have the decimal value 97.

You have to be careful when calling printf. It has no way of knowing how many arguments you've passed it or what their types are other than by looking for the format specifiers in the format string. If there are more format specifiers (that is, more % signs) than there are arguments, or if the arguments have the wrong types for the format specifiers, printf can misbehave badly, often printing nonsense numbers or (even worse) numbers which mislead you into thinking that some other part of your programme is broken.

Because of some automatic conversion rules which we haven't covered yet, you have a small amount of latitude in the types of the expressions you pass as arguments to printf. The argument for %c may be of type char or int, and the argument for %d may be of type char or int.

The string argument for %s may be a string constant, an array of characters, or a pointer to some characters (though we haven't really covered strings or pointers yet). Finally, the arguments corresponding to %e, %f, and %g may be of types float or double.

But other combinations do *not* work reliably: %d will not print a long int or a float or a double; %ld will not print an int; %e, %f, and %g will not print an int.

CHARACTER INPUT AND OUTPUT

Unless a programme can read some input, it's hard to keep it from doing exactly the same thing every time it's run, and thus being rather boring after a while.

The most basic way of reading input is by calling the function getchar. getchar reads one character from the "standard input," which is usually the user's keyboard, but which can sometimes be redirected by the operating system. getcharreturns the character it reads, or, if there are no more characters available, the special value **EOF**. A companion function is putchar, which writes one character to the "standard output."

(The standard output is, again not surprisingly, usually the user's screen, although it, too, can be redirected. printf, like putchar, prints to the standard output; in fact, you can imagine that printf calls putchar to actually print each of the characters it formats.) Using these two functions, we can write a very basic programme to copy the input, a character at a time, to the output:

```
#include <stdio.h>
```

```
/* copy input to output */
main()
{
  int c;
  c = getchar();
  while(c != EOF)
{
  putchar(c);
  c = getchar();
}
  return 0;
}
```

This code is straightforward, and I encourage you to type it in and try it out. It reads one character, and if it is not the **EOF**code, enters a while loop, printing one character and reading another, as long as the character read is not **EOF**. This is a straightforward loop, although there's one mystery surrounding the declaration of the variable c: if it holds characters, why is it an int?

We said that a char variable could hold integers corresponding to character set values, and that an int could hold integers of more arbitrary values. Since most character sets contain a few hundred characters, an int variable can in general comfortably hold all char values, and then some. Therefore, there's nothing wrong with declaring c as an int. But in fact, it's important to do so, because getchar can return every character value,*plus* that special, non-character value **EOF**, indicating that there are no more characters.

Type char is only guaranteed to be able to hold all the character values; it is *not* guaranteed to be able to hold this "no more characters" value without possibly mixing it up with some actual character value. Therefore, you should always remember to use an int for anything you assigngetchar's return value to.

When you run the character copying programme, and it begins copying its input (your typing) to its output (your screen), you may find yourself wondering how to stop it. It stops when it receives end-of-file (**EOF**), but how do you send

EOF? The answer depends on what kind of computer you're using. On Unix and Unix-related systems, it's almost always control-D. On **MS-DOS** machines, it's control-Z followed by the **RETURN** key. Under Think C on the Macintosh, it's control-D, just like Unix. On other systems, you may have to do some research to learn how to send **EOF**.

(Note, too, that the character you type to generate an end-of-file condition from the keyboard is *not* the same as the special **EOF** value returned by getchar. The **EOF** value returned by getchar is a code indicating that the input system has detected an end-of-file condition, whether it's reading the keyboard or a file or a magnetic tape or a network connection or anything else. In a disk file, at least, there is not likely to be any character *in* the file corresponding to **EOF**; as far as your programme is concerned, **EOF** indicates the absence of any more characters to read.)

Another excellent thing to know when doing any kind of programming is how to terminate a runaway programme. If a programme is running forever waiting for input, you can usually stop it by sending it an end-of-file, as above, but if it's running forever *not* waiting for something, you'll have to take more drastic measures. Under Unix, control-C (or, occasionally, the **DELETE** key) will terminate the current programme, almost no matter what. Under **MS-DOS**, control-C or control-**BREAK** will sometimes terminate the current programme, but by default **MS-DOS** only checks for control-C when it's looking for input, so an infinite loop can be unkillable. There's a **DOS** command,

```
break on
```

which tells **DOS** to look for control-C more often, and I recommend using this command if you're doing any programming. (If a programme is in a really tight infinite loop under **MS-DOS**, there can be no way of killing it short of rebooting.) On the Mac, try command-period or command-option-**ESCAPE**.

You'll type a character, and see it on the screen right away, and assume it's your programme working, but it's only your computer echoing every key you type, as it always does. When you hit **RETURN**, a full line of characters is made available to your programme. It then zips several times through its loop, reading and printing all the characters in the line in quick succession. In other words, when you run this programme, it will probably seem to copy the input a line at a time, rather than a character at a time. You may wonder how a programme could instead read a character right away, without waiting for the user to hit **RETURN**. That's an excellent question, but unfortunately the answer is rather complicated, and beyond the scope of our discussion here. (Among other things, how to read a character right away is one of the things that's not defined by the C language, and it's not defined by any of the standard library functions, either.

Stylistically, the character-copying programme above can be said to have one minor flaw: it contains two calls to getchar, one which reads the first character and one which reads (by virtue of the fact that it's in the body of the loop) all the other characters. This seems inelegant and perhaps unnecessary, and it can also be risky: if there were more things going on within the loop, and if we ever changed the way we read characters, it would be easy to change one of the getchar calls but forget to change the other one. Is there a way to rewrite the loop so that there is only one call to getchar, responsible for reading all the characters? Is there a way to read a character, test it for **EOF**, and assign it to the variable c, all at the same time?

There is. It relies on the fact that the assignment operator, =, is just another operator in C. An assignment is not (necessarily) a standalone statement; it is an expression, and it has a value (the value that's assigned to the variable on the left-hand side), and it can therefore participate in a larger, surrounding expression. Therefore, most C programmers would write the character-copying loop like this:

```
while((c = getchar()) != EOF)
putchar(c);
```

The function getchar is called, as before, and its return value is assigned to the variable c. Then the value is immediately compared against the value **EOF**. Finally, the true/false value of the comparison controls the whileloop: as long as the value is not EOF, the loop continues executing, but as soon as an EOF is received, no more trips through the loop are taken, and it exits. The net result is that the call to getchar happens inside the test at the top of the whileloop, and doesn't have to be repeated before the loop and within the loop (more on this in a bit).

Stated another way, the syntax of a while loop is always

```
while( expression )...
```

A comparison (using the != operator) is of course an expression; the syntax is

```
expression != expression
```

And an assignment is an expression; the syntax is

```
expression = expression
```

What we're seeing is just another example of the fact that expressions can be combined with essentially limitless generality and therefore infinite variety. The left-hand side of the != operator (its first *expression*) is the (sub)expression c = getchar(), and the combined expression is the *expression* needed by the while loop.

The extra parentheses around

```
(c = getchar())
```

are important, and are there because because the *precedence* of the != operator is higher than that of the = operator.

If we (incorrectly) wrote

```
while(c = getchar() != EOF)  /* WRONG */
```

the compiler would interpret it as

```
while(c = (getchar() != EOF))
```

That is, it would assign the result of the != operator to the variable c, which is *not* what we want.

The line

```
while((c = getchar()) != EOF)
```

epitomizes the cryptic brevity which C is notorious for. You may find this terseness infuriating (and you're not alone!), and it can certainly be carried too far, but bear with me for a moment while I defend it.

The simple example we've been discussing illustrates the tradeoffs well. We have four things to do:

- Call getchar,
- Assign its return value to a variable,
- Test the return value against **EOF**, and
- Process the character (in this case, print it out again).

We can't eliminate any of these steps. We have to assign getchar's value to a variable because we have to do two different things with it (test, and print). Therefore, compressing the assignment and test into the same line is the only good way of avoiding two distinct calls to getchar. You may not agree that the compressed idiom is better for being more compact or easier to read, but the fact that there is now only one call to getchar *is* a real virtue.

Don't think that you'll have to write compressed lines like

```
while((c = getchar()) != EOF)
```

right away, or in order to be an "expert C programmer." But, for better or worse, most experienced C programmers do like to use these idioms (whether they're justified or not), so you'll need to be able to at least recognize and understand them when you're reading other peoples' code.

READING LINES

It's often convenient for a programme to process its input not a character at a time but rather a line at a time, that is, to read an entire line of input and then act on it all at once.

The standard C library has a couple of functions for reading lines, but they have a few awkward features, so we're going to learn more about character input (and about writing functions in general) by writing our own function to read one line. Here it is:

```
#include <stdio.h>
/* Read one line from standard input, */
/* copying it to line array (but no more than
max chars). */
/* Does not place terminating \n in line array.
*/
/* Returns line length, or 0 for empty line,
or EOF for end-of-file. */
int getline(char line[], int max)
```

```
{
  int nch = 0;
  int c;
  max = max - 1; /* leave room for '\0' */
  while((c = getchar()) != EOF)
{
  if(c == '\n')
  break;
  if(nch < max)
{
    line[nch] = c;
    nch = nch + 1;
  }
}
  if(c == EOF && nch == 0)
  return EOF;
  line[nch] = '\0';
  return nch;
}
```

As the comment indicates, this function will read one line of input from the standard input, placing it into the line array. The size of the line array is given by the max argument; the function will never write more than max characters into line. The main body of the function is a getchar loop, much as we used in the character-copying programme. In the body of this loop, however, we're storing the characters in an array. Also, we're only reading one line of characters, then stopping and returning.

First of all, the getline function accepts an array as a parameter. As we've said, array parameters are an exception to the rule that functions receive copies of their arguments—in the case of arrays, the function *does* have access to the actual array passed by the caller, and *can* modify it. Since the function is accessing the caller's array, not creating a new one to hold a copy, the function does not have to declare the argument array's size; it's set by the caller.

However, so that we won't overflow the caller's array by reading too long a line into it, we allow the caller to pass along the size of the array, which we promise not to exceed. Second, we see an example of the break statement. The top of the loop looks like our earlier character-copying loop—it stops when it reaches EOF—but we only want this loop to read one line, so we also stop (that is, break out of the loop) when we see the \n character signifying end-of-line. An equivalent loop, without the break statement, would be

```
  while((c = getchar()) != EOF && c != '\n')
{
  if(nch < max)
{
  line[nch] = c;
  nch = nch + 1;
}
}
```

We haven't learned about the internal representation of strings yet, but it turns out that strings in C are simply arrays of characters, which is why we are reading the line into an array of characters. The end of a string is marked by the special character, '\0'.

To make sure that there's always room for that character, on our way in we subtract 1 from max, the argument that tells us how many characters we may place in the line array. When we're done reading the line, we store the end-of-string character '\0' at the end of the string we've just built in the line array.

Finally, there's one subtlety in the code which isn't too important for our purposes now but which you may wonder about: it's arranged to handle the possibility that a few characters (i.e. the apparent beginning of a line) are read, followed immediately by an **EOF**, without the usual \n end-of-line character.

In any case, the function returns the length (number of characters) of the line it read, not including the \n. (Therefore, it returns 0 for an empty line.) Like getchar, it returns **EOF** when there are no more lines to read. (It happens that **EOF** is a negative number, so it will never match the length of a line that getline has read.) Here is an example of a test programme which calls getline, reading the input a line at a time and then printing each line back out:

```
#include <stdio.h>
extern int getline(char [], int);
main()
{
  char line[256];
  while(getline(line, 256) != EOF)
  printf("you typed \"%s\"\n", line);
  return 0;
}
```

The notation char [] in the function prototype for getline says that getline accepts as its first argument an array ofchar. When the programme calls getline, it is careful to pass along the actual size of the array. You might notice a potential problem: since the number 256 appears in two places, if we ever decide that 256 is too small, and that we want to be able to read longer lines, we could easily change one of the instances of 256, and forget to change the other one.

READING NUMBERS

The getline function of the previous section reads one line from the user, as a *string*. What if we want to read a number? One straightforward way is to read a string as before, and then immediately convert the string to a number. The standard C library contains a number of functions for doing this.

The simplest to use are atoi(), which converts a string to an integer, and atof(), which converts a string to a floating-point number. (Both of these functions are declared in the header<stdlib.h>, so you should #include that header at the top of any file using these functions.) You could read an integer from the user like this:

```
#include <stdlib.h>
char line[256];
int n;
printf("Type an integer:\n");
getline(line, 256);
n = atoi(line);
```

Now the variable n contains the number typed by the user. (This assumes that the user *did* type a valid number, and thatgetline did not return EOF.)

Reading a floating-point number is similar:

```
#include <stdlib.h>
char line[256];
double x;
printf("Type a floating-point number:\n");
getline(line, 256);
x = atof(line);
```

(atof is actually declared as returning type double, but you could also use it with a variable of type float, because in general, C automatically converts between float and double as needed.) Another way of reading in numbers, which you're likely to see in other books on C, involves the scanf function, but it has several problems, so we won't discuss it for now. (Superficially, scanf seems simple enough, which is why it's often used, especially in textbooks. The trouble is that to perform input reliably using scanf is not nearly as easy as it looks, especially when you're not sure what the user is going to type.)

FORMATTED I/O

There are a number of related functions used for formatted I/O, each one determining the format of the I/O from a *format string*. For output, the format string consists of plain text, which is output unchanged, and embedded *format specifications* which call for some special processing of one of the remaining arguments to the function. On input, the plain text must match what is seen in the input stream; the format specifications again specify what the meaning of remaining arguments is.

Each format specification is introduced by a % character, followed by the rest of the specification.

OUTPUT: PRINT F FAMILY

For those functions performing output, the format specification takes the following form, with optional parts enclosed in brackets:

%<*flags*><*field width*><*precision*>
<*length*>*conversion*

The meaning of *flags, field width, precision, length,* and *conversion* are given below, although tersely. For more detail, it is worth looking at what the Standard says.

Flags

Zero or more of the following:

-

Left justify the conversion within its field.

+

A signed conversion will always start with a plus or minus sign.

Space

If the first character of a signed conversion is not a sign, insert a space. Overridden by + if present.

#

Forces an alternative form of output. The first digit of an octal conversion will always be a 0; inserts 0X in front of a non-zero hexadecimal conversion; forces a decimal point in all floating point conversions even if one is not necessary; does not remove trailing zeros from g and G conversions.

0

Pad d, i, o, u, x, X, e, E, f, F and G conversions on the left with zeros up to the field width. Overidden by the - flag. If a precision is specified for the d, i, o, u, x or X conversions, the flag is ignored. The behaviour is undefined for other conversions.

Field Width

A decimal integer specifying the minimum output field width. This will be exceeded if necessary. If an asterisk is used here, the next argument is converted to an integer and used for the value of the field width; if the value is negative it is treated as a - flag followed by a positive field width.

Output that would be less than the field width is padded with spaces (zeros if the*field width* integer starts with a zero) to fit. The padding is on the left unless the left-adjustment flag is specified.

Precision

This starts with a period '.'. It specifies the minimum number of digits for d,i, o, u, x, or X conversions; the number of digits after the decimal point for e,E, f conversions; the maximum number of digits for g and G conversions; the number of characters to be printed from a string for s conversion.

The amount of padding overrides the field width. If an asterisk is used here, the next argument is converted to an integer and used for the value of the field width. If the value is negative, it is treated as if it were missing. If only the period is present, the precision is taken to be zero.

Length

h preceding a specifier to print an integral type causes it to be treated as if it were a short. (Note that the various sorts of short are always promoted to one of the flavours of int when passed as an argument.) l works like h but applies to a long integral argument. L is used to indicate that a long doubleargument is to be printed, and only applies to the floating-point specifiers. These are cause undefined behaviour if they are used with the 'wrong' type of conversion.

Conversion

Table. Conversions

Specifier	**Effect**	**Default**
	Precision	
d	signed decimal	1
i	signed decimal	1
u	unsigned decimal	1
–	unsigned octal	1
x	unsigned hexadecimal (0–f)	1
X	unsigned hexadecimal (0–F)	1
	Precision specifies minimum number of digits, expanded with leading zeros if necessary.	

	Printing a value of zero with zero precision outputs no characters.	
f	Print a double with *precision* digits (rounded) after the decimal point. To suppress the decimal point use a *precision* of explicitly zero. Otherwise, at least one digit appears in front of the point.	6
e, E	Print a double in exponential format, rounded, with one digit before the decimal point, *precision* after it. A *precision* of zero suppresses the decimal point. There will be at least two digits in the exponent, which is printed as 1.23e15 in e format, or 1.23E15 inE format.	6
g,G	Use style f, or e (E with G) depending on the exponent. If the exponent is less than "4 or e"*precision,* f is not used. Trailing zeros are suppressed, a decimal point is only printed if there is a following digit.	Unspecified
c	The int argument is converted to an unsigned char and the resultant character printed.	
s	Print a string up to *precision* digits long. If *precision*is not specified, or is greater than the length of the string, the string must be NUL terminated.	Infinite
p	Display the value of a (void *) pointer in a system-dependent way.	
n	The argument must be a pointer to an integer. The number of characters output so far by this call will be written into the integer.	
%	A %	—

The functions that use these formats are described in Programming.

All need the inclusion of <stdio.h>. Their declarations are as shown.

```
#include <stdio.h>
int fprintf(FILE *stream, const char
*format,...);
int printf(const char *format,...);
int sprintf(char *s, const char *format,...);
#include <stdarg.h>/* as well as stdio.h */
int vfprintf(FILE *stream, const char *format,
va list arg);
int vprintf(const char *format, va list arg);
int vsprintf(char *s, const char *format, va
list arg);
```

Table. Functions Performing Formatted Output

Name	Purpose
fprintf	General formatted output as described. Output is written to the file indicated by stream.
printf	Identical to fprintf with a first argument equal to stdout.
sprintf	Identical to fprintf except that the output is not written to a file, but written into the character array pointed to by s.
vfprintf	Formatted output as for fprintf, but with the variable argument list replaced by arg which must have been initialized by va_start.va_end is not called by this function.
vprintf	Identical to vfprintf with a first argument equal to stdout.
vsprintf	Formatted output as for sprintf, but with the variable argument list replaced by arg which must have been initialized by va_start.va_end is not called by this function.

All of the above functions return the number of characters output, or a negative value on error. The trailing null is *not* counted by sprintf and vsprintf. Implementations must permit at least 509 characters to be produced by any single conversion.

INPUT SCANF

A number of functions exist analogous to the printf family, but for the purposes of input instead. The most immediate difference between the two families is that thescanf group needs to be passed *pointers* to their arguments, so that the values read can be assigned to the proper destinations. Forgetting to pass a pointer is a very common error, and one which the compiler cannot detect—the variable argument list prevents it.

The format string is used to control interpretation of a stream of input data, which generally contains values to be assigned to the objects pointed to by the remaining arguments to scanf. The contents of the format string may contain:

White Space

This causes the input stream to be read up to the next non-white-space character.

Ordinary Character

Anything except white-space or % characters. The next character in the input stream *must* match this character.

Conversion Specification

This is a % character, followed by an optional * character (which suppresses the conversion), followed by an optional nonzero decimal integer specifying the maximum field width, an optional h, l or L to control the length of the conversion and finally a non-optional conversion specifier. Note that use ofh, l, or L will affect the type of pointer which must be used.

Except for the specifiers c, n and [, a field of input is a sequence of non-space characters starting at the first non-space character in the input. It terminates at the first conflicting character or when the input field width is reached. The result is put into wherever the corresponding argument points, unless the assignment is suppressed using the * mentioned already. The following conversion specifiers may be used:

`d i o u x`

Convert a signed integer, a signed integer in a form acceptable to strtol, an octal integer, an unsigned integer and a hexadecimal integer respectively.

`e f g`

Convert a float (*not* a double).

`s`

Read a string, and add a null at the end. The string is terminated by whitespace on input (which is not read as part of the string).

`[`

Read a string. A list of characters, called the *scan set* follows the [. A]delimits the list. Characters are read until (but not including) the first character which is *not* in the scan set. If the first character in the list is a circumflex ^, then the scan set includes any character not in the list. If the initial sequence is [^] or [], the] is not a delimiter, but part of the list and another] will be needed to end the list. If there is a minus sign (-) in the list, it must be either the first or the last character; otherwise the meaning is implementation defined.

`c`

Read a single character; white space is significant here. To read the first non-white space character, use %1s. A field width indicates that an array of characters is to be read.

`p`

Read a (void *) pointer previously written out using the %p of one of theprintfs.

`%`

A % is expected in the input, no assignment is made.

`n`

Return as an integer the number of characters read by this call so far.

The size specifiers have the effect shown in Table.

Table. Size Specifiers

Specifier	Modifies	Converts
l	d i o u x	long int

h	d i o u x	short int
l	e f	double
L	e f	long double

The functions are described below, with the following declarations:

```
#include <stdio.h>
int fscanf(FILE *stream, const char
*format,...);
int sscanf(const char *s, const char
*format,...);
int scanf(const char *format,...);
```

Fscanf takes its input from the designated stream, scanf is identical to fscanfwith a first argument of stdin, and sscanf takes its input from the designated character array.

If an input failure occurs before any conversion, **EOF** is returned. Otherwise, the number of successful conversions is returned: this may be zero if no conversions are performed.

An input failure is caused by reading **EOF** or reaching the end of the input string (as appropriate). A conversion failure is caused by a failure to match the proper pattern for a particular conversion.

Chapter 5

JAVA Programming Language

DEFINITION

The Java programming language is a general-purpose, concurrent, class-based, object-oriented language. It is designed to be simple enough that many programmers can achieve fluency in the language. The Java programming language is related to C and C++ but is organized rather differently, with a number of aspects of C and C++ omitted and a few ideas from other languages included. It is intended to be a production language, not a research language, and so, as C. A. R. Hoare suggested in his classic paper on language design, the design has avoided including new and untested features.

The Java programming language is strongly typed. This specification clearly distinguishes between the *compile-time errors* that can and must be detected at compile time, and those that occur at run time.

Compile time normally consists of translating programmes into a machine-independent byte code representation. Run-time activities include loading and linking of the classes needed to execute a programme, optional machine code generation and dynamic optimization of the programme, and actual programme execution.

The Java programming language is a relatively high-level language, in that details of the machine representation are not available through the language. It includes automatic storage management, typically using a garbage collector, to avoid the safety problems of explicit deallocation (as in C's free or C++'s delete). High-performance garbage-collected imple-mentations can have bounded pauses to support systems programming and real-time applications.

The language does not include any unsafe constructs, such as array accesses without index checking, since such unsafe constructs would cause a programme to behave in an unspecified way.

After initialization, class methods and class variables may be used. Some classes may be instantiated to create new objects of the class type. Objects that are class instances also contain an instance of each superclass of the class, and object creation involves recursive creation of these superclass instances.

When an object is no longer referenced, it may be reclaimed by the garbage collector. If an object declares a finalizer, the finalizer is executed before the object is reclaimed to give the object a last chance to clean up resources that would not otherwise be released. When a class is no longer needed, it may be unloaded.

EXAMPLE PROGRAMMES

Most of the example programmes given in the text are ready to be executed and are similar in form to:

```
class Test {
public static void main(String[] args) {
for (int i = 0; i < args.length; i++)
System.out.print(i == 0 ? args[i]: " " +
args[i]);
  System.out.println();
  }
}
```

On a Sun workstation using Sun's Java 2 Platform Standard Edition Develpment Kit software, this class, stored in the file Test.java, can be compiled and executed by giving the commands:

```
javac Test.java
java Test Hello, world.
```

producing the output:

```
Hello, world.
```

NOTATION

Throughout this book we refer to classes and interfaces drawn from the Java and Java 2 platforms. Whenever we refer to a class or interface which is not defined in an example in this book using a single identifier N, the intended reference is to the class or interface named N in the package java.lang. We use the canonical name for classes or interfaces from packages other than java.lang.

CLASSES AND INTERFACES

As noted above, this specification often refers to classes of the Java and Java 2 platforms. In particular, some classes have a special relationship with the Java programming language. Examples include classes such as Object, Class, ClassLoader, String, Thread, and the classes and interfaces in package java.lang.reflect, among others.

The language definition constrains the behaviour of these classes and interfaces, but this document does not provide a complete specification for them. The reader is referred to other parts of the Java platform specification for such detailed API specifications.

CONTEXT-FREE GRAMMARS

A context-free grammar consists of a number of productions. Each production has an abstract symbol called a nonterminal as its left-hand side, and a sequence of one or more nonterminal and terminal symbols as its right-hand side.

For each grammar, the terminal symbols are drawn from a specified *alphabet*. Starting from a sentence consisting of a single distinguished nonterminal, called the goal symbol, a given context-free grammar specifies a language, namely, the set of possible sequences of terminal symbols that can result from repeatedly replacing any nonterminal in the sequence with a right-hand side of a production for which the nonterminal is the left-hand side.

THE LEXICAL GRAMMAR

A lexical grammar for the Java programming language is

given in. This grammar has as its terminal symbols the characters of the Unicode character set. It defines a set of productions, starting from the goal symbol Input, that describe how sequences of Unicode characters are translated into a sequence of input elements. These input elements, with white space and comments discarded, form the terminal symbols for the syntactic grammar for the Java programming language and are called tokens. These tokens are the identifiers, keywords, literals, separators, and operators of the Java programming language.

SYNTACTIC GRAMMAR

The syntactic grammar for the Java programming language is given in later Chapters. This grammar has tokens defined by the lexical grammar as its terminal symbols. It defines a set of productions, starting from the goal symbol *CompilationUnit,* that describe how sequences of tokens can form syntactically correct programmes.

GRAMMAR NOTATION

Terminal symbols are shown in fixed width font in the productions of the lexical and syntactic grammars, and throughout this specification whenever the text is directly referring to such a terminal symbol. These are to appear in a programme exactly as written.

Nonterminal symbols are shown in *italic* type. The definition of a nonterminal is introduced by the name of the nonterminal being defined followed by a colon. One or more alternative right-hand sides for the nonterminal then follow on succeeding lines. For example, the syntactic definition:

```
IfThenStatement:
if ( Expression ) Statement
```

states that the nonterminal *IfThenStatement* represents the token if, followed by a left parenthesis token, followed by an *Expression,* followed by a right parenthesis token, followed by a *Statement.*

As another example, the syntactic definition:

```
ArgumentList:
Argument
```

```
ArgumentList , Argument
```

states that an *ArgumentList* may represent either a single *Argument* or an *ArgumentList*, followed by a comma, followed by an *Argument*. This definition of *ArgumentList* is *recursive*, that is to say, it is defined in terms of itself. The result is that an *ArgumentList* may contain any positive number of arguments. Such recursive definitions of nonterminals are common.

The subscripted suffix "opt", which may appear after a terminal or nonterminal, indicates an optional symbol. The alternative containing the optional symbol actually specifies two right-hand sides, one that omits the optional element and one that includes it.

This means that:

```
BreakStatement:
break Identifieropt ;
```

is a convenient abbreviation for:

```
BreakStatement:
break ;
break Identifier ;
```

and that:

```
BasicForStatement:
for ( ForInitopt ; Expressionopt ; ForUpdateopt
) Statement
```

is a convenient abbreviation for:

```
BasicForStatement:
for (; Expressionopt ; ForUpdateopt ) Statement
for ( ForInit ; Expressionopt ; ForUpdateopt
) Statement
```

which in turn is an abbreviation for:

```
BasicForStatement:
for (;; ForUpdateopt ) Statement
for (; Expression ; ForUpdateopt ) Statement
for ( ForInit ;; ForUpdateopt ) Statement
for ( ForInit ; Expression ; ForUpdateopt )
Statement
```

which in turn is an abbreviation for:

```
BasicForStatement:
```

```
for (;; ) Statement
for (;; ForUpdate ) Statement
for (; Expression ; ) Statement
for (; Expression ; ForUpdate ) Statement
for ( ForInit ;; ) Statement
for ( ForInit ;; ForUpdate ) Statement
for ( ForInit ; Expression ; ) Statement
for ( ForInit ; Expression ; ForUpdate )
Statement
```

so the nonterminal *BasicForStatement* actually has eight alternative right-hand sides. A very long right-hand side may be continued on a second line by substantially indenting this second line, as in:

```
ConstructorDeclaration:
ConstructorModifiersopt ConstructorDeclarator
Throwsopt ConstructorBody
```

which defines one right-hand side for the nonterminal **ConstructorDeclaration.**

When the words "one of" follow the colon in a grammar definition, they signify that each of the terminal symbols on the following line or lines is an alternative definition. For example, the lexical grammar contains the production:

```
ZeroToThree: one of
0 1 2 3
```

which is merely a convenient abbreviation for:

```
ZeroToThree:
0 1 2 3
```

When an alternative in a lexical production appears to be a token, it represents the sequence of characters that would make up such a token. Thus, the definition:

```
BooleanLiteral: one of
true false
```

in a lexical grammar production is shorthand for:

```
BooleanLiteral:
t r u e
f a l s e
```

The right-hand side of a lexical production may specify that certain expansions are not permitted by using the phrase "but not" and then indicating the expansions to be excluded, as in the productions for *InputCharacter* and *Identifier*

```
InputCharacter:
UnicodeInputCharacter but not CR or LF
Identifier:
IdentifierName but not a Keyword or
BooleanLiteral or NullLiteral
```

Finally, a few nonterminal symbols are described by a descriptive phrase in roman type in cases where it would be impractical to list all the alternatives:

```
RawInputCharacter:
any Unicode character
```

UNICODE

Programmes are written using the Unicode character set. Information about this character set and its associated character encodings. The Java platform tracks the Unicode specification as it evolves. The precise version of Unicode used by a given release is specified in the documentation of the class Character.

Versions of the Java programming language prior to 1.1 used Unicode version 1.1.5. Upgrades to newer versions of the Unicode Standard occurred in JDK 1.1 (to Unicode 2.0), JDK 1.1.7 (to Unicode 2.1), J2SE 1.4 (to Unicode 3.0), and J2SE 5.0. The Unicode standard was originally designed as a fixed-width 16-bit character encoding.

It has since been changed to allow for characters whose representation requires more than 16 bits. The range of legal code points is now U+0000 to U+10FFFF, using the hexadecimal U+n notation.

Characters whose code points are greater than U+FFFF are called supplementary characters. To represent the complete range of characters using only 16-bit units, the Unicode standard defines an encoding called **UTF-16**.

In this encoding, supplementary characters are represented as pairs of 16-bit code units, the first from the high-surrogates range, (U+D800 to U+DBFF), the second from the low-surrogates range (U+DC00 to U+DFFF). For characters in the range U+0000 to U+FFFF, the values of code points and **UTF**-16 code units are the same.

LEXICAL TRANSLATIONS

A raw Unicode character stream is translated into a sequence of tokens, using the following three lexical translation steps, which are applied in turn:

1. A translation of Unicode escapes in the raw stream of Unicode characters to the corresponding Unicode character. A Unicode escape of the form \u*xxxx*, where *xxxx* is a hexadecimal value, represents the **UTF**-16 code unit whose encoding is *xxxx*. This translation step allows any programme to be expressed using only **ASCII** characters.
2. A translation of the Unicode stream resulting from step 1 into a stream of input characters and line terminators.
3. A translation of the stream of input characters and line terminators resulting from step 2 into a sequence of input elements which, after white space and comments are discarded, comprise the tokens that are the terminal symbols of the syntactic grammar.

The longest possible translation is used at each step, even if the result does not ultimately make a correct programme while another lexical translation would. Thus the input characters a—b are tokenized as a, —, b, which is not part of any grammatically correct programme, even though the tokenization a, -, -, b could be part of a grammatically correct programme.

UNICODE ESCAPES

Implementations first recognize *Unicode escapes* in their input, translating the **ASCII** characters \u followed by four hexadecimal digits to the **UTF**-16 code unit with the indicated hexadecimal value, and passing all other characters unchanged. Representing supplementary characters requires two consecutive Unicode escapes. This translation step results in a sequence of Unicode input characters:

```
UnicodeInputCharacter:
UnicodeEscape
RawInputCharacter
UnicodeEscape:
\ UnicodeMarker HexDigit HexDigit HexDigit
HexDigit
UnicodeMarker:
u
UnicodeMarker u
RawInputCharacter:
any Unicode character
HexDigit: one of
0 1 2 3 4 5 6 7 8 9 a b c d e f A B C D E F
```

The \, u, and hexadecimal digits here are all **ASCII** characters.

In addition to the processing implied by the grammar, for each raw input character that is a backslash \, input processing must consider how many other \ characters contiguously precede it, separating it from a non-\ character or the start of the input stream. If this number is even, then the \ is eligible to begin a Unicode escape; if the number is odd, then the \ is not eligible to begin a Unicode escape. For example, the raw input "\\u2297=\u2297" results in the eleven characters " \ \ u 2 2 9 7 = ⊗ " (\u2297 is the Unicode encoding of the character "⊗").

If an eligible \ is not followed by u, then it is treated as a *RawInputCharacter* and remains part of the escaped Unicode stream. If an eligible \ is followed by u, or more than one u, and the last u is not followed by four hexadecimal digits, then a compile-time error occurs.

The character produced by a Unicode escape does not participate in further Unicode escapes. For example, the raw input \u005cu005a results in the six characters \ u 0 0 5 a, because 005c is the Unicode value for \. It does not result in the character Z, which is Unicode character 005a, because the \ that resulted from the \u005c is not interpreted as the start of a further Unicode escape. The Java programming language specifies a standard way of transforming a programme written in Unicode into **ASCII** that changes a programme into a form that can be processed by **ASCII**-based tools. The transformation involves converting any Unicode escapes in the source text of the programme to **ASCII** by adding an extra u-for example, *uxxxx* becomes \uu*xxxx*-while simultaneously converting non-**ASCII** characters in the source text to Unicode escapes containing a single u each.

This transformed version is equally acceptable to a compiler for the Java programming language ("Java compiler") and represents the exact same programme. The exact Unicode source can later be restored from this **ASCII** form by converting each escape sequence where multiple u's are present to a sequence of Unicode characters with one fewer u, while simultaneously converting each escape sequence with a single u to the corresponding single Unicode character.

Implementations should use the *uxxxx* notation as an output format to display Unicode characters when a suitable font is not available.

LINE TERMINATORS

Implementations next divide the sequence of Unicode input characters into lines by recognizing *line terminators*. This definition of lines determines the line numbers produced by a Java compiler or other system component. It also specifies the termination of the // form of a comment.

```
LineTerminator:
the ASCII LF character, also known as "newline"
the ASCII CR character, also known as "return"
the ASCII CR character followed by the ASCII
LF character
InputCharacter:
UnicodeInputCharacter but not CR or LF
```

Lines are terminated by the **ASCII** characters CR, or LF, or CR LF. The two characters CR immediately followed by LF are counted as one line terminator, not two.

The result is a sequence of line terminators and input characters, which are the terminal symbols for the third step in the tokenization process.

INPUT ELEMENTS AND TOKENS

The input characters and line terminators that result from escape processing and then input line recognition are reduced to a sequence of *input elements*. Those input elements that are not white space or comments are *tokens*. The tokens are the terminal symbols of the syntactic grammar.

This process is specified by the following productions:

```
Input:
InputElementsopt Subopt
InputElements:
InputElement
InputElements InputElement
InputElement:
WhiteSpace
Comment
Token
Token:
Identifier
Keyword
Literal
Separator
Operator
Sub:
the ASCII SUB character, also known as
"control-Z"
```

White space and comments can serve to separate tokens that, if adjacent, might be tokenized in another manner. For example, the ASCII characters - and = in the input can form the operator token -= only if there is no intervening white space or comment.

As a special concession for compatibility with certain operating systems, the ASCII SUB character (\u001a, or control-Z) is ignored if it is the last character in the escaped input stream.

Consider two tokens *x* and *y* in the resulting input stream. If *x* precedes *y*, then we say that *x* is *to the left of y* and that *y* is *to the right of x*.

For example, in this simple piece of code:

```
class Empty {
}
```

we say that the } token is to the right of the { token, even though it appears, in this two-dimensional representation on paper, downward and to the left of the { token. This convention about the use of the words left and right allows us to speak, for example, of the right-hand operand of a binary operator or of the left-hand side of an assignment.

WHITE SPACE

White space is defined as the **ASCII** space, horizontal tab, and form feed characters, as well as line terminators.

```
WhiteSpace:
the ASCII SP character, also known as "space"
the ASCII HT character, also known as
"horizontal tab"
the ASCII FF character, also known as "form
feed"
LineTerminator
```

IDENTIFIERS

An *identifier* is an unlimited-length sequence of *Java letters* and *Java digits*, the first of which must be a Java letter. An identifier cannot have the same spelling (Unicode character sequence) as a keyword, boolean literal, or the null literal.

```
Identifier:
IdentifierChars but not a Keyword or
BooleanLiteral or NullLiteral
IdentifierChars:
JavaLetter
IdentifierChars JavaLetterOrDigit
JavaLetter:
any Unicode character that is a Java letter
JavaLetterOrDigit:
any Unicode character that is a Java letter-
or-digit.
```

Letters and digits may be drawn from the entire Unicode

character set, which supports most writing scripts in use in the world today, including the large sets for Chinese, Japanese, and Korean. This allows programmers to use identifiers in their programmes that are written in their native languages.

A "Java letter" is a character for which the method Character.is JavaIdentifierStart(int) returns true. A "Java letter-or-digit" is a character for which the method Character .isJavaIdentifierPart(int) returns true.

The Java letters include uppercase and lowercase **ASCII** Latin letters A-Z (\u0041-\u005a), and a-z (\u0061-\u007a), and, for historical reasons, the **ASCII** underscore (_, or \u005f) and dollar sign ($, or \u0024). The $ character should be used only in mechanically generated source code or, rarely, to access preexisting names on legacy systems. The "Java digits" include the **ASCII** digits 0-9 (\u0030-\u0039).

LITERALS

A *literal* is the source code representation of a value of a primitive type, the String type, or the null type:

```
Literal:
IntegerLiteral
FloatingPointLiteral
BooleanLiteral
CharacterLiteral
StringLiteral
NullLiteral
```

INTEGER LITERALS

For a general discussion of the integer types and values.

An *integer literal* may be expressed in decimal (base 10), hexadecimal (base 16), or octal (base 8):

```
IntegerLiteral:
DecimalIntegerLiteral
HexIntegerLiteral
OctalIntegerLiteral
DecimalIntegerLiteral:
DecimalNumeral IntegerTypeSuffixopt
HexIntegerLiteral:
```

```
HexNumeral IntegerTypeSuffixopt
OctalIntegerLiteral:
OctalNumeral IntegerTypeSuffixopt
IntegerTypeSuffix: one of
l L
```

An integer literal is of type long if it is suffixed with an **ASCII** letter L or l (ell); otherwise it is of type int. The suffix L is preferred, because the letter l (ell) is often hard to distinguish from the digit 1 (one).

A decimal numeral is either the single **ASCII** character 0, representing the integer zero, or consists of an **ASCII** digit from 1 to 9, optionally followed by one or more **ASCII** digits from 0 to 9, representing a positive integer:

```
DecimalNumeral:
  0
NonZeroDigit Digitsopt
Digits:
Digit
Digits Digit
Digit:
  0
NonZeroDigit
NonZeroDigit: one of
  1 2 3 4 5 6 7 8 9
```

A hexadecimal numeral consists of the leading **ASCII** characters 0x or 0X followed by one or more **ASCII** hexadecimal digits and can represent a positive, zero, or negative integer.

Hexadecimal digits with values 10 through 15 are represented by the **ASCII** letters a through f or A through F, respectively; each letter used as a hexadecimal digit may be uppercase or lowercase.

```
HexNumeral:
  0 x HexDigits
  0 X HexDigits
HexDigits:
HexDigit
HexDigit HexDigits
```

The following production from is repeated here for clarity:

```
HexDigit: one of
0 1 2 3 4 5 6 7 8 9 a b c d e f A B C D E F
```

An octal numeral consists of an **ASCII** digit 0 followed by one or more of the **ASCII** digits 0 through 7 and can represent a positive, zero, or negative integer.

```
OctalNumeral:
  0 OctalDigits
OctalDigits:
OctalDigit
OctalDigit OctalDigits
OctalDigit: one of
 0 1 2 3 4 5 6 7
```

Note that octal numerals always consist of two or more digits; 0 is always considered to be a decimal numeral-not that it matters much in practice, for the numerals 0, 00, and 0x0 all represent exactly the same integer value.

The largest decimal literal of type int is 2147483648 (2^{31}). All decimal literals from 0 to 2147483647 may appear anywhere an int literal may appear, but the literal 2147483648 may appear only as the operand of the unary negation operator..

FLOATING-POINT LITERALS

A *floating-point literal* has the following parts: a whole-number part, a decimal or hexadecimal point (represented by an **ASCII** period character), a fractional part, an exponent, and a type suffix. A floating point number may be written either as a decimal value or as a hexadecimal value. For decimal literals, the exponent, if present, is indicated by the **ASCII** letter e or E followed by an optionally signed integer. For hexadecimal literals, the exponent is always required and is indicated by the **ASCII** letter p or P followed by an optionally signed integer.

For decimal floating-point literals, at least one digit, in either the whole number or the fraction part, and either a decimal point, an exponent, or a float type suffix are required. All other parts are optional. For hexadecimal floating-point literals, at least one digit is required in either the whole number or fraction part, the exponent is mandatory, and the float type suffix is optional.

A floating-point literal is of type float if it is suffixed with an ASCII letter F or f; otherwise its type is double and it can optionally be suffixed with an ASCII letter D or d.

```
FloatingPointLiteral:
DecimalFloatingPointLiteral
HexadecimalFloatingPointLiteral
DecimalFloatingPointLiteral:
Digits . Digitsopt ExponentPartopt
FloatTypeSuffixopt
. Digits ExponentPartopt FloatTypeSuffixopt
  Digits ExponentPart FloatTypeSuffixopt
  Digits ExponentPartopt FloatTypeSuffix
ExponentPart:
ExponentIndicator SignedInteger
ExponentIndicator: one of
e E
SignedInteger:
Signopt Digits
Sign: one of
+ -
FloatTypeSuffix: one of
f F d D
HexadecimalFloatingPointLiteral:
HexSignificand BinaryExponent FloatTypeSuffixopt
HexSignificand:
HexNumeral
HexNumeral .
0x HexDigitsopt . HexDigits
0X HexDigitsopt . HexDigits
BinaryExponent:
BinaryExponentIndicator SignedInteger
BinaryExponentIndicator:one of
  p P
```

The elements of the types float and double are those values that can be represented using the IEEE 754 32-bit single-precision and 64-bit double-precision binary floating-point formats, respectively. The details of proper input conversion from a Unicode string representation of a floating-point number to the internal **IEEE** 754 binary floating-point representation are described for the methods valueOf of class Float and class Double of the package java.lang.

The largest positive finite float literal is 3.4028235e38f. The smallest positive finite nonzero literal of type float is 1.40e-45f. The largest positive finite double literal is 1.7976931348623157e308. The smallest positive finite nonzero literal of type double is 4.9e-324.

A compile-time error occurs if a nonzero floating-point literal is too large, so that on rounded conversion to its internal representation it becomes an **IEEE** 754 infinity. A programme can represent infinities without producing a compile-time error by using constant expressions such as 1f/0f or -1d/0d or by using the predefined constants **POSITIVE_INFINITY** and **NEGATIVE_INFINITY** of the classes Float and Double.

A compile-time error occurs if a nonzero floating-point literal is too small, so that, on rounded conversion to its internal representation, it becomes a zero. A compile-time error does not occur if a nonzero floating-point literal has a small value that, on rounded conversion to its internal representation, becomes a nonzero denormalized number.

BOOLEAN LITERALS

The boolean type has two values, represented by the literals true and false, formed from **ASCII** letters.

A *boolean literal* is always of type boolean.

```
BooleanLiteral: one of
true false
```

CHARACTER LITERALS

A *character literal* is expressed as a character or an escape sequence, enclosed in **ASCII** single quotes. (The single-quote, or apostrophe, character is \u0027.)

Character literals can only represent **UTF**-16 code units, i.e., they are limited to values from \u0000 to \uffff. Supplementary characters must be represented either as a surrogate pair within a char sequence, or as an integer, depending on the API they are used with.

A character literal is always of type char.

```
CharacterLiteral:
' SingleCharacter '
' EscapeSequence '
SingleCharacter:
InputCharacter but not ' or \
```

The escape sequences are described in.

As specified in, the characters CR and LF are never an *InputCharacter*; they are recognized as constituting a *LineTerminator*. It is a compile-time error for the character following the *SingleCharacter* or *EscapeSequence* to be other than a '. It is a compile-time error for a line terminator to appear after the opening ' and before the closing '.

The following are examples of char literals:

```
'a'
'%'
'\t'
'\\'
'\''
'\u03a9'
'\uFFFF'
'\177'
'W'
'Ä'
```

Because Unicode escapes are processed very early, it is not correct to write '\u000a' for a character literal whose value is linefeed (LF); the Unicode escape \u000a is transformed into an actual linefeed in translation step 1 and the linefeed becomes a *LineTerminator* in step 2, and so the character literal is not valid in step 3.

Instead, one should use the escape sequence '\n'.Similarly, it is not correct to write '\u000d' for a character literal whose value is carriage return (CR). Instead, use '\r'.

In C and C++, a character literal may contain representations of more than one character, but the value of such a character literal is implementation-defined. In the Java programming language, a character literal always represents exactly one character.

STRING LITERALS

A *string literal* consists of zero or more characters enclosed in double quotes. Characters may be represented by escape sequences - one escape sequence for characters in the range U+0000 to **U+FFFF**, two escape sequences for the **UTF-16** surrogate code units of characters in the range U+010000 to U+10FFFF.

A string literal is always of type String. A string literal always refers to the same instance of class String.

```
StringLiteral:
" StringCharactersopt "
StringCharacters:
  StringCharacter
  StringCharacters StringCharacter
StringCharacter:
  InputCharacter but not " or \
  EscapeSequence
```

The escape sequences are described in.

As specified in, neither of the characters CR and LF is ever considered to be an *InputCharacter*; each is recognized as constituting a *LineTerminator*.

It is a compile-time error for a line terminator to appear after the opening " and before the closing matching ". A long string literal can always be broken up into shorter pieces and written as a (possibly parenthesized) expression using the string concatenation operator +.

The following are examples of string literals:

```
"" // the empty string
"\"" // a string containing " alone
"This is a string" // a string containing 16
characters
"This is a " + // actually a string-valued
constant expression,
"two-line string" //  formed from two string
literals
```

Because Unicode escapes are processed very early, it is not correct to write "\u000a" for a string literal containing a single linefeed (LF); the Unicode escape \u000a is transformed into an actual linefeed in translation step 1 and the linefeed becomes a *LineTerminator* in step 2, and so the string literal is not valid in step 3.

Instead, one should write "\n". Similarly, it is not correct to write "\u000d" for a string literal containing a single carriage return (CR). Instead use "\r".

Each string literal is a reference to an instance of class String. String objects have a constant value. String literals-or, more generally, strings that are the values of constant expressions -are "interned" so as to share unique instances, using the method String.intern.

Thus, the test programme consisting of the compilation unit:

```
package testPackage;
class Test {
  public static void main(String[] args) {
  String hello = "Hello", lo = "lo";
  System.out.print((hello == "Hello") + " ");
  System.out.print((Other.hello == hello) + "
  ");
  System.out.print((other.Other.hello == hello)
  + " ");
  System.out.print((hello == ("Hel"+"lo")) + "
  ");
 System.out.print((hello == ("Hel"+lo)) + " ");
  System.out.println(hello ==
  ("Hel"+lo).intern());
  }
}
class Other { static String hello = "Hello";}
```

and the compilation unit:

```
package other;
public class Other { static String hello =
"Hello";}
```

produces the output:

```
true true true true false true
```

This example illustrates six points:

- Literal strings within the same class in the same package represent references to the same `String` object.
- Literal strings within different classes in the same package represent references to the same `String` object.
- Literal strings within different classes in different packages likewise represent references to the same `String` object.
- Strings computed by constant expressions are computed at compile time and then treated as if they were literals.
- Strings computed by concatenation at run time are newly created and therefore distinct.

The result of explicitly interning a computed string is the same string as any pre-existing literal string with the same contents.

NULL LITERAL

The null type has one value, the null reference, represented by the literal null, which is formed from **ASCII** characters. A *null literal* is always of the null type.

```
NullLiteral:
null
```

SEPARATORS

The following nine **ASCII** characters are the *separators* (punctuators):

```
Separator: one of
( ) {} [];,.
```

OPERATORS

The following 37 tokens are the operators, formed from **ASCII** *characters:*

```
Operator: one of
= > < ! ~ ? :
== <= >= != && || ++ --
```

```
+ - * / & | ^ % << >> >>>
+= -= *= /= &= |= ^= %= <<= >>= >>>=
```

The Java programming language is a *strongly typed* language, which means that every variable and every expression has a type that is known at compile time. Types limit the values that a variable can hold or that an expression can produce, limit the operations supported on those values, and determine the meaning of the operations. Strong typing helps detect errors at compile time.

The types of the Java programming language are divided into two categories: primitive types and reference types. The primitive types are the boolean type and the numeric types. The numeric types are the integral types byte, short, int, long, and char, and the floating-point types float and double.

The reference types are class types, interface types, and array types. There is also a special null type. An object is a dynamically created instance of a class type or a dynamically created array. The values of a reference type are references to objects. All objects, including arrays, support the methods of class Object. String literals are represented by String objects. Types exist at compile-time. Some types correspond to classes and interfaces, which exist at run-time. The correspondence between types and classes or interfaces is incomplete for two reasons:

1. At run-time, classes and interfaces are loaded by the Java virtual machine using class loaders. Each class loader defines its own set of classes and interfaces. As a result, it is possible for two loaders to load an identical class or interface definition but produce distinct classes or interfaces at run-time.
2. Type arguments and type variables are not reified at run-time. As a result, different parameterized types are implemented by the same class or interface at run time. Indeed, all invocations of a given generic type declaration share a single run-time implementation.

A consequence of is the possibility of heap pollution. Under certain conditions, it is possible that a variable of a parameterized type refers to an object that is not of that parameterized type. The variable will always refer to an object that is an instance of a class that implements the parameterized type.

TYPES AND VALUES

There are two kinds of *types* in the Java programming language: primitive types and reference types. There are, correspondingly, two kinds of data values that can be stored in variables, passed as arguments, returned by methods, and operated on: primitive values and reference values.

```
Type:
  PrimitiveType
  ReferenceType
```

There is also a special *null type,* the type of the expression null, which has no name. Because the null type has no name, it is impossible to declare a variable of the null type or to cast to the null type. The null reference is the only possible value of an expression of null type. The null reference can always be cast to any reference type. In practice, the programmer can ignore the null type and just pretend that null is merely a special literal that can be of any reference type.

PRIMITIVE TYPES AND VALUES

A *primitive type* is predefined by the Java programming language and named by its reserved keyword:

```
PrimitiveType:
  NumericType
  boolean
NumericType:
  IntegralType
  FloatingPointType
IntegralType: one of
  byte short int long char
FloatingPointType: one of
  float double
```

Primitive values do not share state with other primitive values. A variable whose type is a primitive type always holds a primitive value of that same type. The value of a variable of primitive type can be changed only by assignment operations on that variable including increment and decrement operators.

The *numeric types* are the integral types and the floating-point types. The *integral types* are byte, short, int, and long, whose values are 8-bit, 16-bit, 32-bit and 64-bit signed two's-complement integers, respectively, and char, whose values are 16-bit unsigned integers representing **UTF**-16 code units.

The *floating-point types* are float, whose values include the 32-bit **IEEE** 754 floating-point numbers, and double, whose values include the 64-bit **IEEE** 754 floating-point numbers. The boolean type has exactly two values: true and false.

INTEGRAL TYPES AND VALUES

The values of the integral types are integers in the following ranges:

- For byte, from -128 to 127, inclusive
- For short, from -32768 to 32767, inclusive
- For int, from -2147483648 to 2147483647, inclusive
- For long, from -9223372036854775808 to 922337203 6854775807, inclusive
- For char, from '\u0000' to '\uffff' inclusive, that is, from 0 to 65535

INTEGER OPERATIONS

The Java programming language provides a number of operators that act on integral values:

- The comparison operators, which result in a value of type boolean:
  - The numerical comparison operators <, <=, >, and >=
  - The numerical equality operators == and !=
  - The numerical operators, which result in a value of type int or long:
    a. The unary plus and minus operators + and -
    b. The multiplicative operators *,/, and %
    c. The additive operators + and - – The increment operator ++, both prefix and postfix

   d. The decrement operator --, both prefix and postfix
   e. The signed and unsigned shift operators <<, >>, and >>>
   f. The bitwise complement operator ~
   g. The integer bitwise operators &, |, and ^
- The conditional operator ?:
- The cast operator, which can convert from an integral value to a value of any specified numeric type
- The string concatenation operator + which, when given a String operand and an integral operand, will convert the integral operand to a String representing its value in decimal form, and then produce a newly created String that is the concatenation of the two strings

Other useful constructors, methods, and constants are predefined in the classes Byte, Short, Integer, Long, and Character.

If an integer operator other than a shift operator has at least one operand of type long, then the operation is carried out using 64-bit precision, and the result of the numerical operator is of type long. If the other operand is not long, it is first widened to type long by numeric promotion. Otherwise, the operation is carried out using 32-bit precision, and the result of the numerical operator is of type int. If either operand is not an int, it is first widened to type int by numeric promotion.

The built-in integer operators do not indicate overflow or underflow in any way. Integer operators can throw a NullPointerException if unboxing conversion of a null reference is required. Other than that, the only integer operators that can throw an exception are the integer divide operator / and the integer remainder operator %, which throw an ArithmeticException if the right-hand operand is zero, and the increment and decrement operators ++ and -- which can throw an OutOfMemoryError if boxing conversion is required and there is not sufficient memory available to perform the conversion.

The example:

```
class Test {
public static void main(String[] args) {
int i = 1000000;
System.out.println(i * i);
long l = i;
System.out.println(l * l);
System.out.println(20296 / (l - i));
}
}
```

produces the output:

```
-727379968
1000000000000
```

and then encounters an ArithmeticException in the division by l - i, because l - i is zero. The first multiplication is performed in 32-bit precision, whereas the second multiplication is a long multiplication. The value -727379968 is the decimal value of the low 32 bits of the mathematical result, 1000000000000, which is a value too large for type int.

Any value of any integral type may be cast to or from any numeric type. There are no casts between integral types and the type boolean.

Floating-Point Types, Formats, and Values

The floating-point types are float and double, which are conceptually associated with the single-precision 32-bit and double-precision 64-bit format **IEEE** 754 values and operations as specified in **IEEE** *Standard for Binary Floating-Point Arithmetic*, **ANSI/IEEE** Standard 754-1985 (**IEEE**, New York).

The **IEEE** 754 standard includes not only positive and negative numbers that consist of a sign and magnitude, but also positive and negative zeros, positive and negative *infinities*, and special *Not-a-Number* values (hereafter abbreviated **NaN**).

A **NaN** value is used to represent the result of certain invalid operations such as dividing zero by zero. NaN constants of both float and double type are predefined as Float.**NaN** and Double.**NaN**. Every implementation of the Java programming language is required to support two standard sets of floating-point values, called the *float value set* and the *double value set*. In addition, an implementation of the Java programming language may support either or both of two extended-exponent floating-point value sets, called the *float-extended-exponent value set* and the *double-extended-exponent value set*. These extended-exponent value sets may, under certain circumstances, be used instead of the standard value sets to represent the values of expressions of type float or double.

The finite nonzero values of any floating-point value set can all be expressed in the form $s \cdot m \cdot 2^{(e-N+1)}$, where s is +1 or -1, m is a positive integer less than 2^N, and e is an integer between $E_{min} = -(2^{K-1}-2)$ and $E_{max} = 2^{K-1}-1$, inclusive, and where N and K are parameters that depend on the value set. Some values can be represented in this form in more than one way; for example, supposing that a value v in a value set might be represented in this form using certain values for s, m, and e, then if it happened that m were even and e were less than 2^{K-1}, one could halve m and increase e by 1 to produce a second representation for the same value v.

A representation in this form is called *normalized* if $m \geq 2^{(N-1)}$; otherwise the representation is said to be *denormalized.* If a value in a value set cannot be represented in such a way that $m \geq 2^{(N-1)}$, then the value is said to be a *denormalized value,* because it has no normalized representation.

FLOATING-POINT OPERATIONS

The Java programming language provides a number of operators that act on floating-point values:

- The comparison operators, which result in a value of type boolean:
  - The numerical comparison operators <, <=, >, and >=
  - The numerical equality operators == and !=
- The numerical operators, which result in a value of type float or double:
  - The unary plus and minus operators + and -

  - The multiplicative operators *,/, and %
  - The additive operators + and -
  - The increment operator ++, both prefix and postfix
  - The decrement operator —, both prefix and postfix
- The conditional operator ?:
- The cast operator, which can convert from a floating-point value to a value of any specified numeric type)
- The string concatenation operator + which, when given a String operand and a floating-point operand, will convert the floating-point operand to a String representing its value in decimal form (without information loss), and then produce a newly created String by concatenating the two strings

Cther useful constructors, methods, and constants are predefined in the classes Float, Double, and Math. If at least cne of the operands to a binary operator is of floating-point type, then the operation is a floating-point operation, even if the other is integral.

If at least one of the operands to a numerical operator is of type double, then the operation is carried out using 64-bit floating-point arithmetic, and the result of the numerical operator is a value of type double. (If the other operand is not a double, it is first widened to type double by numeric promotion Otherwise, the operation is carried out using 32-bit floating-point arithmetic, and the result of the numerical operator is a value of type float.

If the other operand is not a float, it is first widened to type float by numeric promotion. Operators on floating-point numbers behave as specified by IEEE 754 (with the exception of the remainder operator. In particular, the Java programming language requires support of IEEE 754 *denormalized* floating-point numbers and *gradual underflow,* which make it easier to prove desirable properties of particular numerical algorithms. Floating-point operations do not "flush to zero" if the calculated result is a denormalized number.

The Java programming language requires that floating-point arithmetic behave as if every floating-point operator rounded its floating-point result to the result precision. *Inexact* results must be rounded to the representable value nearest to the infinitely precise result; if the two nearest representable values are equally near, the one with its least significant bit zero is chosen. This is the IEEE 754 standard's default rounding mode known as *round to nearest*. The language uses *round toward zero* when converting a floating value to an integer, which acts, in this case, as though the number were truncated, discarding the mantissa bits.

Rounding toward zero chooses at its result the format's value closest to and no greater in magnitude than the infinitely precise result. Floating-point operators can throw a NullPointerException if unboxing conversion of a null reference is required. Other than that, the only floating-point operators that can throw an exception are the increment and decrement operators ++ and —, which can throw an OutOfMemoryError if boxing conversion is required and there is not sufficient memory available to perform the conversion.

An operation that overflows produces a signed infinity, an operation that underflows produces a denormalized value or a signed zero, and an operation that has no mathematically definite result produces NaN. All numeric operations with NaN as an operand produce NaN as a result. As has already been described, NaN is unordered, so a numeric comparison operation involving one or two NaNs returns false and any != comparison involving NaN returns true, including x!=x when x is NaN.

The example programme:

```
class Test {
public static void main(String[] args) {
// An example of overflow:
double d = 1e308;
System.out.print("overflow produces infinity:
");
  System.out.println(d + "*10==" + d*10);
// An example of gradual underflow:
d = 1e-305 * Math.PI;
System.out.print("gradual underflow: " + d +
"\n  ");
```

```
for (int i = 0; i < 4; i++)
System.out.print(" " + (d /= 100000));
System.out.println();
// An example of NaN:
System.out.print("0.0/0.0 is Not-a-Number: ");
d = 0.0/0.0;
System.out.println(d);
// An example of inexact results and rounding:
System.out.print("inexact results with
float:");
for (int i = 0; i < 100; i++) {
float z = 1.0f / i;
if (z * i != 1.0f)
System.out.print(" " + i);
}
System.out.println();
// Another example of inexact results and
rounding:
System.out.print("inexact results with
double:");
for (int i = 0; i < 100; i++) {
double z = 1.0 / i;
if (z * i != 1.0)
System.out.print(" " + i);
}
System.out.println();
// An example of cast to integer rounding:
System.out.print("cast to int rounds toward
0: ");
d = 12345.6;
System.out.println((int)d + " " + (int)(-d));
}
}
```

produces the output:

```
overflow produces infinity: 1.0e+308*10= =Infinity
gradual underflow: 3.141592653589793E-305
3.1415926535898E-310 3.141592653E-315 3.142E-320
0.0
```

```
0.0/0.0 is Not-a-Number: NaN
inexact results with float: 0 41 47 55 61 82 83
94 97
inexact results with double: 0 49 98
cast to int rounds toward 0: 12345 -12345
```

This example demonstrates, among other things, that gradual underflow can result in a gradual loss of precision. The results when i is 0 involve division by zero, so that z becomes positive infinity, and z * 0 is NaN, which is not equal to 1.0.

THE BOOLEAN TYPE AND VALUES

The boolean type represents a logical quantity with two possible values, indicated by the literals true and false. The boolean operators are:

- The relational operators == and !=
- The logical-complement operator !
- The logical operators &, ^, and |
- The conditional-and and conditional-or operators && and ||
- The conditional operator ?:
- The string concatenation operator +, which, when given a String operand and a boolean operand, will convert the boolean operand to a String (either "true" or "false"), and then produce a newly created String that is the concatenation of the two strings.

Boolean expressions determine the control flow in several kinds of statements:

- The if statement
- The while statement
- The do statement
- The for statement

A boolean expression also determines which sub expression is evaluated in the conditional ?

Operator: Only boolean or Boolean expressions can be used in control flow statements and as the first operand of the conditional operator ? An integer x can be converted to a boolean, following the C language convention that any nonzero value is true, by the expression x!=0. An object reference obj can be converted to a boolean, following the C language convention that any reference other than null is true, by the expression obj!=null.

A cast of a boolean value to type boolean or Boolean is allowed; no other casts on type boolean are allowed. A boolean can be converted to a string by string conversion.

REFERENCE TYPES AND VALUES

There are three kinds of *reference types*: class types, interface types, and array types. Reference types may be parameterized with type arguments.

```
ReferenceType:
ClassOrInterfaceType
TypeVariable
ArrayType
ClassOrInterfaceType:
ClassType
InterfaceType
ClassType:
TypeDeclSpecifier TypeArgumentsopt
InterfaceType:
TypeDeclSpecifier TypeArgumentsopt
TypeDeclSpecifier:
TypeName
ClassOrInterfaceType . Identifier
TypeName:
Identifier
TypeName . Identifier
TypeVariable:
Identifier
ArrayType:
Type []
```

A class or interface type consists of a type declaration specifier, optionally followed by type arguments (in which case it is a parameterized type). Type arguments are described in. A type declaration specifier may be either a type name, or a class or interface type followed by "." and an identifier. In the latter case, the specifier has the form *T.id,* where *id* must be the simple name of an accessible member type of *T,* or a compile-time error occurs. The specifier denotes that member type.

The sample code:

```
class Point { int[] metrics;}
interface Move { void move(int deltax, int
deltay);}
```

declares a class type Point, an interface type Move, and uses an array type int[] (an array of int) to declare the field metrics of the class Point.

OBJECTS

An object is a class instance or an array. The reference values (often just *references*) are *pointers* to these objects, and a special null reference, which refers to no object. A class instance is explicitly created by a class instance creation expression. An array is explicitly created by an array creation expression. A new class instance is implicitly created when the string concatenation operator + is used in a non-constant expression, resulting in a new object of type String.

A new array object is implicitly created when an array initializer expression is evaluated; this can occur when a class or interface is initialized, when a new instance of a class is created, or when a local variable declaration statement is executed. New objects of the types Boolean, Byte, Short, Character, Integer, Long, Float and Double may be implicitly created by boxing conversion.

Many of these cases are illustrated in the following example:

```
class Point {
int x, y;
Point() { System.out.println("default");}
Point(int x, int y) { this.x = x; this.y = y;}
// A Point instance is explicitly created at
class initialization time:
static Point origin = new Point(0,0);
// A String can be implicitly created by a +
  operator:
```

```
  public String toString() {
  return "(" + x + "," + y + ")";
  }
}
class Test {
public static void main(String[] args) {
  // A Point is explicitly created using
  newInstance:
  Point p = null;
  try {
  p =
(Point)Class.forName("Point").newInstance();
} catch (Exception e) {
System.out.println(e);
}
// An array is implicitly created by an array
constructor:
Point a[] = { new Point(0,0), new Point(1,1)};
// Strings are implicitly created by + operators:
System.out.println("p: " + p);
System.out.println("a: {" + a[0] + ", "
+ a[1] + "}");
// An array is explicitly created by an array
creation expression:
String sa[] = new String[2];
sa[0] = "he"; sa[1] = "llo";
System.out.println(sa[0] + sa[1]);
}
}
```

which produces the output:

```
default
p: (0,0)
a: {(0,0), (1,1)}
hello
```

The operators on references to objects are:

- Field access, using either a qualified name or a field access expression
- Method invocation

- The cast operator
- The string concatenation operator + which, when given a String operand and a reference, will convert the reference to a String by invoking the to String method of the referenced object (using "null" if either the reference or the result of to String is a null reference), and then will produce a newly created String that is the concatenation of the two strings
- The instanceof operator
- The reference equality operators == and !=
- The conditional operator ?:.

There may be many references to the same object. Most objects have state, stored in the fields of objects that are instances of classes or in the variables that are the components of an array object. If two variables contain references to the same object, the state of the object can be modified using one variable's reference to the object, and then the altered state can be observed through the reference in the other variable.

The example programme:

```
class Value { int val;}
class Test {
public static void main(String[] args) {
  int i1 = 3;
  int i2 = i1;
  i2 = 4;
  System.out.print("i1==" + i1);
  System.out.println(" but i2==" + i2);
  Value v1 = new Value();
  v1.val = 5;
  Value v2 = v1;
  v2.val = 6;
  System.out.print("v1.val==" + v1.val);
  System.out.println(" and v2.val==" + v2.val);
 }
}
```

```
produces the output:
i1==3 but i2==4
v1.val==6 and v2.val==6
```

because v1.val and v2.val reference the same instance variable in the one Value object created by the only new expression, while i1 and i2 are different variables. for examples of the creation and use of arrays.

Each object has an associated lock, which is used by synchronized methods and the synchronized statement to provide control over concurrent access to state by multiple threads.

THE CLASS OBJECT

The class Object is a superclass of all other classes. A variable of type Object can hold a reference to the null reference or to any object, whether it is an instance of a class or an array All class and array types inherit the methods of class Object, which are summarized here:

```
package java.lang;
public class Object {
public final Class<?> getClass() {...}
public String toString() {...}
public boolean equals(Object obj) {...}
public int hashCode() {...}
protected Object clone()
throws CloneNotSupportedException {...}
public final void wait()
throws IllegalMonitorStateException,
InterruptedException {...}
 public final void wait(long millis)
throws IllegalMonitorStateException,
InterruptedException {...}
 public final void wait(long millis, int nanos)
{...}
throws IllegalMonitorStateException,
InterruptedException {...}
public final void notify() {...}
throws IllegalMonitorStateException
public final void notifyAll() {...}
throws IllegalMonitorStateException
protected void finalize()
```

```
throws Throwable {...}
}
```

The members of Object are as follows:

- The method getClass returns the Class object that represents the class of the object. A Class object exists for each reference type. It can be used, for example, to discover the fully qualified name of a class, its members, its immediate superclass, and any interfaces that it implements. A class method that is declared synchronized synchronizes on the lock associated with the Class object of the class. The method Object.getClass() must be treated specially by a Java compiler. The type of a method invocation e.getClass(), where the expression e has the static type T, is Class<? extends |T|>.
- The method toString returns a String representation of the object.
- The methods equals and hashCode are very useful in hashtables such as java.util.Hashtable. The method equals defines a notion of object equality, which is based on value, not reference, comparison.
- The method clone is used to make a duplicate of an object.
- The methods wait, notify, and notifyAll are used in concurrent programming using threads, as described in.
- The method finalize is run just before an object is destroyed and is described in.

TYPE VARIABLES

A type variable is an unqualified identifier. Type variables are introduced by generic class declarations generic interface declarations generic method declarations and by generic constructor declarations.

```
TypeParameter:
TypeVariable TypeBoundopt
TypeBound:
extends
```

```
ClassOrInterfaceType AdditionalBoundListopt
AdditionalBoundList:
AdditionalBound AdditionalBoundList
AdditionalBound
AdditionalBound:
& InterfaceType
```

Type variables have an optional bound, T & I_1 ... I_n. The bound consists of either a type variable, or a class or interface type T possibly followed by further interface types I_1 ,..., I_n. If no bound is given for a type variable, Object is assumed. It is a compile-time error if any of the types I_1 ... I_n is a class type or type variable.

The erasures of all constituent types of a bound must be pairwise different, or a compile-time error occurs. The order of types in a bound is only significant in that the erasure of a type variable is determined by the first type in its bound, and that a class type or type variable may only appear in the first position. A type variable may not at the same time be a subtype of two interface types which are different parameterizations of the same generic interface. The members of a type variable X with bound T & I_1 ... I_n are the members of the intersection type T & I_1 ... I_n appearing at the point where the type variable is declared.

Discussion

The following example illustrates what members a type variable has.

```
package TypeVarMembers;
class C {
  void mCDefault() {}
  public void mCPublic() {}
  private void mCPrivate() {}
  protected void mCProtected() {}
}
  class CT extends C implements I {}
  interface I {
  void mI();}
    <T extends C & I> void test(T t) {
```

```
        t.mI();// OK
        t.mCDefault();// OK
        t.mCPublic();// OK
        t.mCPrivate();// compile-time error
        t.mCProtected();// OK
    }
}
```

The type variable T has the same members as the intersection type C & I, which in turn has the same members as the empty class CT, defined in the same scope with equivalent supertypes. The members of an interface are always public, and therefore always inherited (unless overridden). Hence mI is a member of CT and of T.

Among the members of C, all but mCPrivate are inherited by CT, and are therefore members of both CT and T. If C had been declared in a different package than T, then the call to mCDefault would give rise to a compile-time error, as that member would not be accessible at the point where T is declared.

PARAMETERIZED TYPES

A parameterized type consists of a class or interface name C and an actual type argument list $<T_1,..., T_n>$. It is a compile time error if C is not the name of a generic class or interface, or if the number of type arguments in the actual type argument list differs from the number of declared type parameters of C. In the following, whenever we speak of a class or interface type, we include the generic version as well, unless explicitly excluded. Throughout this section, let $A_1,..., A_n$ be the formal type parameters of C, and let be B_i be the declared bound of A_i. The notation $[A_i := T_i]$ denotes substitution of the type variable A_i with the type T_i, for $1 \leq i \leq n$, and is used throughout this specification.

Let $P = G<T_1,..., T_n>$ be a parameterized type. It must be the case that, after P is subjected to capture conversion resulting in the type $G<X1,..., Xn>$, for each actual type argument X_i, $1 \leq i \leq n$, $X_i <: B_i[A_1 := X_1,..., A_n := X_n]$, or a compile time error occurs.

Example: Parameterized types.

```
Vector<String>
Seq<Seq<A>>
Seq<String>.Zipper<Integer>
Collection<Integer>
Pair<String,String>
// Vector<int> – illegal, primitive types cannot
be arguments
// Pair<String> – illegal, not enough arguments
// Pair<String,String,String> – illegal, too
many arguments
```

Two parameterized types are provably distinct if either of the following conditions hold:

- They are invocations of distinct generic type declarations.
- Any of their type arguments are provably distinct.

Index